Pan Breakthrough Books

Pan Breakthrough Books open the door to successful self-education. The series provides essential knowledge using the most modern self-study techniques.

Expert authors have produced clear explanatory texts on business subjects to meet the particular needs of people at work and of those studying for relevant examinations.

A highly effective learning pattern, enabling readers to measure progress step-by-step, has been devised for Breakthrough Books by the National Extension College, Britain's leading specialists in home study.

John Gillespie is a member of a mathematics research project, based at the University of Nottingham. He was formerly Head of Mathematics at Carlton-le-Willows School, and Deputy Headmaster at Christ the King School, Arnold, Nottinghamshire. He is the author of Numbers at Work, *published jointly by the National Extension College and Channel 4 Television, and of other National Extension College texts.*

Pan Breakthrough Books

Other books in the series

Pan Breakthrough Books

Examination Mathematics 1

John Gillespie

A Pan Original
Pan Books London and Sydney

Acknowledgements I should like to thank the many colleagues and pupils who have contributed ideas. In particular, I wish to thank my family for their help and support, and Jean Winfield, who typed the manuscript.

First published 1986 by Pan Books Ltd,
Cavaye Place, London SW10 9PG
9 8 7 6 5 4 3 2 1
© John Gillespie 1986

ISBN 0 330 29129 3

Published in collaboration with the
National Extension College

Photoset by Parker Typesetting Service, Leicester
Printed and bound in Great Britain by
Cox & Wyman Ltd, Reading

Contents

Introduction

Who this book is written for

You may be studying maths at college – meeting topics in your course for the first time, or revising them following studies in previous years. Or you may be studying at home. You may be preparing for an exam like 'O' level maths, or RSA Stage 1 maths, or you may simply be trying to improve your understanding of mathematics. In all these situations, I hope this book will help you.

About this book

On its own, this book covers nearly all the topics in syllabuses like RSA Stage 1, and BTEC-1 mathematics. Together with Volume 2, it covers the syllabuses of several popular GCE 'O' level examinations, such as AEB syllabus C, London B361 and JMB syllabus A, as well as several pilot '16+' syllabuses.

A feature of this Breakthrough book is the importance attached to the pocket calculator. I believe that using a calculator helps in understanding key ideas in mathematics more clearly and easily. You'll find a section on buying a calculator in Chapter 1.

There are 15 chapters in this book, with a further 17 chapters in Volume 2. You will find a topics list at the beginning of each chapter.

How to use this book

I believe you will understand mathematical ideas more fully by putting them into practice. So make sure you work through the questions in the self-checks, and go through calculations again if you don't get correct answers first time. Understanding is more important than speed.

- Get into the habit of writing things down as you go. It helps you get things clear in your mind and gives you something to look back on when you come to revise. And in any case, nearly all exam papers tell you to show working – you can lose marks if you don't.
- Don't give up if you face problems. Everyone finds things difficult at times. Maybe you didn't read a question carefully enough, or perhaps you find a particular topic hard to follow. Put it on one side and return to it later – often a fresh mind helps to make things easier a second time around. Trying to explain a problem to someone else can also help to clear your own mind.

What you need

- A notebook, pen, pencil, ruler and rubber.
- Some squared paper (2 mm or 5 mm squares are best).
- A protractor and compasses.
- Some tracing paper (typing copy paper will do).
- A pocket calculator (and maybe a book of mathematical tables).

Answers to questions

The self-checks have answers immediately below the questions. There are also longer Review exercises with answers at the end of the book.

1 | Introducing decimals and fractions

Everyday problems involving adding, subtracting and checking

Most everyday uses of mathematics involve no more than adding or subtracting. For example:

- seeing if we can afford something (involving **adding** what money we have, then **subtracting** all the amounts we know we'll need to spend and seeing what's left;
- not arriving late for an appointment (involving **subtracting** the journey time from the appointment time to find when we should leave home).

Activity

Make a note of five more everyday situations involving maths. Which of these require no more than adding or subtracting?

In real life, many subtraction calculations get changed into addition calculations. This shows a good way of **checking** that subtractions are correct.

- I give a £5 note in a shop for goods worth £4.23. What is my change? You work out the change by **adding on** enough money to the £4.23 to come to £5.00, like this:

  £4.23 + 2p + 5p + 20p + 50p = £5.00

  so the change is 77p.

- I have to be at an appointment at 9.35 a.m. The journey from home takes 50 minutes. When should I leave home? You can solve this by making a **guess** at the leaving time and then checking and improving it. I guess that I have to leave at 8.55. Then I **add on** 50 minutes, reaching 9.45 a.m. – 10 minutes late. So I **improve my guess** – I have to leave 10 minutes earlier, at 8.45, to arrive on time.

You can see how the awkward subtractions of:

$$
\begin{array}{c} 5.00 \\ -\,4.23 \\ \hline ? \end{array}
\quad \text{and} \quad
\begin{array}{c} 9\,\text{h.}\ 35\,\text{min.} \\ -\,50\,\text{min.} \\ \hline ? \end{array}
$$

are changed into easier additions, and how poor estimates can be improved by checking. It also shows there is no single correct method of subtracting; you'll probably have chosen a different method than I did with the 'time' problem. What *is* important is the checking by adding.

> ### Self-check
>
> Try these and **check your answers by adding**.
>
> Example:
> $$
> \begin{array}{r} 1731 \\ -\ 846 \\ \hline 885 \end{array}
> $$
>
> Check:
> $$
> \begin{array}{r} 885 \\ +\ 846 \\ \hline 1731 \end{array}
> $$

1 143 − 62
2 1079 − 864
3 2135 − 378
4 2047 − 1788
5 60097 − 4278
6 Take 473 from 2045.
7 What change is given after buying a train tricket at £12.87 using a £20 note?
8 A bus journey to town takes 27 minutes. It takes you 8 minutes to walk to the bus stop, and the buses pass the stop at 10-minute intervals from 8 o'clock onwards. When should you leave home if you have to be in town by 8.45 a.m.?

ANSWERS

1 81. 2 215. 3 1757. 4 259. 5 55819. 6 1572. 7 £7.13.
8 You have to catch the 8.10, so you leave home not later than 2 minutes past 8.

Did that last question put you in a panic? Don't worry if you're not sure you are correct first time; just take your answer and **check it by adding on** − first the 8 minutes, then the 27 minutes. Are you on the right side of 8.45? Don't forget to take into account the times at which the buses pass the stop near your home.

Calculators and this book

As I mentioned in the introduction, this book reflects new approaches and opportunities made available by the **pocket calculator**.

You'll find that some topics occur in a different order from normal; this is because it is only natural to make use of the calculator as soon as possible. I am not saying 'traditional' methods can be left behind now; rather that you can gain an understanding of some key topics in mathematics by using a calculator.

Choosing a calculator

There are so many models on the market, and they change so often, that it's impossible to recommend one in particular.

However, it's probably worth choosing one with **auto power off**, which avoids battery wastage – it switches off the calculator after a few minutes of non-use.

Simple or scientific?

You will have to choose between 'simple' and 'scientific' types. If you are studying for an exam like RSA Stage 1 mathematics, the simple type of four function (+, −, ×, ÷) plus memory calculator will be suitable. If you are studying for GCE 'O' level or equivalent, the scientific type may be worth getting.

Instructions Can you understand the instructions? Some are easier to follow than others, though you'll learn a lot by experimenting with the calculator, trying out calculations whose answers you know already.

Percentages If you're following a course like 'O' level mathematics, you will find that the % key is useful but not essential. You can calculate percentages quite easily without it.

Place value and the decimal number line

'Place value' refers to the way our numbers are written in figures, where different places stand for units, tens, hundreds, thousands, etc.

Key in the number seven hundred and forty-eight on your calculator:

748

Now press:

and you obtain:

7480

Each single number or 'digit' has moved one place to the left. The 8 now stands for 8 tens, not 8 units, the 4 for 4 hundreds, not 4 tens, and so on.

Now press:

÷	1	0	=

and you return to:

| 748 |

Press:

again and you obtain:

| 74.8 |

showing that 74.8 is a **tenth** of 748. The 8 now stands for 8 tenths of a unit, whilst the 4 now stands for 4 units, instead of the 4 tens in 748. Press:

| × | 1 | 0 | = |

and you return to:

| 748 |

The decimal point has disappeared now, because the right-hand digit, 8, stands for 8 **units** once again. You only need to use a decimal point to show the position of the units digit when it is **not** at the right-hand end of a number.

Showing decimals in the number line

Figure 1 shows part of a line with whole number and decimal positions on it. We call it a '**number line**'. 74.8 comes between 74 and 75, nearer 75 than 74. The 8 stands for 8 **tenths** – the space between 74 and 75 is divided into **ten** equal parts.

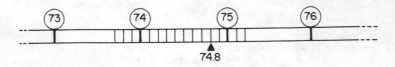

Figure 1. Part of the number line

Let's look at the section between 74 and 75 in more detail (see Figure 2). *a* is at 74.8 and *b* is at 74.3.

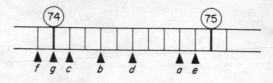

Figure 2. The number line between 74 and 75

> ## Self-check
>
> **1** Write down the position of c.
> **2** Write down the position of d.
> **3** Write down the position of e.
> **4** Write down the position of f.
> **5** Write down the position of g.
> Without using your calculator, write down the answers to these calculations.
> **6** 74.1 × 10
> **7** 74.5 × 10
> **8** 74.9 × 10
> Now check them on your calculator.

ANSWERS

1 74.1. **2** 74.5, halfway between 74 and 75.
3 74.9. **4** 73.9.
5 74 or 74.0. Both numbers stand for the same position.
6 741. **7** 745. **8** 749.

Figure 3 shows the number line again. *k* is midway between 74.8 and 74.9 – we say that *k* is at 74.85. The digit 5 stands for **5 hundredths**.

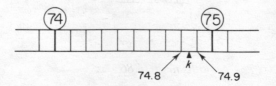

Figure 3. The number line between 74.8 and 74.9

Imagine the space between 74.8 and 74.9 cut into 10 parts (see Figure 4). *k* is at 74.85 and *h* is at 74.87.

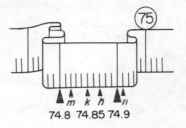

Figure 4.

Self-check

1 Write down the position of *m*.
2 Write down the position of *n*.

ANSWERS

1 74.82. **2** 74.91.

We can carry on dividing each part into smaller and smaller amounts (see Figure 5). Each time we divide by 10, we use another place to the right of the decimal point, e.g. *p* is at 74.857 and *q* is at 74.864, where the right-hand '7' stands for **7 thousandths** and the right-hand '4' stands for **4 thousandths**.

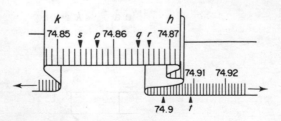

Figure 5. Thousandths near 74.86

Self-check

1 Write down the position of r.
2 Write down the position of s.
3 Write down the position of t.
4 What does the '6' stand for in 74.864?
What number should go in the box to make each of these calculations correct?

5 $74.864 \times \boxed{} = 748.64$

6 $74.864 \times \boxed{} = 74\,864$

Check these with your calculator.

7 Continue experimenting with your calculator, multiplying other decimal numbers by 10, 100, 1000, etc. Notice what happens.

8 Now try dividing a number by 10, 100, 1000, etc. Notice what happens.

Write down these calculations and, **without using your calculator**, write down the correct numbers that should go in the boxes.

9 $3.2 \times \boxed{} = 32$

10 $3.14 \times \boxed{} = 314$

11 $314 \div \boxed{} = 3.14$

12 $2.83 \div \boxed{} = 0.283$

13 $4700 \div \boxed{} = 4.7$

Now check these using your calculator.

ANSWERS

1 74.866. 2 74.854. 3 74.909. 4 6 hundredths. 5 10. 6 1000.
9 10. 10 100. 11 100. 12 10. 13 1000.

Activity

Make up some more questions like these and check the answers with your calculator. Write down what you notice.

ANSWER

Each time you multiply by 10, the decimal point moves 1 step right. When you divide by 10, the decimal point moves one place left. With × or ÷ by 100, the decimal point moves 2 places. With × or ÷ by 1000, the decimal point moves 3 places.

Improving guesses

This section is based on a calculator activity. Follow the start of the activity, then continue it yourself in the self-check below.

> *Activity*
>
> Choose any whole number you like from 1 to 12. Now **multiply** it by another number, with or without decimals, and end up at 12, e.g. if you choose 4, you can **multiply** it by 3:
>
> | 4 | × | 3 | = |
>
> giving 12; if you choose 2, you can multiply it by 6:
>
> | 2 | × | 6 | = |
>
> giving 12.
>
> Use your calculator to find how to solve this problem for all the other whole numbers from 1 to 12. Do not read on until you have solved the problem as far as you can.

ANSWER

You probably solved this problem for many of the numbers, but you probably still have 5, 7, 8, 9, 10 and 11 to deal with.

Let's look at 5. You have to solve the problem $5 \times ? = 12$. You know that $4 \times 3 = 12$ and $6 \times 2 = 12$, so ? must be a number less than 3 but more than 2. Could it be 2.5? Press:

| 5 | × | 2 | . | 5 | = |

and you obtain 12.5, so 2.5 is too large. The unknown number must be between 2 and 2.5. You've probably found it by now – it's 2.4.

Now try to find the number that matches 7, to solve $7 \times ? = 12$. You'll find it's between 1.7 and 1.73.

You can see how each guess, even though it is not the exact solution, gives you more information about where the exact solution might be. After each guess you can narrow down further the possible range for that solution. The closer you get to 12, the longer the numbers become, with more and more digits after the decimal point. For example:

$7 \times 1.71 = 11.97$ which is 0.03 below 12;

$7 \times 1.7143 = 12.0001$ which is 0.0001 above 12.

Thus it is sensible to decide in advance what accuracy is sufficient. We look at this in more detail in the next section.

Approximating and rounding up

Look at Figure 6 showing the section of a number line around 12. Numbers within the shaded part are closer to 12 than 11 or 13. We say that these numbers are approximately equal to 12, **to the nearest whole number**.

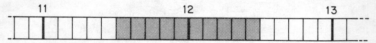

Figure 6. Numbers within shaded region approximately equal to 12 (to nearest whole number)

> ### Self-check
>
> **1** Which of the following numbers are approximately 12 (to nearest whole number)?
>   11.8, 12.07, 11.36, 12.7, 12.083, 12.245, 11.097, 11.97, 13.63, 1.217.
>
> **2** State the nearest whole number to each of these:
>   9.1, 7.04, 8.48, 36.19, 39.73, 41.86, 1.08, 0.69, 0.43, 0.219.

ANSWERS

1 11.8, 12.07, 12.083, 12.245, 11.97 (see Figure 7).
2 9, 7, 8, 36, 40, 42, 1, 1, 0, 0.

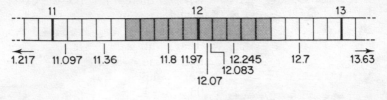

Figure 7.

Look at Figure 8, showing a smaller section of the number line around 12. Numbers in the shaded part are closer to 12.0 than to 11.8, 11.9, 12.1 or 12.2, etc. We say that these numbers (in the shaded part) are approximately equal to 12.0 'to the nearest tenth' or 'correct to 1 decimal place'. In short, we can write:

11.97 $\simeq$ 12.0 (1 dec. pl.)
11.951 $\simeq$ 12.0 (1 dec. pl.)
12.16 $\simeq$ 12.2 (1 dec. pl.)
12.052 $\simeq$ 12.1 (1 dec. pl.) and so on

where $\simeq$ means 'is approximately equal to'.

11.95, on the border between 11.9 and 12.0, is normally counted as $\simeq$ 12.0 (1 dec. pl.), while 12.05, on the border between 12.0 and 12.1, is normally counted as $\simeq$ 12.1 (1 dec. pl.). This is called **rounding up**.

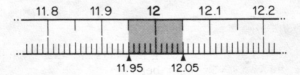

Figure 8. Numbers within shaded region approximately equal to 12.0

Self-check

Write down each of these sentences and fill in the missing figures.

1 11.98 $\simeq$ ... (1 dec. pl.).
2 11.914 $\simeq$ ... (1 dec. pl.).
3 11.914 $\simeq$ ... (2 dec. pl.).
4 11.9671 $\simeq$ ... (2 dec. pl.).

> **5** 12.197 $\simeq$ ... (2 dec. pl.).
> **6** 12.008 $\simeq$ ... (2 dec. pl.).
> **7** 12.091 $\simeq$ ... (1 dec. pl.).
> **8** 12.901 $\simeq$ ... (2 dec. pl.).

ANSWERS

1 12.0. **2** 11.9. **3** 11.91. **4** 11.97. **5** 12.20.
6 12.01. **7** 12.1. **8** 12.90.

Introducing fractions of amounts

Finding a fraction of something involves cutting it into **equal parts**. Thus a third ($\frac{1}{3}$) of £18 involves dividing £18 into **three equal amounts** of £6 each, a quarter ($\frac{1}{4}$) of £18 involves dividing £18 into **four equal amounts** of £4.50 each, and a fifth ($\frac{1}{5}$) of £18 involves dividing £18 into **five equal amounts** of £3.60 each.

Don't worry if you can't see how to calculate these yet – we come to that later in this chapter. Just check with your calculator that these fractions of £18 are correctly worked out. For instance, if a fifth of £18 is £3.60, then five lots of £3.60 should give £18. You can check this either by calculating:

$$\boxed{3}\ \boxed{.}\ \boxed{6}\ \boxed{0}\ \boxed{\times}\ \boxed{5}\ \boxed{=}$$

or by adding five £3.60s together.

> *Self-check*
>
> **1** Check if an eighth ($\frac{1}{8}$) of £18 is £2.25. How did you carry out the check?
> **2** Check if a twelfth ($\frac{1}{12}$) of £18 is £1.60. How did you carry out the check?
> **3** Check if a fifteenth ($\frac{1}{15}$) of £18 is £1.20. How did you carry out the check?

ANSWERS

1 2.25 × 8 = 18.00, so £2.25 is $\frac{1}{8}$ of £18.00.
2 1.60 × 12 = 19.20, so £1.60 is *not* $\frac{1}{12}$ of £18.00. The correct amount is £1.50.
3 1.20 × 15 = 18.00, so £1.20 is $\frac{1}{15}$ of £18.00.

You can extend this method to finding other fractions of amounts. For instance, to find three-fifths ($\frac{3}{5}$) of £18, you find the total of three lots of one-fifth of £18, i.e. £3.60 × 3. To find $\frac{4}{5}$ of £18 you find the total of four lots of $\frac{1}{5}$ of £18, i.e. £3.60 × 4, and so on.

Self-check

1 Calculate $\frac{3}{8}$ of £18.
2 Calculate $\frac{5}{12}$ of £18.
3 Calculate $\frac{7}{8}$ of £18.
4 Calculate $\frac{4}{15}$ of £18.
5 Calculate $\frac{1}{3}$ of £12.
6 Calculate $\frac{2}{3}$ of £12.
7 Calculate $\frac{1}{5}$ of £30.
8 Calculate $\frac{2}{5}$ of £30.

ANSWERS

1 £6.75. **2** £7.50 (note that 7.5 is the same as 7.50). **3** £15.75. **4** £4.80. **5** £4.00. **6** £8.00. **7** £6.00. **8** £12.00.

Figure 9 shows a length of wood cut into fifths, while Figure 10 shows the total of $2\frac{2}{5}$ of these lengths of wood.

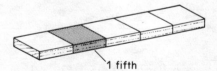

1 fifth

Figure 9.

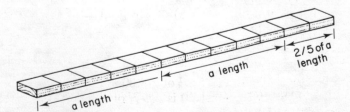

a length

a length

2/5 of a length

Figure 10. $2\frac{2}{5}$ lengths of wood

Suppose each length of wood is 1 metre long, then the total length of all the pieces in Figure 10 is $2\frac{2}{5}$ metres. But how could you write this length using decimals of a metre instead of fractions?

Figure 11 shows the wood laid beside a decimal metre scale. You can see how $2\frac{2}{5} = 2.4$; 2.4 means two and four tenths $(2\frac{4}{10})$, so the diagram shows how:

$$\tfrac{2}{5} = \tfrac{4}{10} \text{ or } 0.4$$

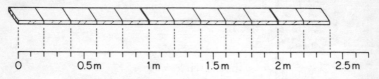

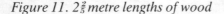

Figure 11. $2\frac{2}{5}$ metre lengths of wood

Figure 12 shows a long piece of timber marked in thirds $(\frac{1}{3})$ of a metre. Thus if the wood is cut at the arrow, the amount cut off is $1\frac{2}{3}$ metres. As before, there is a decimal metre scale below the wood and you can see that:

$$1\tfrac{2}{3}\text{m} \simeq 1.7\text{m (1 dec. pl.)}$$

although, in fact, 1.7 is a little more than $1\frac{2}{3}$.

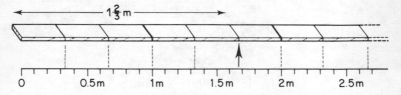

Figure 12. Wood cut at $1\frac{2}{3}$m

Self-check

Use the scales in Figures 11 and 12 to answer these questions.

1 Convert these fractions to decimals (correct to 1 decimal place):
   $1\frac{1}{3}$m; $2\frac{1}{5}$m; $2\frac{3}{5}$m; $2\frac{2}{3}$m; $\frac{4}{5}$m; $2\frac{1}{3}$m.
2 What decimal length is the same as $2\frac{1}{2}$m?

3 Using only ½s, ⅓s or ⅕s, which fraction lengths are closest to:
2.8 m; 0.7 m; 1.5 m; 2.2 m; 1.4 m; 2.3 m?

ANSWERS

1 1.3 m; 2.2 m; 2.6 m; 2.7 m; 0.8 m; 2.3 m.
2 2.5 m. **3** $2\frac{4}{5}$ m; $\frac{2}{3}$ m; $1\frac{1}{2}$ m; $2\frac{1}{5}$ m; $1\frac{2}{5}$ m; $2\frac{1}{3}$ m.

Multiplication and division

Activity

Can you repeat the activity on page 17 if you started with the number 15, say, which is larger than 12? Do not read on until you have tried this on your calculator.

You are trying to solve the problem 15 × ? = 12. If you can't solve it, try:

| 1 | 5 | × | 0 | . | 9 | = |

It is not correct but it will give you a hint.

Self-check

Find decimal numbers which give 12 (correct to 2 dec. pl.) when you multiply them by the whole numbers from 13 to 20 inclusive.

ANSWER

13 × 0.92; 14 × 0.86; 15 × 0.80; 16 × 0.75;
17 × 0.71; 18 × 0.67; 19 × 0.63; 20 × 0.60.

This last self-check will show you that multiplying doesn't always make things larger. When you solve the problem 15 × ? = 12, you're saying '15 lots of **something** make 12' and the **something** must be less than 1 (see how the 'of' stands for ×).

You can see a connection between these results and the fraction diagrams on page 22 in Figures 11 and 12. After all, saying '15 × ? = 12' is really asking the same question as 'if I divide this line 12 metres long into 15 pieces, how long is each piece?' So you could calculate the unknown number straight-away by calculating:

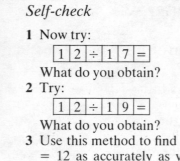

Try it and see what you obtain.

Self-check

1 Now try:

What do you obtain?
2 Try:

What do you obtain?
3 Use this method to find the unknown number in 23 × ? = 12 as accurately as you can. Then check by multi-plying this number by 23 and making sure you come back to 12.

ANSWERS

1 0.7058... 2 0.6315... 3 12 ÷ 23 = 0.5217...

Thus you can see how multiplying and dividing are closely connected, just like adding and subtracting, and how you can use this to help you check that answers are correct on your calculator.

Self-check

Solve the following problems on your calculator, giving missing numbers correct to 3 decimal places. Make sure you check your answers.
1 8 × ? = 15
2 8 × ? = 5
3 15 ÷ ? = 6
4 15 ÷ ? = 14
5 15 ÷ ? = 21

ANSWERS

1 1.875. **2** 0.625. **3** 2.5. **4** 1.071. **5** 0.714.

You can see from **4** and **5** that dividing doesn't always make things smaller, just as multiplying doesn't always make things larger.

Some everyday problems involving × and ÷; finding a method

Suppose you know your car uses 1 gallon of petrol for every 34 miles. How much petrol will you need to cover 185 miles?

Faced with a problem like this, all sorts of thoughts go through your mind. Do you multiply or divide, add or subtract? Which number do you start with? How accurate an answer do you want?

The calculator will carry out the arithmetic, but you've got to know what to do to obtain a correct answer. As before, making **guesses** or **estimates** and **carrying out checks** will greatly help. For example, you can:

- **Simplify** the numbers in the problem, see how you solve it with these simpler numbers, then use the same method to solve the given problem, e.g. 34 miles is roughly 30 miles and 185 miles is a little more than 180 miles, so see how to solve the problem if the car covers 30 miles on a gallon and the journey is 180 miles;
- write down exactly what you did to solve the simpler problem, then:
- use your calculator to find a method of carrying out the calculation which will give the solution you expect (note down how you used the calculator);
- use the same method with the real numbers, to obtain the real answer;
- afterwards **check** that the answer 'fits', and round it to a sensible accuracy.

In this case, 30 × 6 = 180, so a **rough answer** is 6 gallons. How can you obtain the answer '6' starting with 30 and 180? Maybe

by finding 180 ÷ 30. Write this down. Now replace the simpler
numbers by the real numbers, and calculate:

| 1 | 8 | 5 | ÷ | 3 | 4 | = |

obtaining something like 5.4411765. Go back to your first calculation and **check** this: you use 5.44... gallons and each gallon
takes you 34 miles, so you cover:

$34 \times 5.4411765 = 185$ miles

as you hoped.

Finally, though the distance may be exact, the distance the
car travels on 1 gallon is only accurate to the nearest mile or so,
so round your answer sensibly to about $5\frac{1}{2}$ gallons.

Self-check

Calculate the amount of petrol needed for the 185 miles if
the car used 1 gallon for every 38 miles.

ANSWER

$185 \div 38 \simeq 4.9$ gallons, i.e. about $\frac{1}{2}$ gallon less than before.

Here's another problem. You'll need your calculator as before,
and you'll find the steps on page 25 worth following.

It costs about 48p to run an electric shower for an hour. You
reckon to have a shower lasting 4 minutes – how much does it
cost?

It's tempting to say $4 \times 12 = 48$, so the cost is 12p for 4
minutes, but this means that 48p gives only 16 minutes' shower,
so 12p can't be correct. Do not read on until you have tried to
solve this problem.

Try simplifying the numbers. Suppose it cost 60p an hour to
run; that works out at a penny a minute, so 4 minutes would
cost about 4p. The correct answer should be less, because 48p is
less than 60p. Thus you can solve the problem by saying:

Cost of a shower for 1 minute × No. of minutes = Cost of
shower.

Each minute costs a little less than a penny, which fits with
calculating $48 \div 60 = 0.8$, so the cost of the 4-minute shower is

$0.8 \times 4 = 3.2$p

You can check this in a variety of ways. Here are two possibilities.
1 If 4 min. costs 3.2p
  40 min. costs 32p
  20 min. costs 16p
 so 1 hour costs 48p
2 If 4 min. costs 3.2p
  8 min. costs 6.4p
 16 min. costs 12.8p
 32 min. costs about 25p
and an hour costs about 50p

Self-check

Give all your answers correct to 1 decimal place, unless otherwise stated.
1 Calculate the total cost of two showers a day for 13 weeks if each shower costs 3.2p.
2 How many showers could you have for £1?
3 A gallon is about 4.546 litres. If a car uses 5.4 gallons of petrol, how many litres is this?
4 Bread contains about 2.5 calories in each gram. How many calories are contained in a slice of 18 grams?
5 Cheese contains about 4.2 calories per gram. How many grams of cheese will give 200 calories?
6 Suppose you are paid at £1.80 per hour for casual work. How many complete hours do you work before you've earned £20?
7 A courier on a coach trip knows the coach travels at about 35 mph. It's now 3 p.m. and the group are stopping for afternoon tea. When should they be on the road again if they have to cover 84 miles by 6.30 p.m.? Answer the question to the nearest 10 minutes on the 'right' side.

ANSWERS

Your calculator will take the drudgery out of the work, leaving you free to have several attempts at each question if you need to. Always check at the end to see that the answer makes sense, using your calculator again if you need to.

In these answers, I've given some steps to help you if you are stuck, but there are different, equally good, methods for each question – don't worry if your method is not the same as these.

Notice that it's worth **writing down** what you are doing and what the numbers stand for.

1 Two showers cost 6.4p a day, which gives $6.4 \times 7 = 44.8$p a week and $13 \times 44.8 = 582.4$p for 13 weeks, so cost $\simeq$£6.00.

2 How many 3.2s are there in 100? Given by $100 \div 3.2 = 31.25$. Thus you could have 31 showers. **Check:** $31 \times 3.2 = 99.2$p.

3 5.4 gallons gives $5.4 \times 4.546 = 24.5484 \simeq 24.5$ litres.

4 45 calories (18×2.5).

5 How many 4.2s in 200? Given by $200 \div 4.2 = 47.61... \simeq 48$ grams. **Check**: $47.6 \times 4.2 = 199.92 \simeq 200$.

6 How many 1.80s in 20? Given by $20 \div 1.8 = 11.11...$ hours. Thus you'll have to work 12 hours. **Check:** $12 \times 1.8 = 21.60$, i.e. £21.60.

7 You have to 'work back' with this one. First find how many hours it will take to cover 84 miles by finding how many 35s there are in 84, i.e. $84 \div 35 = 2.4$ hours. Each $\frac{1}{10}$ of the hour is 6 minutes ($6 \times 10 = 60$), so journey will take approximately 2 hr. 24 min. Thus you could leave at 4.06 at the latest – say 4 o'clock to be on the safe side.

Looking at division

You've seen how **finding a fraction of** something and **dividing by** are closely connected. For instance, a third ($\frac{1}{3}$) of 12 corresponds to **dividing** 12 **by** 3, i.e. $12 \div 3$. Similarly, a quarter ($\frac{1}{4}$) of 28 corresponds to **dividing** 28 **by** 4, i.e. $28 \div 4$. Thus to find $\frac{1}{5}$ of 28 on your calculator you press:

$\boxed{2}\ \boxed{8}\ \boxed{\div}\ \boxed{5}\ \boxed{=}$

Do this now. Did you obtain 5.6? Similarly, to find $\frac{3}{5}$ of 28 you multiply 5.6 by 3 or, in a single calculation, press:

$\boxed{2}\ \boxed{8}\ \boxed{\div}\ \boxed{5}\ \boxed{\times}\ \boxed{3}\ \boxed{=}$

Try this now. Did you obtain 16.8?

You can also think of division as saying **how many of one number will make another number**, e.g. how many 3s make 12, how many 4s make 28, etc. Thus a calculation like:

$12 \div \frac{1}{2}$ means 'How many $\frac{1}{2}$s are there in 12?'
$15 \div \frac{1}{3}$ means 'How many $\frac{1}{3}$s are there in 15?'
Think back to the length of wood in Figure 12. Imagine you had lots of pieces of wood $\frac{1}{3}$ m long. How many of them are needed to make a total length of 15 m? Not 5 at any rate.

Self-check

1 You have strips of wood 4 m long. How many pieces $\frac{1}{5}$ metre long can you cut from each strip?
2 A small milk bottle holds $\frac{1}{3}$ pint. How many of these bottles contain 7 pints altogether?

ANSWERS

1 20. **2** 21.

Talking about numbers large and small

Up to now we have used large and small numbers on the calculator, but we haven't said **what** they are. Here's a reminder.

As an example, let's start with 48 = forty-eight units (or 4 tens, 8 units). If you multiply by 10 again and again, you obtain:

$48 \times 10 =$	480	Four hundred and eighty
$480 \times 10 =$	4 800	Four thousand eight hundred
$4 800 \times 10 =$	48 000	Forty-eight thousand
$48 000 \times 10 =$	480 000	Four-hundred-and-eighty thousand
$480 000 \times 10 =$	4 800 000	Four million, eight-hundred thousand
$4 800 000 \times 10 =$	48 000 000	Forty-eight million

Going back to 48, but this time dividing by 10 again and again or multiplying by 0.1 again and again, you obtain:

$48 \div 10 \,(= 48 \quad \times 0.1) = 4.8$	Four units and eight tenths, or 48 tenths
$4.8 \div 10 \,(= 4.8 \quad \times 0.1) = 0.48$	Four tenths and eight hundredths, or 48 hundredths
$0.48 \div 10 \,(= 0.48 \times 0.1) = 0.048$	Four hundredths and eight thousandths, or 48 thousandths

Self-check

Write these numbers in figures.
  1 Two thousand and sixty-three.
  2 Forty-one and eight thousandths.
  3 Seven million, sixty-one thousand.
  4 Thirty-nine hundredths.
  5 Thirty-nine thousandths.
Write these numbers in words.
  6 26 007
  7 0.103
  8 64 000 000
  9 20.078
  10 184 269

ANSWERS

  1 2063. **2** 41.008. **3** 7 061 000. **4** 0.39. **5** 0.039.
  6 Twenty-six thousand and seven.
  7 One tenth and three thousandths, or one-hundred-and-three thousandths.
  8 Sixty-four million.
  9 Twenty and seventy-eight thousandths.
  10 One-hundred-and-eighty-four thousand, two hundred and sixty-nine.

Self-check

Fill in the missing numbers in each of the boxes.

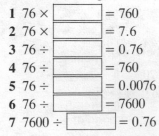

  1 76 × ☐ = 760
  2 76 × ☐ = 7.6
  3 76 ÷ ☐ = 0.76
  4 76 ÷ ☐ = 760
  5 76 ÷ ☐ = 0.0076
  6 76 ÷ ☐ = 7600
  7 7600 ÷ ☐ = 0.76

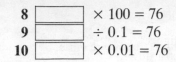

8 ⬚ × 100 = 76
9 ⬚ ÷ 0.1 = 76
10 ⬚ × 0.01 = 76

ANSWERS

1 10. **2** 0.1. **3** 10. **4** 0.1. **5** 10000. **6** 0.01. **7** 10000. **8** 0.76.
9 7.6. **10** 7600.

I hope you've reached this far without too much trouble and that you've found the answers helpful.

Maybe this is the right time to emphasize a few points which apply to the whole course.

- **Take the time to puzzle things out,** working back from the answers if you need to.
- **Write down calculations and results** as you go.
- **Keep what you've written down** – it could help you later.
- **Go back over** parts you've found hard (after a little rest).

Finally, here is a review exercise covering the work of this chapter. First see how much you can do without looking back through the chapter, then refer back for help with the rest.

Review

1 Your supermarket bill is £18.37. What is your change from £20?

2 What numbers are midway between these pairs?

61 and 62
16.96 and 17.08

3 Fill in the missing numbers in the boxes.

26.7 × ⬚ = 2670
26.7 ÷ ⬚ = 2.67
19 ÷ ⬚ = 190

$$\boxed{} \times 100 = 4.2$$

4 Round these figures correct to one decimal place.

17.49
36.038

5 Figure 13 shows a decimal and $\frac{1}{7}$ths scales, side by side. Use the scales to estimate (to 1 decimal place) the decimal numbers closest to:

$2\frac{3}{7}$
$4\frac{5}{7}$

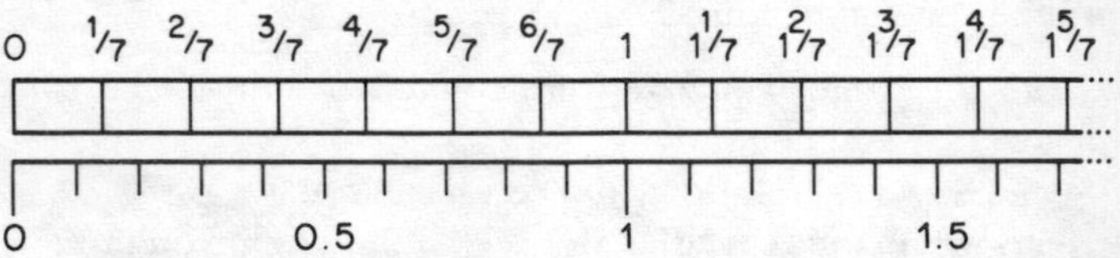

Figure 13. Sevenths and decimal (tenths) scales

6 A 539g tin of baked beans costs 28p. How many grams of beans cost 1p?

7 You need to serve 12 people with baked beans and each person's helping is at least 200g. Use the information in **6** to find the number of tins required.

8 A car covers 31 miles for each gallon of petrol used. If petrol costs 204p a gallon, find the cost of the petrol used in travelling 1 mile (to 1 decimal place).

Answers on page 359.

2 | Introducing formulae, coordinates and graphs

You will need squared or graph paper for the second half of the chapter.

Topics covered

- Introducing sequences.
- Describing rules for sequences.
- Number pairs and relations.
- Rules for number pairs using words and letters.
- Precedence.
- Finding values with a calculator.
- Formula, variable.
- Plotting points on a coordinate grid, showing formulae on a graph.
- Negative numbers.
- Evaluating simple formulae with negative numbers.
- Adding and subtracting negative numbers.

Introducing sequences

Activity

Here's a puzzle. Can you tell what the next number is in this sequence?

1, 2, 4, ...

It could be 7 (add one more each time) or 8 (double each time). You can't be sure because you haven't enough information.

Self-check

Now try these. In each case look at the numbers and find the **pattern** which tells you how the sequence is built up. **Check** that the pattern fits **all** the numbers in the sequence, then you can be sure of the missing number in each box. I'll start with the two sequences above.

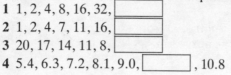

1 1, 2, 4, 8, 16, 32,
2 1, 2, 4, 7, 11, 16,
3 20, 17, 14, 11, 8,
4 5.4, 6.3, 7.2, 8.1, 9.0,   , 10.8

ANSWERS

1 64. **2** 22. **3** 5. **4** 9.9.

Describing rules for sequences

Look back at **1** in the self-check above. You could say 'start at 1, then double, double again and keep on doubling', or you could say 'start at 1, add on 1 to make 2, add on 2 to make 4, add on 4 to make 8, and so on'. How would *you* describe the pattern or **rule** for this sequence?

Question 3 is easier to describe. You could say 'start at 20, then subtract 3 each time'.

Self-check

In your own words, write down the rule for each of the sequences in the last self-check.

ANSWERS

1 Start at 1, then add on last number *or* double last number.
2 Start at 1, then add on one more each time.
3 Start at 20, then subtract three each time.
4 Start at 5.4, then add on 0.9 each time.

The numbers which make up a sequence are called **terms**. In the following self-check see if you can find the next four terms in the sequences, using the given rules.

Self-check

Write down the next four terms in these sequences.
1 Start at 3. Double any term to obtain the next term.
2 Start at 6. Add on 4 each time.
3 Start at 80. Halve any term to obtain the next term.
4 Start at 5. Double any term and add 1 to obtain the next term.
5 Start at 5. Subtract 3 from any term, then multiply by 3 to obtain the next term.

ANSWERS

1 3, 6, 12, 24, 48.   4 5, 11, 23, 47, 95.
2 6, 10, 14, 18, 22.   5 5, 6, 9, 18, 45.
3 80, 40, 20, 10, 5.

Introducing number pairs and relations

Figure 14 shows part of a fence made from concrete posts spaced 2 metres apart, with six wires between them. To make a fence 8 m long, how many posts and how much wire do you need?

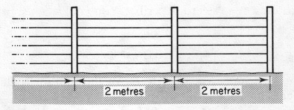

Figure 14. Post and wire fence

You can see from the diagram that you need five posts (one at each end) and 6 × 8 = 48 m of wire.

How many posts and how much wire do you need for a 14 m fence? Work it out now before you read further.

You can collect all this information in a table.

Fence length (metres)	Number of posts	Wire length (metres)
2	2	12
4	3	24
6	4	36
8	5	48
10		
12		
14		
16		

You can thus see how an 8-metre length of fence needs five posts and 48 m of wire (line 4 of the table).

Self-check

1 Copy the table and fill in the missing numbers.
2 If you have a fence 100 m long, how many posts and how much wire do you need?

ANSWERS

1

Fence length (metres)	Number of posts	Wire length (metres)
2	2	12
4	3	24
6	4	36
8	5	48
10	6	60
12	7	72
14	8	84
16	9	96

2 51 posts, 600 m.

How did you work out your answers to 2 above? One way is to look at the patterns in each column of numbers:

2, 4, 6, 8, 10, 12, 14, 16...
2, 3, 4, 5, 6, 7, 8, 9...
12, 24, 36, 48, 60, 72, 84, 96...

then **carry on these sequences** till you reach 100m in the *Length of fence* column.

Another method is to spot a way of working out the number of posts needed from the length of fence. You can then use this method for any length of fence you like. Maybe you can also spot a way of working out the length of wire needed for a fence of any length you like.

Activity

See if you can spot these two ways now.

ANSWER

Got them? The posts are spaced every 2m, so you have to halve the fence length, then add 1 for the extra post at the end. This gives the number of posts, *whatever* the fence length. In other words:

Number of posts = $\frac{1}{2}$ (Fence length in metres) + 1   **Relation 1**

You probably spotted that the six wires in the fence mean that:

Length of wire in metres = 6 × (Fence length in metres)

Relation 2

Using these relations for a fence 100m long:

Number of posts = $\frac{1}{2}$ of 100 + 1
$$= 50 + 1$$
$$= 51$$

Length of wire in metres = 6 × 100
$$= 600$$

For a fence 200m long you need 101 posts and 1200m of wire.

Self-check

Using relations **1** and **2** above, find the following.
1 Number of posts for a fence 150m long.
2 Length of wire for a fence 150m long.
3 Number of posts for an 84m fence.
4 Length of wire for an 84m fence.
5 Length of fence if you have 28 posts.

6 Length of fence if you have 240m of wire.
7 Length of fence if you have 36 posts and 400m of wire.

ANSWERS

1 76. **2** 900m. **3** 43. **4** 504m. **5** 54m. **6** 40m. **7** 70m (posts), 66m (wire), so maximum length is 66m.

Imagine you are setting out tables for à wedding reception. Each table can fit two people at each side and one at an end. The tables are arranged in lines as in Figure 15.

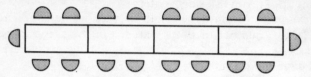

Figure 15. Wedding table plan

Activity

Copy and complete the following table.

Number of tables	Number of guests
1	6
2	
4	
8	

Self-check

1 How many guests can be seated round a line of 24 tables?
2 Find the number of guests who can be seated around two lines, each consisting of 12 tables.
3 You rearrange the 24 tables into six lines. How many **extra** guests can you fit in?

ANSWERS

1 98. **2** 100. **3** 8 more.

You probably found a relation like:
Number of guests = 4 × (number of tables) + 2 **Relation 3**
Thus, for a line of 24 tables:
$$\text{Number of guests} = 4 \times 24 + 2$$
$$= 96 + 2$$
$$= 98$$

You can make each of these relations quicker and neater to write down if you use **single letters** to stand for groups of words, like 'number of guests', 'length of wire in metres'. Thus if p stands for 'number of posts' and f stands for 'fence length in metres':

Relation 1 becomes $p = \frac{1}{2}$ of $f + 1$
or simply $p = \frac{1}{2}f + 1$
or $p = 0.5f + 1$ (because $\frac{1}{2} = 0.5$)

If w stands for 'length of wire in metres':

Relation 2 becomes $w = 6 \times f$
or simply $w = 6f$

See how the 'of' or '×' can be left out:
$\frac{1}{2}$ of f is written $\frac{1}{2}f$
$6 \times f$ is written $6f$

If g stands for 'number of guests' and t stands for 'number of tables in the line':

Relation 3 becomes $g = 4 \times t + 2$
or simply $g = 4t + 2$

Self-check

1 Calculate the value of g when $t = 5$.
2 Calculate the value of g when $t = 10$.
3 Calculate the value of w when $f = 15$.
4 Calculate the value of w when $f = 120$.
5 Calculate the value of p when $f = 16$.
6 Calculate the value of p when $f = 120$.
7 Calculate the value of f when $p = 20$.
8 Calculate the value of t when $g = 26$.

ANSWERS

1 22. **2** 42. **3** 90. **4** 720.
5 9. **6** 61. **7** 38. **8** 6.

Finding fractions and 'dividing by'

Look back to relation **1**. Halving the fence length is the same as dividing the fence length by 2, just as finding a $\frac{1}{7}$th of something is the same as dividing it by 7, and so on. So you could write relation **1** as:

$p = f \div 2 + 1$

so when $f = 100$:

$p = 100 \div 2 + 1$
$= 50 + 1$
$= 51$ as before

You can also write:

$p = \frac{f}{2} + 1$ (read as f halves plus one)

Again, when $f = 100$:

$p = \frac{100}{2} + 1$ (because 2 halves make 1 unit, so 100 halves
                  make 50 units)

$= 50 + 1$
$= 51$

Finally, fractions like $\frac{f}{2}$ are sometimes written $f/2$ to save space.

So all these have the same value if you start with the same number for f:

- $\frac{1}{2}f$
- $0.5f$
- $f \div 2$
- $\frac{f}{2}$
- $f/2$

Self-check

1 Calculate the value of $f/2$ when $f = 16$.
2 Calculate the value of $\frac{1}{2}f$ when $f = 26$.
3 Calculate the value of $f \div 3$ when $f = 24$.
4 Calculate the value of $f/3$ when $f = 30$.
5 Calculate the value of $0.5f$ when $f = 14$.

ANSWERS

1 8. **2** 13. **3** 8. **4** 10. **5** 7.

Precedence

Think back to the wedding problem. You could work out the number of guests in a line of tables by saying:

Total number of guests $\Big\}$ = $\Big\{$ 1 at each end, making 2 altogether, plus 4 more for each table.

Using letters:

$g = 2 + 4 \times t$

Then someone might say 'Oh I see . . . When you have five tables, there are 30 guests.' Is that correct? Can you see how this number was calculated? It's 2 + 4 (that's 6), then multiply by t (that's 5), so guest total is $6 \times 5 = 30$.

But that's wrong, because there are guests at each end of the line only, plus four more on each table (see Figure 16), i.e.:

$2 + 20 = 22$

Can you see what you have to do to obtain 22, not 30? You have to work out 4×5 first, *then* find 2 + 20, giving 22 altogether. So in working out $2 + 4 \times 5$, you **multiply** first, then add. You don't just read from left to right.

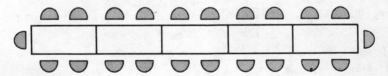

Figure 16. Five tables in a line

We say that $\times$ and $\div$ **have precedence over** + and $-$; that means you carry out $\times$ or $\div$ **before** + or $-$. For example:

- $4 \times 5 + 7$ = 20 + 7   = 27
  but $4 + 5 \times 7$ = 4 + 35   = 39
- $30 \times 2 - 9$ = 60 - 9   = 51
  but $30 - 2 \times 9$ = 30 - 18   = 12
- $6 \div 2 + 2$ = 3 + 2   = 5
  but $6 + 2 \div 2$ = 6 + 1   = 7

- $27 \div 3 + 6 - 2$ $\qquad = 9 + 6 - 2 = 13$
  but $27 + 6 \div 3 - 2$ $\quad = 27 + 2 - 2 = 27$

Self-check

Find the value of the following.
1 $4 + 5 - 8$
2 $6 \times 3 - 4$
3 $6 + 3 \times 4$
4 $14 - 6 \div 2$
5 $4 \times 3 + 5 \times 2$
6 $8 \div 2 + 9 \times 3$
7 $3 + 14 \div 7 + 4$
8 $8 - 2 \times 3$
9 $7 + 4 \times 5 - 1$
10 $24 + 0.5 \times 16$
11 $36 + 0.1 \times 40$
12 $2 \times 17 - 51 \div 3$

ANSWERS

1 1. **2** 14. **3** 18. **4** 11. **5** 22. **6** 31. **7** 9. **8** 2. **9** 26. **10** 32. **11** 40.
12 17.

Using your calculator

When you are only having to work with simple whole numbers, you'll find that a calculator may not save you much time; you may have to rearrange the calculation to carry it out on your calculator, maybe using the memory. However, it is worth using your calculator with simple examples – then you can use it confidently when the numbers are more complicated.

In this section:

- obtain results without your calculator with the 'simple number' examples;
- make sure you can obtain the same results with your calculator; then
- use the method you *now* know is correct to carry out more complicated calculations.

In the relation $y = 100 - 6z$, find the missing values of y in the following table.

z	y
3	82
8	
7.3	
11.86	

$6z$ means $6 \times z$, so to calculate $100 - 6z$ you have to find the value of $6z$ first, then take your answer from 100 to find the matching value of y. Thus when $z = 3$, $6z = 18$ and $100 - 6z = 100 - 18 = 82$, as shown in the table.

Self-check

1 Copy the table above and use your calculator to complete it.
2 There is another relation:
   $$x = z/4 + 7$$
   Copy the following table and complete it.

z	x
3	7.75
8	
7.3	8.825
11.86	

ANSWERS

z	y	x
3	18	7.75
8	52	9
7.3	56.2	8.825
11.86	28.84	9.965

Using brackets

Look back at the fence problem at the beginning of the chapter. Suppose you have 40 posts – how long a fence can you make? There are posts at both ends of the fence, and the posts are spaced 2 metres apart. That means there will be 39 spaces of 2 metres (see Figure 17). So the fence length (*f*) will be:

$39 \times 2 = 78\,\text{m}$

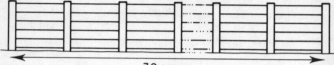

39 spaces

Figure 17. Fence with 40 posts

You have to subtract 1 from the number of posts, then multiply by the spacing of 2 metres, so, whatever the number of posts (*p*), the fence length (*f*) = number of posts minus 1, then multiply by 2. We write this as:

$f = (p - 1) \times 2$

or just

$f = (p - 1)2$

The brackets mean 'work out this part first', so you find $p - 1$ first, **then** multiply the result by 2. Without brackets, '$p - 1 \times 2$' means 'calculate 1×2 first, then subtract this from *p*', so if $p = 40$:

$p - 1 \times 2 = 40 - 2 = 38$

If the spacing between posts is extended to 3 metres, then:

$f = (p - 1)3 \text{ or } f = 3(p - 1)$

so if you had 50 posts you could make a fence of:

$(50 - 1)3 = 49 \times 3 = 147\,\text{m}$

Self-check

1 Copy the following table and use the relation $f = (p - 1)3$ to find the missing numbers.

p	f
10	
20	
30	
50	147
100	

2 Make another table for a fence with a post spacing of 2.5 m and these numbers of posts:

    10, 20, 60, 100

Calculate the values of the following:

3 $(31 - 2)6$

4 $31 - 2 \times 6$

5 $6 \times 31 - 2$

6 $6(31 - 2)$

ANSWERS

1

p	f
10	27
20	57
30	87
100	297

2

p	f
10	22.5
20	47.5
60	147.5
100	247.5

3 174. **4** 19. **5** 184. **6** 174.

Does the order matter?

Activity

Use your calculator to find the results of the calculations below. Make a note of the questions and answers as you go.

7×36	5×14.3	9×12.3
$6 + 13$	$4 \div 8$	$6 - 8$
$2 \div 5$	$17 - 8$	$13 + 6$
$8 \div 4$	36×7	$30 \div 7.5$
14.3×5	$8 - 17$	12.3×9
$8 - 6$	$5 \div 2$	$7.5 \div 30$

Suppose you choose two different numbers – we'll call them *a* and *b*. Which of the statements below is true, whatever values you choose for *a* and *b*?

1 Does $a + b = b + a$ always?
2 Does $a - b = b - a$ always?
3 Does $a \times b = b \times a$ always?
4 Does $a \div b = b \div a$ always?

You'll probably agree that $a + b$ **always equals** $b + a$. For instance:

  $6 + 13 \ = 19$, and so does $13 + 6$
  $29 + 4.6 = 33.6$, and so does $4.6 + 29$

But $8 - 6 = 2$, while $6 - 8$ means 'start with 6, then take away 8', which is certainly **not** 2, so $a - b$ **does not equal** $b - a$. $7 \times 13 = 91$, and so does 13×7; other examples will confirm that $a \times b$ **always equals** $b \times a$. Finally $8 \div 4 = 2$, but $4 \div 8 = 0.5$, so $a \div b$ **does not equal** $b \div a$.

All this shows that you **can interchange two numbers** when you are **adding** or **multiplying**, but **not** when you are **subtracting** or **dividing**.

Self-check

Look at the calculations below, lettered **1** to **12**. Write down the pairs of question numbers for any two calculations which have the same values as each other.

  1 $16.89 + 4.231$
  2 $17.9 \div 5$
  3 $16 - 48.3$
  4 914×0.73
  5 $48.3 - 16$
  6 $21.9 + 84$
  7 $4.231 + 16.89$
  8 $84 \div 21.9$

9 $5 \div 17.9$
10 0.73×914
11 84×21.9
12 $21.9 - 84$

ANSWERS

Check on your calculator that **1** and **7** give the same result, as do **4** and **10**.

Review

Find the missing numbers in these sequences.

1 $1, 3, 5, 7, \boxed{}, 11$
2 $2, 5, 9, \boxed{}, \boxed{}, 27$
3 $13.5, 12.75, 12, 11.25, \boxed{}, 9.75$
4 $1, 3, 9, \boxed{}, \boxed{}, 243$
5 Complete the following table for the relations:
$y = 2x + 3$
$z = \frac{1}{2}(x + 4)$

x	y	z
4		
6		
7		
10.4		
12.8		

Insert brackets or signs in the spaces of the following to make them true statements.

6 $20 \quad 3 = 17$
7 $20 \quad 3 \quad 2 \quad = 14$
8 $20 \quad 3 \quad 2 \quad = 34$
9 $20 \quad 3 \quad 2 \quad = 20$
10 $20 \quad 3 \quad 2 \quad = 11.5$
11 $20 \quad 3 \quad 2 \quad = 30$

Formulae and variables

The relations you have met in the first half of this chapter have described the connections between pairs of **variables**. For instance, in the relation:

$f = (p - 1)2$

p can have many different values (different numbers of fencing posts), so p is a **variable**. In the same way, f is also a **variable**; the relation is arranged so that you can work out a value of f if you know a value for p, i.e. it is a **formula for f in terms of p**. The relation:

$p = \frac{1}{2}f + 1$

is a **formula for p in terms of f**.

Of course, the numbers involved may be more awkward, and again you'll find your calculator a help. Here is a formula for electricity costs:

$e = 0.05u + 6.25$

where u is the number of units of electricity used and e is the cost of the bill in pounds. Even if you use no electricity (when $u = 0$), with this formula you still have to pay £6.25 (the 'standing charge'). Each unit costs about 5p (£0.05).

> ### *Self-check*
>
> Use the formula for e to do the following.
> 1 Calculate e when $u = 513$.
> 2 Calculate e when $u = 436$.
> 3 Suppose that a unit of electricity now costs 6p and the standing charge is £7.30. Write down a revised formula for e.
> 4 Use your formula to calculate e when $u = 513$.
> 5 A family can afford to spend no more than £32 on their electricity bill. Using the formula in 3, make guesses to find the largest number of units they can use. Give your answer to the nearest 10 units.

ANSWERS

1 31.9 (£31.90). **2** 28.05 (£28.05). **3** $e = 0.06u + 7.3$. **4** 38.08 (£38.08).

5 400 units cost £31.30, 410 units cost £31.90, 420 units cost £32.50, so they can use up to 410 units.

Coordinates and graphs

Activity

Consider the formula:

$y = 2x - 3$

Complete the following table for x and y, c.g.:

when $x = 2, y = 1$
when $x = 3, y = 3$
when $x = 4, y = 5$

and so on.

x	y
2	1
3	
4	
5	
6	
7	

You can write the matching pairs of (x, y) values like this:

(2, 1), (3,3), (4,5).

Note that the **x value is given first**, then the **y value**, as in the general pattern (x, y).

Self-check

1 Write down the remaining three pairs of values from the table above, using brackets as above to show number pairs.
2 Check to see which of these pairs fit the formula:
   $y = 3x + 1$
   (2, 7), (5,16), (9,28), (4,1), (1.5, 5.5), (4, 15), (6,17).

ANSWERS

1 (5, 7), (6, 9), (7, 11).
2 $3 \times 2 + 1 = 7$, so (2,7) fits. In the same way, you'll find that these fit as well:
   (5, 16), (9,28), (1.5, 5.5).

You can **plot** number pairs on a **grid** or **graph** (see Figure 18). The point A has an *x* value of 2 (2 steps **right** from the **origin**) and a *y* value of 1 (1 step **up** from the **origin**). We say that 'the **coordinates** of A are (2,1)', so the point A corresponds to the pair in the table above where $x = 2$ and $y = 1$.

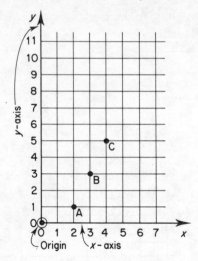

Figure 18. Graph of $y = 2x - 3$

See how:

● the grid is built around the **origin** where the two **axes** cross;
● the **coordinates** of a point tell you the (steps right, steps up) from the origin;
● the **grid lines** are equally spaced and numbered from **zero**.

Note that the coordinates of origin are (0,0).

Activity

Copy Figure 18 on to squared paper.

Self-check

1 What are the coordinates of B?
2 What are the coordinates of C?
3 Plot three other points on the grid to show the remaining number pairs from the table for $y=2x-3$.
4 Plot the points $(8,13)$ and $(9,14)$ on the grid. Do they fit the formula $y = 2x - 3$? How can you be sure you are correct?
5 Complete the following tables for the formula:
$y = 10 - x$

x	y
0	10
2	
4	
6	4
8	
10	

Copy the diagram of the grid in Figure 19.

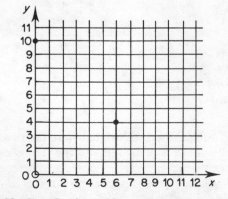

Figure 19. Graph of y = 10 − x

6 Plot points on the diagram for each of the number-pairs in the table.

7 Plot two extra points with *x* coordinates of 1 and 5 which fit the formula.

ANSWERS

1 (3, 3). 2 (4, 5). 3 See Figure 20.

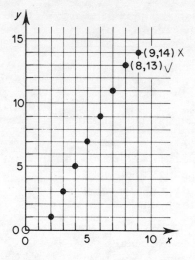

Figure 20.

4 (8, 13) fits because $2 \times 8 - 3 = 13$ and because the point (8, 13) is in line with the other points on the graph.

5

x	*y*
0	10
2	8
4	6
6	4
8	2
10	0

6 and 7 See Figure 21.

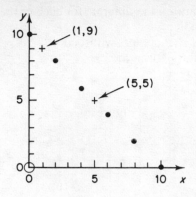

Figure 21. Points on graph of y=10−x

See how you can spot more number pairs which 'fit' a particular formula by.

- plotting some points which you already know will fit;
- joining the points with a line;
- choosing other points on the line;
- reading off their coordinates.

Finally it is always worthwhile **checking** that the new coordinates fit the formula.

Activity

Figure 22 is a copy of Figure 18 with the first two steps above completed. Look along the line where $y = 4$ until you meet the sloping graph line. 'Dot' in the point on the line at this position. Look down and you'll see that the x coordinate of this point is 3.5 or $3\frac{1}{2}$, so the point (3.5, 4) is on the line for $y = 2x - 3$.

Does it fit the formula though?

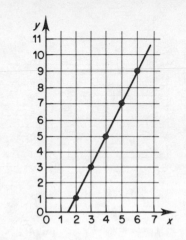

Figure 22. Graph of y =2x − 3

ANSWER

When $x = 3.5$:
$$2x - 3 = 2 \times 3.5 - 3 = 4$$
so y does equal 4, as we expected from the graph line.

Activity

Choose some other points on the graph line in Figure 22. Check, as above, that the coordinates of these points are number pairs which fit the formula:
$$y = 2x - 3$$

You can plot graphs for any of the formulae we've met so far – you'll see a selection in Figure 23. Note that:

● the numbers on the scales (**axes**) go in equal steps (are spaced **uniformly**);
● the spacing of the numbers in the axes is adjusted to fit the numbers in the results tables;
● you can read off further results from the graph lines.

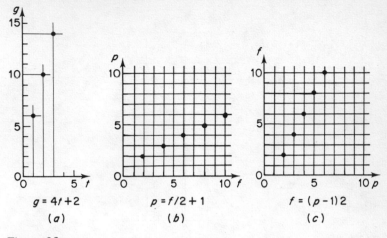

Figure 23.

Negative and positive numbers

Figure 24 shows a thermometer marked in degrees Celsius (°C), sometimes called centigrade. You are probably used to this temperature scale from TV weather forecasts.

- 0°C is freezing.
- 25°C is the temperature of a warm summer's day.
- It rarely gets above 30°C in Britain.

The temperature can fall below freezing point, of course. To describe these temperatures we use **negative** numbers, below zero. Thus ⁻7°C stands for 7 degrees below zero, i.e. 32 degrees below the summer temperature of 25°C. The ⁻ sign stands for **negative**. The thermometer is showing ⁻7°C. Sometimes you'll see ⁻7° written as −7°, but as this can cause confusion with subtracting, we'll write it with the negative sign at the top.

In the same way, when you need to avoid confusion we will use ⁺ to stand for **positive**, though often it can be omitted, as positive numbers behave in the same way as ordinary counting numbers.

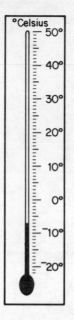

Figure 24. Thermometer showing degrees Celsius

Look at the table below showing midday temperatures in degrees Celsius on 28 January 1984 in different cities in Europe. If you had flown from London to Helsinki the temperature would have dropped from 8°C to ⁻5°C – that is, by 13 degrees altogether. In the opposite direction it would have risen by 13 degrees, of course.

City	Temperature
Frankfurt	2°C
Helsinki	⁻5°C
London	8°C
Oslo	⁻8°C

Self-check

How did the temperature change on 28 January 1984 after the following flights?
1 London to Helsinki.
2 Helsinki to Oslo.
3 Oslo to Frankfurt.

ANSWERS

1 Down 13°. 2 Down 3°. 3 Up 10°.

Figure 25 shows these flights and the temperature changes.

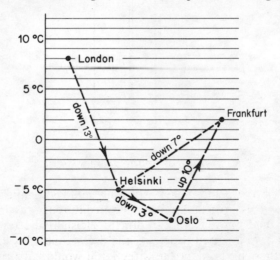

Figure 25. Temperature changes between cities on 28 January 1984

Suppose the temperature in Oslo fell by 2°C. The temperature there would then be ⁻10°C, 2 degrees below ⁻8°C.

Self-check

Write down the new temperature at:
1 Helsinki after a fall of 5°C;

  2 Frankfurt after a fall of 3°C;
  3 London after a rise of 2°C.

ANSWERS

1 ⁻10°C. **2** ⁻1°C. **3** 10°C.

- You can see how 'going down' corresponds to 'going in a **negative direction**'.
- 'going up' corresponds to 'going in a **positive direction**'.

Extending axes of graphs

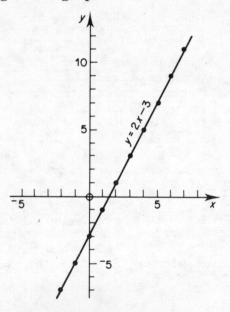

Figure 26. Graph of y = 2x − 3

Here is the table for y=2x−3 again, though re-written upside down.

x	y
7	11
6	9
5	7
4	5
3	3
2	1
1	‑1
0	‑3
‑1	‑5
‑2	‑7

See how the sequence of x values is 7, 6, 5, 4, 3, 2..., going down 1 each time. You can extend this below zero as ...1, 0, ‑1, ‑2, etc.

In the same way the sequence of y values is 11, 9, 7, 5, 3, 1, ‑1, ‑3, ‑5, ‑7..., going down 2 each time.

You can see what the graph looks like in Figure 26. See how the x and y axes are extended to the left of and below the origin to show negative values.

Now return to the formula:

$$y = 2x - 3$$

You can see from the table that when $x = {}^-1$, $y = {}^-5$. You can also **calculate** it like this:

$$2 \times {}^-1 - 3 = {}^-2 - 3 = {}^-5$$

You can see how subtracting 3 takes you further down, from ‑2 to ‑5. You can also see how $2 \times {}^-1$ is really 2 steps of '1 down', giving ‑2.

In the same way, when $x = {}^-2$:

$$y = 2 \times {}^-2 - 3 = {}^-4 - 3 = {}^-7$$

Self-check

Copy and complete the following table using these formulae:

$$y = 3x + 1$$
$$z = x - 2$$
$$w = 3(x - 2)$$

x	6	5	4	3	2	1	0	⁻1	⁻2	⁻3
y	19			10					⁻2	
z						0	⁻1	⁻2		
w		9								⁻15

ANSWER

x	6	5	4	3	2	1	0	⁻1	⁻2	⁻3
y	19	16	13	10	7	4	1	⁻2	⁻5	⁻8
z	4	3	2	1	0	⁻1	⁻2	⁻3	⁻4	⁻5
w	12	9	6	3	0	⁻3	⁻6	⁻9	⁻12	⁻15

Self-check

Look back to the table on page 52 with the formula:
$$y = 10 - x$$
Extend the table with larger and smaller x values, as follows.

x	⁻6	⁻4	⁻2	0	2	4	6	8	10	12	14	16
y				10	8	6	4	2	0			

ANSWER

x	⁻6	⁻4	⁻2	0	2	4	6	8	10	12	14	16
y	16	14	12	10	8	6	4	2	0	⁻2	⁻4	⁻6

You can see how these results show that:

- $10 - 12 = {}^-2$
- $10 - 14 = {}^-4$
- $10 - 16 = {}^-6$
  etc.

and how:

- $10 - {}^-2 = 12$
- $10 - {}^-4 = 14$
- $10 - {}^-6 = 16$

And don't forget, from Chapter 1, that you can always convert subtraction problems into addition ones, using the 'adding back' idea. Just as you can find $5.00 - 4.73$ by saying 'What do I add back to 4.73 to make 5.00?', so you can find $10 - {}^-6$ by saying 'What do I add back to $^-6$ to make 10?' In other words, how many 'steps up' are there from $^-6$ to 10?

This explains why:

$10 - {}^-6 = 16$

and

$10 - {}^-4 = 14$

etc.

You'll see the graph of the formula in Figure 27.

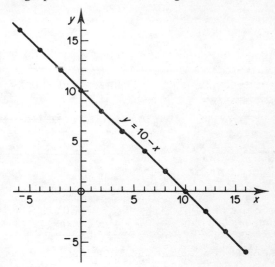

Figure 27. Graph of $y = 10 - x$

Adding and subtracting negative numbers

So far we have looked at simple formulae to help us see how negative numbers behave. We have thought of increases and decreases in temperature or moves up and down a scale.

Let's look at some of these results again. From the self-check on page 57 we can re-write question **1** as:

$8 - 13 = {}^-5$

i.e. from 8° reduce the temperature by 13° to give ⁻5°, or as:

$8 + {}^-13 = {}^-5$

i.e. from 8°, add on a change of ⁻13° to give ⁻5°.

2 can be written as:

$^-5 - \quad 3 = {}^-8$

or

$^-5 + \quad {}^-3 = {}^-8$

3 can be written as:

$^-8 + 10 = \quad 2$

or

$^-8 + {}^+10 = {}^+2$

From the self-check on page 60 we see that:

$10 - {}^-2 = 12$

and

$10 + \quad 2 = 12$

$10 - {}^-6 = 16$

$10 + \quad 6 = 16$, etc.

You'll probably notice some general patterns in the results. Again we can use letters to show these patterns as before, using a and b to stand for any number we wish:

$a + {}^-b = a - b$ (e.g. $6 + {}^-2 = 6 - 2$; $^-3 + {}^-5 = {}^-3 - 5$)

and

$a - {}^-b = a + b$ (e.g. $10 - {}^-3 = 10 + 3$; $^-8 - {}^-2 = {}^-8 + 2$)

Self-check

Find the values of the following.

  1 $4 - \quad 6$

  2 $4 + {}^-7$

  3 $^-2 - \quad 6$

  4 $^-2 + {}^-7$

  5 $8 + {}^-5$

  6 $6 - \quad 9$

  7 $9 + {}^-7$

  8 $9 - {}^-7$

  9 $^-3 + {}^-4$

10 $^-1 - {}^-5$

11 $5 - \quad 7$

12 $^-3 - {}^-7$

|| **13** $^-8 - ^-3$
|| **14** $^-8 - \ \ 3$

ANSWERS

1 $^-2$. **2** $^-3$. **3** $^-8$. **4** $^-9$. **5** 3. **6** $^-3$. **7** 2. **8** 16. **9** $^-7$. **10** 4. **11** $^-2$.
12 4. **13** $^-5$. **14** $^-11$.

Negative numbers and your calculator

If your calculator has a $+/-$ key you will be able to carry out calculations involving negative numbers directly. If your calculator does not have a $+/-$ key it may not show negative numbers. In this case you'll have to re-think some calculations and insert the $^-$ sign yourself where required. You will find that re-arranging the questions using the general results on page 62 can make things clearer. For example:

  $9 - \ ^-7$ becomes $9 + 7$
  $= 16$

From your answers to the last self-check you may have noticed that pairs of calculations like $4 - 6$ and $6 - 4$, $3 - 8$ and $8 - 3$ give similar-sized answers, except that one answer is positive and the other negative. In general:

- $a - b = \ ^-(b - a)$

for instance:

- $4 - 6 = \ ^-2$ and $^-(6 - 4) = \ ^-(2) = \ ^-2$

Thus if you want to find the value of something like $3.7 - 8.15$, you say that $3.7 - 8.15 = \ ^-(8.15 - 3.7)$, and then use your calculator.

  Activity

  Use your calculator to find the values of the calculations in
  the previous self-check.

Looking at temperature again

Although we introduced negative numbers through temperature in degrees Celsius, many people are more used to temperatures in degrees Fahrenheit. Here is an approximate formula for converting degrees Celsius (c) into degrees Fahrenheit (f):

$f = 2c + 30$

Self-check

Complete this table for number pairs of c and f, using the formula:

$f = 2c + 30$

c	40	25	10	0	⁻10	⁻25	⁻40
f							

ANSWER

c	40	25	10	0	⁻10	⁻25	⁻40
f	110	80	50	30	10	⁻20	⁻50

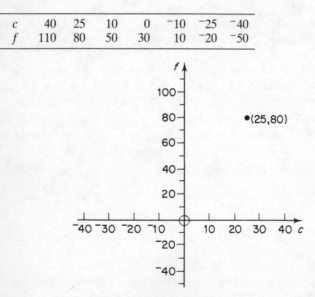

Figure 28. Grid for f = 2c + 30

You can see that c values run from ⁻40 to 40, while f values run from ⁻50 to 110, so your graph will have to show positive and negative values of both c and f, with the numbers spaced uniformly along both axes. The origin will be near the middle of your graph paper, with negative values to the left of it and below it (see Figure 28). You'll also see that the c-axis runs from left to right and the f-axis from bottom to top. (If you are drawing your graph on A4 paper, a possible spacing of the numbers on the axes is $1\,\text{cm} = 5\,°\text{C}$ and $1\,\text{cm} = 10\,°\text{F}$.)

> *Activity*
>
> Copy the axes on to a sheet of graph paper and label them as in Figure 28. Now plot points on your graph of each of the number pairs in the table (the point (25,80) is shown in Figure 28).

Because you can have any temperature you like, so you can also have any point you like on the graph, as long as it lines up with the points you've plotted already. You can show this by joining the points you've plotted with a straight line (see Figure 29). You can check any point on the line by reading off its c and f values and seeing if they fit the formula:

$$f = 2c + 30$$

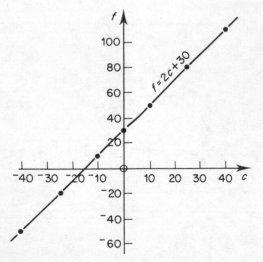

Figure 29

If you want to carry out accurate conversions you can use the exact formula:

$f = 1.8c + 32$

Review

1 Complete the following table from the formula:

$d = 0.8p + 6.1$

p	0	50	75	100	150
d					

2 A person keeps a check on his weight over a 6-week period. At the end of each week he notes how much he has lost or gained, as shown in the table.

Week	1	2	3	4	5	6
Weight change	2 kg Gain	3 kg Loss	4 kg Loss	2 kg Gain	1 kg Gain	4 kg Loss

If his final weight is now 56 kg, what weight was he to start with?

3 Complete the following table for:

$h = 20 - 3m$

m	10	8	6	4	2	0	⁻2	⁻4
h								

4 Write down the values of:

a $9 + {}^-8$

b $9 + {}^-11$

c $12 - 3$

d $12 - {}^-3$

3 | Introducing angles, parallel lines and symmetry

You will need a protractor and tracing paper for this chapter.

Topics covered

- Angles.
- Degrees.
- Angle properties involving parallel lines.
- Simple angle formulae and calculations.
- Types of triangles and quadrilaterals.
- Line symmetry.
- Rotation symmetry.
- Regular polygons.
- Polygons.

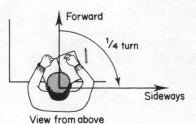

Figure 30.

Angles – measuring in degrees

Angles describe **changes in direction**.

Look forwards (as in Figure 30). Now turn your head to look

sideways. Your head will have turned through a quarter ($\frac{1}{4}$) turn, i.e. a **right-angle**. Four right-angle turns will bring you back to your original direction. You'll have turned through a **complete** or **whole turn**.

For more accurate measuring, whole turns are divided into 360 degrees (written 360°), so a right angle measures:

$\frac{1}{4} \times 360 = 90°$ (see Figure 31).

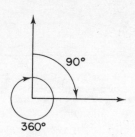

Figure 31.

Self-check

What angles, in degrees, are the same as the following.

1 $\frac{1}{2}$ of a whole turn?
2 $\frac{1}{3}$ of a whole turn?
3 $\frac{1}{5}$ of a whole turn?
4 $\frac{2}{5}$ of a whole turn?
5 $\frac{1}{3}$ of a right angle?
6 $\frac{1}{5}$ of a right angle?

ANSWERS

1 180°. **2** 120°. **3** 72°. **4** 144°. **5** 30°. **6** 18°.

The protractor

Angles are measured with a **protractor**.

Activity

Place your protractor over the angle in Figure 32, as shown. Read off the angle measurement in degrees. Be careful to choose the correct scale on your protractor – the one which has its '0' over one of the direction lines.

This angle measures 34°. Check that you can measure it.

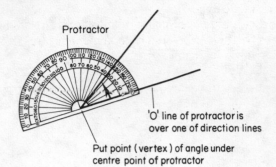

Figure 32. The protractor

Self-check

Measure the angles in Figure 33.

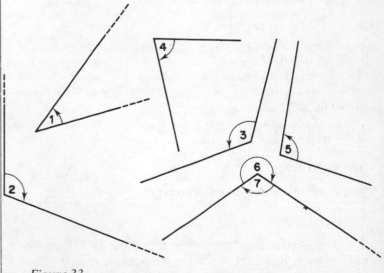

Figure 33.

ANSWERS

1 = 38°. **2** = 112°. **3** = 124°. **4** = 76°. **5** = 99°. **6** = 248°. **7** = 112°.

- Angles like **1** and **4** (less than 90°) are called **acute**.
- Angles like **2**, **3**, **5** and **7** (between 90° and 180°) are called **obtuse**.
- Angles like **6** (between 180° and 360°) are called **reflex**.

You can measure reflex angles with your protractor by finding the matching smaller angle and subtracting from 360°. Thus to measure **6**, measure angle **7** with your protractor, then subtract this from 360°.

Degrees and minutes

For very accurate measuring you may have to deal with angles which include fractions of a degree. You can use decimals or fractions – for example $22\frac{1}{2}°$ or 22.5° – or you can use **minutes**, where 60 minutes (written 60') equals 1 degree.

Parallel lines and connections between angles

Activity

You will need to cut out a cardboard triangle before you start this section. You are going to draw round it on a sheet of plain paper several times over, so don't make the triangle too large or too small – side lengths between 4 cm and 7 cm will be ideal.

Label the angles of your triangle *a*, *b* and *c* and mark the side between *b* and *c* (as in Figure 34).

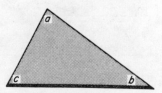

Figure 34.

Now take a sheet of plain paper, draw a line on it near the bottom and place your triangle on the sheet, with the marked edge on the line (see Figure 35). Build up a pattern of triangles by moving your cardboard triangle and repeatedly drawing around it. See how the marked edge is always the bottom edge. Make sure there are no gaps between the triangles.

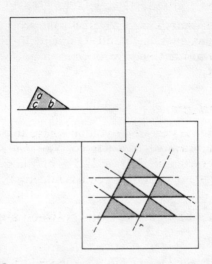

Figure 35.

You'll have produced a grid of three sets of parallel lines, made from the three edges of your triangles.

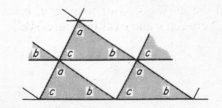

Figure 36.

Now label with an *a* all the angles in the pattern which are in the same position as *a* on your cardboard triangle. Do the same with the drawn angles in positions *b* and *c* (see Figure 36).

Corresponding angles on a parallel line are equal

All the angles you marked *a* are equal to each other. They are called **corresponding angles** because they are in matching or 'corresponding' positions in the diagram. In the same way all the angles you marked *b* form another set of corresponding angles, as do all the angles you marked *c*.

Now take your cardboard triangle and rotate it so that the marked edge is uppermost. You'll find it fits into the gaps in Figure 36. This means that there are many more angles in the diagram which are the same size as *a*, *b* and *c*. Mark them in now (see Figure 37).

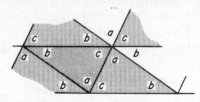

Figure 37.

Vertically opposite angles are equal

At each crossover point you'll find **vertically opposite** pairs of angles of the same size (see Figure 38).

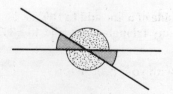

Figure 38. Vertically opposite angles

Alternate angles on parallel lines are equal

Looking at Figure 37 you can see many pairs of equal angles in a 'Z' or 'N' position (see Figure 39). These pairs of equal angles are called **alternate angles**.

(Note that the arrows are used to show that pairs of lines are parallel.)

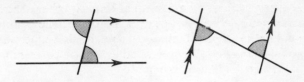

Figure 39. Alternate angles

Angles on a line and in a triangle

Look at any of the crossover points. You'll see that the angles of your cardboard triangle (a, b and c) equal the angles on one side of a line (see Figure 40). These in turn make up half a complete turn ($=180°$). This means that:

$a + b + c = 180°$

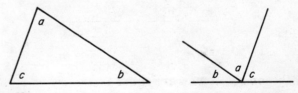

Figure 40.

Thus:

- **angles on one side of a line add to 180°** and
- the **angles of any triangle must add to 180°**, whatever shape the triangle is.

Check this now with your protractor.

Interior angles between parallel lines

Finally look at pairs of angles inside parallel lines (see Figure 41). Such pairs are called **interior angles**. Again, because:

$a + b + c = 180°$

and because in each case pairs of the interior angles add to $a + b + c$, **interior angles between parallel lines add to 180°**.

Figure 41. Interior angles add to 180°

Angle calculations

To summarize:

- pairs of corresponding, vertically opposite or alternate angles are equal;
- pairs of interior angles, angles in a triangle and angles on one side of a straight line add to 180°.

You can use these results to **calculate** unknown angles in shapes or diagrams. Often such sketch diagrams will not be drawn with the angles exactly the correct size, so you cannot find the size of an unknown angle by measuring it. Instead you have to 'work back' from information you are told (**given** information) and use the results above to calculate the required angle sizes. Here are some examples.

1 In Figure 42, x and 104° are interior angles, so:

$$x + 104° = 180°$$
$$x = 76°$$

(because $76 + 104 = 180$).

2 In Figure 42, y and 104° are vertically opposite, so:

$$y = 104°$$

3 Additionally, in Figure 42, z corresponds to 104°, so:

$$z = 104°$$

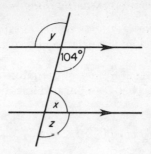

Figure 42.

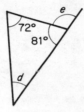

Figure 43.

4 The three angles inside the triangle in Figure 43 add to 180°, so:

$d = 27°$

5 Additionally in Figure 43, because they are on a straight line:

$e + 81° = 180°$

$e = 99°$

When more than one angle in a diagram is marked with the same letter or symbol, it means those angles are equal. Thus in Figure 44:

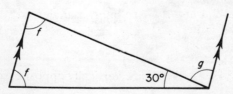

Figure 44.

$$f + f + 30° = 180°$$
$$2f + 30° = 180°$$
$$2f = 150°$$
$$f = 75°$$

f and g are equal (alternate), so $g = 75°$ as well.

Self-check

Look at Figure 45. In each case, using the information in the diagrams, **calculate** the sizes of angles marked with small letters.

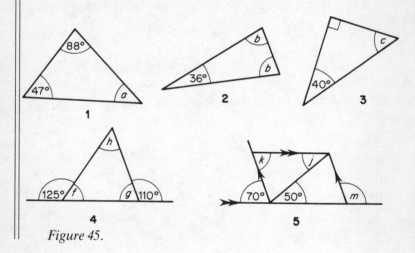

Figure 45.

ANSWERS

1 $a + 135° = 180°$, so $a = 45°$. **2** $2b = 144°$, so $b = 72°$. **3** $c + 40° = 90°$, so $c = 50°$. **4** $f = 55°$, $g = 70°$, so $h = 55°$. **5** $k = 70°$ (alt.), $j = 50°$ (alt.), $m + 70° = 180°$, so $m = 110°$.

Types of triangles

You can classify triangles according to their angles.

- **acute-angled** triangles have all angles less than 90°.
- **obtuse-angled** triangles have one angle greater than 90°.
- **right-angled** triangles have one angle equal to 90°. (Note that

a right angle (90°) is often shown by a small square.)

- Some triangles have all sides and all angles of different sizes. These are **scalene** triangles.
- **Isosceles** triangles have two sides equal and two angles equal. (Equal sides often are shown by small cross marks.)
- **Equilateral** triangles have all sides equal and all angles equal. Because the angles add up to 180°, each angle is 180° ÷ 3 = 60°.

Self-check

Look at the triangles in Figure 46. Describe each triangle as fully as you can, using the classifications above.

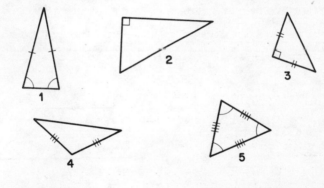

Figure 46.

ANSWERS

1 Acute-angled isosceles. **2** Right-angled scalene. **3** Right-angled isosceles. **4** Obtuse-angled isosceles. **5** Equilateral.

Types of quadrilateral

Triangles are three-sided **plane** (meaning flat) shapes, while quadrilaterals are four-sided plane shapes.

Because every quadrilateral can be cut along a diagonal to form two triangles (see Figure 47), the four corner angles of every quadrilateral must add up to 2 × 180 = 360°.

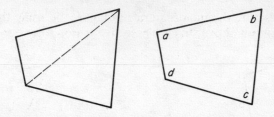

Figure 47. a + b + c + d = *360°*

You can classify quadrilaterals as follows (see Figure 48).

- **Trapezium** – one pair of opposite sides parallel.
- **Parallelogram** – both pairs of opposite sides parallel or equal, and both pairs of opposite angles equal.

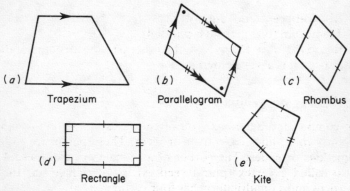

Figure 48.

Special types of parallelogram

- **Rhombus** – all sides equal (Figure 48(*c*)).
- **Rectangle** – all angles equal 90° (Figure 48(*d*)).
- **Square** – all sides equal and all angles 90°.
- **Kite** – adjacent (next door) pairs of sides equal.

Self-check

Describe the quadrilaterals in Figure 49, using the classifications above. In each case give reasons for your answer.

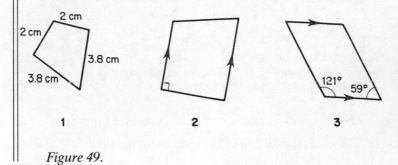

Figure 49.

ANSWERS

1 Kite (adjacent sides equal).
2 Trapezium (one pair sides parallel).
3 Because 121° + 59° = 180°, the other pair of sides are parallel also, so it is a parallelogram.

Labelling diagrams

In complicated diagrams, you often use capital letters to label points where lines cross over or meet. These points are called **junctions** or **nodes**. The corner of a triangle or quadrilateral is also called a **vertex** (plural **vertices**), so a triangle has three vertices and a quadrilateral has four vertices.

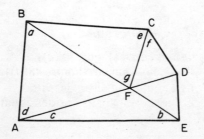

Figure 50.

In Figure 50, AFE is a triangle, as is FDE, but BFE is not. BCDF is a quadrilateral, but AFDC is not. EFA is the same triangle as AFE, of course.

You can also use capital letters to describe angles. Imagine that you are standing at B looking towards A (Figure 50) and turn anti-clockwise to face F. You have turned through angle ABF, written ∠ABF, so ∠ABF stands for the angle marked *a*. You could also describe it as ∠FBA. In the same way ∠BEA stands for the angle marked *b*, and you could also describe *b* as ∠AEB, ∠AEF or ∠FEA.

Self-check

1 Which 'small letter' angles in Figure 50 are the same as ∠BFC, ∠BCF and ∠BAF?
2 Describe angles *c*, *f* and *g* using capital letters.

ANSWERS

1 *g*, *e*, *d*.
2 ∠FAE or ∠DAE or ∠EAF or ∠EAD; ∠FCD or ∠DCF; ∠CFB or ∠BFC.

Review

1 What angle in degrees is the same as $\frac{5}{8}$ of a complete turn?
2 A triangle has angles of 61.4° and 39.8°. What is the size of the third angle, in degrees?

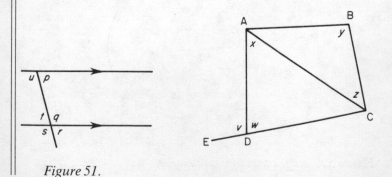

Figure 51.

3 What word describes a triangle with a pair of equal angles?

4 A rhombus has one angle of 102°. What are the sizes of the other angles?

5 A trapezium has two angles of 36° and 74°. What are the sizes of the other angles?

6 In Figure 51, pick out a pair of alternate angles.

7 In Figure 51, which small letter stands for the same angle as ∠ABC?

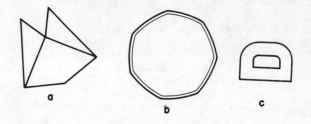

a
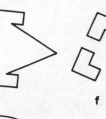
b

c

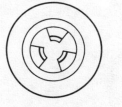
d

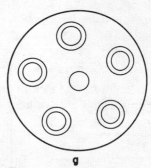
e

f

g

Figure 52. Shapes with line symmetry

Line symmetry

Look at Figure 52. Imagine cutting out one of the shapes and folding it in half, so that one half **fits exactly** over the other half (see Figure 53). Where would you fold each diagram? Sometimes there is only one fold line, in other shapes there are two, three or more.

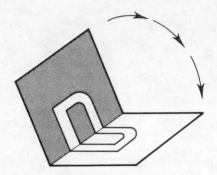

Figure 53.

Activity

1 Trace each shape and fold in half to check if you were correct.
2 Beside each tracing, write down the number of fold lines.

ANSWERS

a 1 line. **b** 7 lines. **c** 1 line. **d** 3 lines. **e** 2 lines. **f** 4 lines. **g** 5 lines (see Figure 54).

Each fold line is called a **line of symmetry** or **mirror line**, and diagrams that have such lines are **symmetrical**.

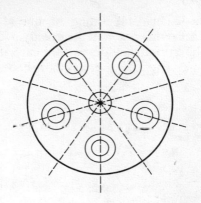

Figure 54.

Activity

In the diagrams in Figure 55 the dotted lines are lines of symmetry, but part of each diagram is missing. Use the symmetry line(s) to complete each diagram. Check by folding or tracing. (There's an example in Figure 55.)

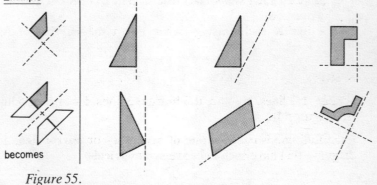

Figure 55.

Congruent shapes

Any two shapes which are the same shape and size as each other are said to be **congruent**. Any symmetrical shape can be cut into two congruent parts by a line of symmetry.

Activity

Mark three points (P, Q and R) on a sheet of paper such that distance PQ = PR. Make sure that the three points are *not* in line.

Join up the three points to form the isosceles triangle PQR. Cut it out and fold it along the symmetry line (that is, so that Q and R are in contact). Label the point S where the fold line crosses QR.

Cut out the two congruent right-angled triangles PQS and PRS. Place the two triangles on a flat surface to make the following shapes:

1 a rectangle;
2 a parallelogram (not rectangle);
3 a kite;
4 another isosceles triangle, different from the original triangle PQR.

Sketch how you made each of the above shapes (see Figure 56).

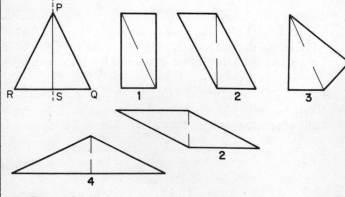

Figure 56.

Cut out two more triangles, each congruent to the original triangles. Fit the four triangles together to make:

5 a rhombus;
6 a kite;
7 a trapezium;
8 a right-angled triangle.

Quadrilaterals and lines of symmetry

You can divide the different quadrilaterals into four sets, depending on the number of lines of symmetry they have.

- Squares have **four** lines of symmetry.
- Rectangles and rhombuses each have **two** lines of symmetry.
- Kites and some trapeziums have **one** line of symmetry.
- Other quadrilaterals (including most trapeziums and parallelograms) have **no** lines of symmetry.

Rotation symmetry

Even though parallelograms in general have no symmetry lines (try folding a parallelogram to find its symmetry line), they have **rotation symmetry**.

Activity

Draw a parallelogram EFGH. Join the diagonals EG and FH and mark the **intersection** (crossover) point. Label it M. Cut out the parallelogram, place it on another sheet of paper and draw round its outline. Now turn (**rotate**) the cutout, keeping M fixed, as in Figure 57. When you've **rotated** – that is, turned – the parallelogram through 180°, so that E is in G's original place, etc., the parallelogram will occupy the same outline as it did to start with.

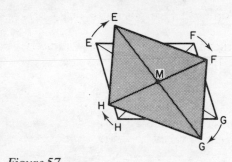

Figure 57.

The parallelogram EFGH has **rotation symmetry of order 2**. The order simply tells you the number of different positions into which you can rotate the shape to fit over the outline. In general:

- a square has rotation symmetry of **order 4**;
- a rectangle has rotation symmetry of **order 2**;
- an equilateral triangle has rotation symmetry of **order 3**.

Activity

1 Trace the outlines of the shapes in Figure 58 on to a sheet of paper. Cut out another tracing of each shape and rotate the tracing about the dot. For each shape, count how many positions it can be rotated to fit over the outline. Use your results to state the order of rotation symmetry for each shape.

2 Look back to Figure 42. What is the order of notation symmetry for each shape?

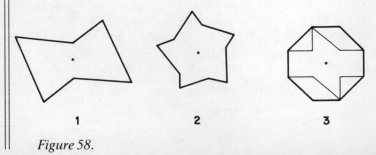

Figure 58.

1 Two positions, order 2. Five positions, order 5. Two positions, order 2.
Note that none of the diagrams have lines of symmetry.
2 b, 7; d, 3; e, 2; f, 4; g, 5.

Polygons

Shapes like triangles or quadrilaterals are particular examples of a larger set of plane shapes called **polygons** – a triangle is a three-sided polygon, a quadrilateral is a four-sided polygon, etc.

Polygons which have all their sides the same length *and* all their angles the same size (like squares or equilateral triangles) are called **regular polygons**.

All polygons have straight edges.

- 5-sided polygons are called **pentagons**.
- 6-sided polygons are called **hexagons**.
- 7-sided polygons are called **heptagons**.
- 8-sided polygons are called **octagons**.
- 9-sided polygons are called **nonagons**.
- 10-sided polygons are called **decagons**.

Self-check

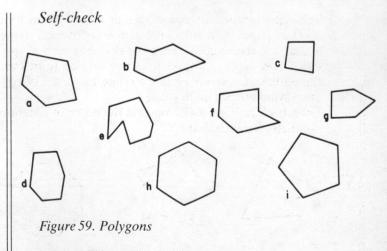

Figure 59. Polygons

Look at Figure 59.

1 Which of these shapes are hexagons?
2 Which of these shapes are pentagons?
3 Measure the angles and side lengths of the polygons, then say which are regular.

ANSWERS

1 Hexagons are **b, d, f, h**.   2 Pentagons are **a, g, i**.
3 The only regular polygons are **h** and **i**.

● Shapes like **a,c,d**, etc. in Figure 59, with all the vertices pointing outwards, are **convex**.
● Shapes like **b,e** in Figure 59, with one or more vertices pointing inwards, are **concave**.

Figure 59 **i** shows a regular pentagon. By tracing the pentagon and rotating it about the dot in the centre (the **centre of rotation**) you can see that it has rotation symmetry of order 5, just as the hexagon **h** has rotation symmetry of order 6.

Drawing a regular polygon

You can draw a regular polygon 'from scratch' using a ruler and protractor (see Figure 60).

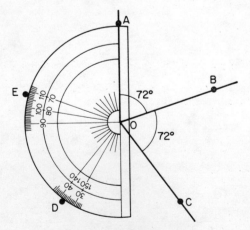

Figure 60. Drawing a rectangular pentagon

Mark a point labelled O in the middle of a sheet of paper, rule a line through it and use your protractor to mark dots around the edge of your protractor, every 72° (A,B,C,D and E). Now join up AB, BC, CD, DE, EA to make a regular pentagon. You can vary the size of the pentagon by measuring different distances from O to the corners (vertices) of your pentagon.

The centre angles for a regular pentagon are 72° because 360° ÷ 5 = 72°. In the same way the centre angle for a regular hexagon is 60° because 360° ÷ 6 = 60°.

Review

1 A shape has rotation symmetry of order 2. How many lines of symmetry can it have?
2 A regular polygon has nine sides. What are the sizes of:
 a its centre angle: and
 b its interior angles?
3 A quadrilateral has all four sides equal and two lines of symmetry. What is it called?
4 What is a concave polygon?

4 | Whole numbers, powers and equations

You will need a calculator for parts of this chapter.

Topics covered

- Prime, rectangle and square numbers.
- Multiples and factors.
- Sets of numbers, shapes, etc.
- Simple set language.
- Powers and indices.
- Brackets.
- Equivalent expressions.
- Factorizing and expanding.
- Solving simple equations by repeated guesses.

Rectangle, square and prime numbers

You can write most whole numbers as a **product** of other whole numbers (the product of two numbers is the result of multiplying them together). For instance, the product of 2 and 6 is 12 because:

$2 \times 6 = 12$

12 is also the product of 3 and 4 because:

$3 \times 4 = 12$

$49 = 7 \times 7$, so 49 is the product of 7 and 7

$51 = 3 \times 17$, so 51 is the product of 3 and 17

You can show this using **rectangle dot patterns** (see Figure 61). In some cases (as with 12 and 36) there are several different rectangle dot patterns. One of these is a **square** (6×6), so 36 is called a **square number**. 49 is also a square number. 12 and 51 are **rectangle numbers**.

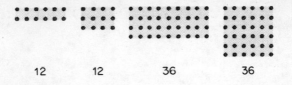

12   12   36   36

Figure 61. Rectangle dot patterns

Activity

Use your calculator if you need help in this activity.

Make a list of the whole numbers from 5 to 30 inclusive. Put a circle round any numbers which have rectangle dot patterns. On the same list put a square round any square number.

You should find that you have eighteen numbers with circles round them, and three of these have squares as well. That means there are three **square** numbers and fifteen more **rectangle** numbers between 5 and 30 inclusive.

The remaining eight numbers (5, 7, 11, 13, 17, 19, 23 and 29) have no rectangle or square dot patterns. Such numbers are called **prime numbers**.

Self-check

1 List the rectangle numbers between 31 and 50 inclusive.
2 List the square numbers betweeen 31 and 50 inclusive.
3 List the prime numbers between 31 and 50 inclusive.

ANSWERS

1 32, 33, 34, 35, 38, 39, 40, 42, 44, 45, 46, 48, 50.
2 36, 49.
3 31, 37, 41, 43, 47.

Factors

Think of the collection of pairs of whole numbers which you can multiply to give 16. Each of these numbers is a **factor** of 16.

- 2 and 8 are factors of 16 because $2 \times 8 = 16$
- 4 is a factor of 16 because $4 \times 4 = 16$
- 1 and 16 are factors of 16 because $1 \times 16 = 16$

Thus 16 has five factors altogether: 1, 2, 4, 8 and 16. In the same way 12 has six factors: 1, 2, 3, 4, 6 and 12. 51 has four factors: 1, 3, 17 and 51.

> ### Self-check
>
> **1** List the factors of 10, 18, 21, 23 and 25.
> **2** List the whole numbers between 1 and 20 inclusive which have exactly four factors.
> **3** How many factors does a prime number have?

ANSWERS

1 1, 2, 5, 10; 1, 2, 3, 6, 9, 18; 1, 3, 7, 21; 1, 23; 1, 5, 25.
2 6 – 1, 2, 3, 6; 8 – 1, 2, 4, 8; 10 – 1, 2, 5, 10; 14 – 1, 2, 7, 14; 15 – 1, 3, 5, 15.
3 Two.

You'll probably have realized that each prime number has just two factors, itself and 1. Other whole numbers will be either rectangle or square numbers. The number 1 counts as a square number ($1 \times 1 = 1$), *not* a prime number; it only has one factor.

Finding factors

You can use your calculator to help find factors of large numbers, Suppose, for instance, you want to find all the factors of 442. You know that 1 and 442 are factors, but are there any others? Remember you're looking for a pair of whole numbers which multiply to give 442. On your calculator, $442 \div 2 = 221$. If you calculate 221×2 you arrive back at 442, so 2 and 221 are factors of 442. You may have spotted that 2 is a factor, as 442 is an even number. Is 3 a factor? $442 \div 3 = 147.33$, so 3 is not a factor. What about 4? $442 \div 4 = 110.5$, so 4 is not a factor, and so on.

It isn't until you reach $442 \div 13 = 34$ that you find two more factors – 13 and 34. Continue further and you find $442 \div 17 =$

26, so 17 and 26 are factors. You don't find factors again until you try 442 ÷ 26 = 17 – but you've found these factors already.

See how your list of factors is growing from each end:

1, 2, 13, 17, 26 and 442, 221, 34, 26

Because you are beginning to find factors for the second time round, you know your list is complete, so the factors of 442 are 1, 2, 13, 17, 26, 34, 221 and 442.

Self-check

1 Find all the factors of 648.
2 Find all the factors of 256.
3 Find all the factors of 317.
4 Say whether each of the numbers in **1–3** is square, rectangle or prime.

ANSWERS

1 1, 2, 3, 4, 6, 8, 9, 12, 18, 24, 27, 36, 54, 72, 81, 108, 162, 216, 324, 648; rectangle.
2 1, 2, 4, 8, 16, 32, 64, 128, 256; square.
3 1, 317; prime.

Multiples

What have 3, 18, 36, 39, 9, 15, 102 and 300 got in common? Try these on your calculator:

- 3 × 1 =
- 3 × 6 =
- 3 × 13 =
- 3 × 3 =
- 3 × 34 =

and so on.

Now can you see it? You can obtain them all by multiplying 3 by different whole numbers; 3, 18, 36, 39, 9, 15, 102 and 300 are all **multiples of 3**. Similarly, 25, 55, 60, 30, 45, 500, etc., are all **multiples of 5**.

Put in order, the complete list of:

- multiples of 2 form this sequence:
    2, 4, 6, 8, 10, 12, 14, 16, 18, etc.
- multiples of 3 form this sequence:
    3, 6, 9, 12, 15, 18, 21, 24, 27, etc.

> ## Self-check
>
> **1** List the multiples of 13 below 100.
> **2** List the multiples of 3 below 100 which are also multiples of 4.

ANSWERS

1 13, 26, 39, 52, 65, 78, 91.
2 12, 24, 36, 48, 60, 72, 84, 96 – all multiples of 12.

Sets and subsets

All the lists of numbers you have met are clearly defined, i.e. it's clear whether a number belongs to any particular list or not.
    Such a list is called a **set**.

- Some sets are **infinite** (go on for ever) like the set of multiples of 3 or the set of all parallelograms.
- Other sets are **finite** (come to an end) like the set of factors of 30 or the set of people you have talked to today.
- The **members** of a set are also called **elements** – 8 is an element (or member) of the set of factors of 16.

Symbols used in sets

You may come across these symbols.

- Curly brackets { } are used to mean 'the set'.
- $\in$ means 'is an element of'.
- $\notin$ means 'is not an element of'.
- = means 'is the same as' or 'stands for', like an ordinary equals sign.

Thus:
    $A = \{$factors of 16$\}$
means 'A stands for the set of factors of 16, i.e. 1, 2, 4, 8 and 16';

$9 \notin A$

means '9 is not an element of the set A';

$9 \in \{\text{multiples of } 3\}$

means '9 is an element of the set of multiples of 3'.

Subsets

Sometimes one set is completely contained within another set. For example if:

$B = \{\text{factors of } 32\} = 1, 2, 4, 8, 16, 32$

then A is a **subset** of B.

In symbols:

$A \subset B$

where $\subset$ is short for 'is a subset of'. Of course it doesn't work the other way round – B is not a subset of A, because 32 is a member of B only. In short:

$B \not\subset A$

You can show this on a **Venn diagram** (see Figure 62).

- A has five elements, written as:
  $n(A) = 5$
- B has six elements, written as:
  $n(B) = 6$

where $n(A)$ is short for 'the number of elements in set A'.

Because of the extra element (32) in B, sets A and B are not the same. In symbols this is written:

$A \neq B$

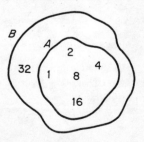

Figure 62. Venn diagram showing factors of 8 and of 16

Self-check

In these questions $F = \{$multiples of 5 below 50$\}$, $G = \{$multiples of 10 below 50$\}$ and $P = \{$factors of 30$\}$.
  What do these statements mean?
1 $15 \in F$
2 $P \not\subset F$
What are the values of the following?
3 $n(P)$
4 List the members of *F* which are also in *P*.

ANSWERS

1 15 is an element of the set of multiples of 5 below 50.
2 The set of factors of 30 are not all members of the set of multiples of 5 below 50.
3 $n(P) = 8$ (30 has eight factors).
4 $\{5, 10, 15, 30\}$.

Answers to questions like **3** above can be seen at a glance if you can show the different sets and their elements in Venn diagrams, as in Figure 63.

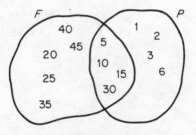

Figure 63. Venn diagram showing factors of 30 and some multiples of 5

Powers and indices

What have these expressions in common?

- $3 \times 3 \times 3 \times 3 \times 3$
- $6 \times 6 \times 6$
- 7×7
- $2.8 \times 2.8 \times 2.8 \times 2.8 \times 2.8$

Each expression shows **repeated multiplying by the same number**. In short, you can write:

- 3^5 instead of $3 \times 3 \times 3 \times 3 \times 3$ (say '3 to the power 5' or just '3 to the 5');
- 7^2 instead of 7×7 (say '7 to the power 2' or just '7 to the 2');
- 6^3 instead of $6 \times 6 \times 6$ (say '6 to the power 3' or just '6 to the 3').

The small raised number is called a **power** or **index**; it tells you how many of the same numbers are being multiplied together. Thus:

- '2 to the 4' means 2^4 which means $2 \times 2 \times 2 \times 2$;
- 3×2^4 means $3 \times 2 \times 2 \times 2 \times 2$;
- $3^2 \times 4^3$ means $3 \times 3 \times 4 \times 4 \times 4$;
- $(7 \times 2)^3$ means $7 \times 2 \times 7 \times 2 \times 7 \times 2$.

Notice that the power only applies to the number immediately to its left, unless it is outside brackets (see above). You'll also find amounts like 3^5, 3^7, 3^4, etc., called 'powers of 3', so the word **power** can refer to either the raised number (index) on its own or to the results of repeated multiplying by a single number.

Evaluating an expression means working it out, i.e. you **evaluate** 3^5 when you find its value:
$$3^5 = 3 \times 3 \times 3 \times 3 \times 3 = 243$$
You can carry out the multiplying in steps, as below, or on your calculator.
$$3^5 = 9 \times 3 \times 3 \times 3$$
$$= 27 \times 3 \times 3$$
$$= 81 \times 3$$
$$= 243$$

In reverse, you can re-write long expressions using powers like this:

- $8 \times 10 \times 10 \times 10 = 8 \times 10^3$
- $6 \times 5 \times 6 \times 5 \times 6 \times 5 = 6 \times 6 \times 6 \times 5 \times 5 \times 5 = 6^3 \times 5^3$

(The order in which you multiply numbers does not matter.)
$$27\,000\,000\,000 = 27 \times 10 \times 10 \times 10 \times 10 \times 10 \times 10 \times 10 \times 10 \times 10$$
$$= 27 \times 10^9$$

You'll find the word **squared** used instead of 'to the power 2' and **cubed** instead of 'to the power 3'. Thus '5 squared' means 5^2 = 25 and '7 cubed' means $7^3 = 343$. The use of squared and cubed is connected with finding areas and volumes of shapes, which in turn are measured in square metres, cubic metres, etc.

Self-check

Re-write the following, using powers as much as possible.
1 $4 \times 5 \times 5 \times 5 \times 5$.
2 $6 \times 7 \times 6 \times 6 \times 6 \times 7$.
Evaluate the following.
3 5^3
4 $6^2 \times 10^3$
5 $7^2 - 5^2$
6 $(4 + 3)^2$

ANSWERS

1 4×5^4. **2** $6^4 \times 7^2$ or $7^2 \times 6^4$. **3** 125. **4** 36 000. **5** 24. **6** 49.

Multiplying powers of the same number

Activity

Copy out these statements and fill in the missing powers in the boxes.
$$3^4 \times 3^2 \quad = 3 \times 3 \times 3 \times 3 \times 3 \times 3 = \quad 3^\square$$
$$7^2 \times 7^3 \quad = 7 \times 7 \times 7 \times 7 \times 7 \qquad = \quad 7^\square$$
$$10^1 \times 10^3 = 10 \times 10 \times 10 \times 10 \qquad = 10^\square$$
Check that you got 3^6, 7^5 and 10^4.

Now look at the powers on their own:

- 4,2 → 6
- 2,3 → 5
- 1,3 → 4

You can see how, **when you multiply powers of the same number, you add the powers**.

> *Self-check*
>
> Write out the statements below, filling in the missing powers in the boxes as you go.
> **1** $3^5 \times 3^8 = 3^\square$
> **2** $2^6 \times 2^\square = 2^{10}$
> **3** $3^{10} = 9 \times 3^\square$

ANSWERS

1 13. **2** 4. **3** 8, because $9 = 3^2$.

You can summarize the rule above by using letters instead of numbers, so that the general pattern is as in Figure 64.

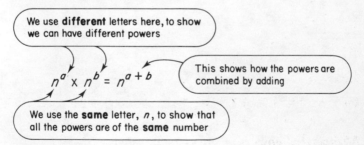

Figure 64. When you multiply powers of the same number you add the powers

Dividing powers of the same number

Starting again with $3^{10} = 59049$, you can find 3^9 from it:

$$3 \times 3^9 = 3^{10}$$

then 3^9 must be $\frac{1}{3}$ of 3^{10}, that is:

$$3^9 = 3^{10} \div 3 = 59049 \div 3 = 19683$$

In the same way:

$3^2 \times 3^8 = 3^{10}$ or $9 \times 3^8 = 3^{10}$

so:

$3^8 = 3^{10} \div 9$
$3^{10} \div 3^2 = 59059 \div 9 = 6561$

Similarly:

$3^9 \div 3^3 = 3^6$
$3^{11} \div 3^7 = 3^4$

See how **when you divide one power by another of the same number, you subtract the second power**.

Self-check

Write out the statements below, filling in the missing powers in the boxes as you go.
1 $3^{14} \div 3^4 = 3^\square$
2 $7^8 \div 7^5 = 7^\square$
3 $2^{20} \div 2^5 = 2^\square$
4 $5^{11} \div 5^{10} = 5^\square$

ANSWERS

1 $3^{14} \div 3^4 = 3^{10}$, so $\square = 10$. **2** 3. **3** 15. **4** 1, 5^1 is simply 5.

You can summarize the rule above, just as in the previous section (see Figure 65).

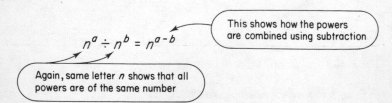

$n^a \div n^b = n^{a-b}$

This shows how the powers are combined using subtraction

Again, same letter *n* shows that all powers are of the same number

Figure 65. When you divide one power by another of the same number you subtract the powers

Zero powers

What does 3^0 mean . . . if anything? Or 2^0 or 8^0?

Remember that: $3^{10} = 59\,049$

so:

$3^{10} \div 3^{10} = 59\,049 \div 59\,049 = 1$

$3^6 \div 3^6 = 729 \div 729 = 1$

You can see that because you're dividing each number by itself, the answers are bound to be 1. If you use the rule on page 100, then:

$3^{10} \div 3^{10} = 3^{10-10} = 3^0$

$3^6 \div 3^6 = 3^{6-6} = 3^0$

So 3^0 must equal 1, and the same goes for 2^0, 5^0 – in fact (anything)^0. They all equal 1, so in general:

- $n^0 = 1$

Negative powers

What does 2^{-1} mean? Using the division rule above:

$2^3 \div 2^4 = 2^{3-4} = 2^{-1}$

so 2^{-1} is the same as $2^3 \div 2^4$. But:

$2^3 \div 2^4 = 8 \div 16 = \frac{8}{16} = \frac{1}{2}$

so 2^{-1} must equal $\frac{1}{2}$. Similarly:

$2^3 \div 2^5 = 8 \div 32 = \frac{8}{32} = \frac{1}{4}$

so 2^{-2} equals $\frac{1}{4}$. You can make up further calculations, leading to this table of results:

Fraction	$\frac{1}{2}$	$\frac{1}{4} = \frac{1}{2^2}$	$\frac{1}{8} = \frac{1}{2^3}$	$\frac{1}{16} = \frac{1}{2^4}$	. . .
Power of 2	2^{-1}	2^{-2}	2^{-3}	2^{-4}	

From the table you can see that:

$2^{-a} = \dfrac{1}{2^a}$

Similarly:

$3^{-a} = \dfrac{1}{3^a}$

$10^{-a} = \dfrac{1}{10^a}$

So, for example:

$$3^{-2} = \frac{1}{3^2} = \frac{1}{9}$$

$$10^{-2} = \frac{1}{10^2} = \frac{1}{100} = 0.01$$

In general:

- $n^{-a} = \dfrac{1}{n^a}$

Self-check

1 Give the values of the following as fractions:
$4^{-1}; 6^{-2}; 10^{-3}$.

2 Express as powers of 5 the following:
$\dfrac{1}{5}, \dfrac{1}{125}$.

3 Give the values of the following as decimals:
$4 \times 10^{-2}; 1.6 \times 10^{-4}$.

4 Express as powers of 10:
$0.0001; 0.000\,000\,1$.

ANSWERS

1 $\dfrac{1}{4}, \dfrac{1}{36}, \dfrac{1}{1000}$. **2** $5^{-1}; 5^{-3}$. **3** $0.04; 0.0016$. **4** $10^{-4}; 10^{-7}$.

Different ways of multiplying: using brackets

You've probably found that *not* using a calculator can make a difference to the way you work things out. Think of what happens when you have to do calculations in your head, without even paper and pencil.

Imagine you are buying eight 28p stamps, or 8 metres of ribbon at 28p a metre, or eight packets of screws at 28p each. On your calculator you'd just press:

| 8 | × | 2 | 8 | = |

But how would you do it in your head? Just see if you can follow this method.

First find eight 30s. You may do this by adding eight 30s

together if you're not too good at tables – 30, 60, 90, 120 . . . Do you get 240?

Each of the 30s is 2 more than 28, so 240 is eight 2s (16) more than 8×28, i.e.:

$8 \times 28 = 8 \times 30 - 8 \times 2 = 240 - 16 = 224$

Figure 66 shows this. Similarly:

$8 \times 32 = 240 + 16 = 256$

and so on.

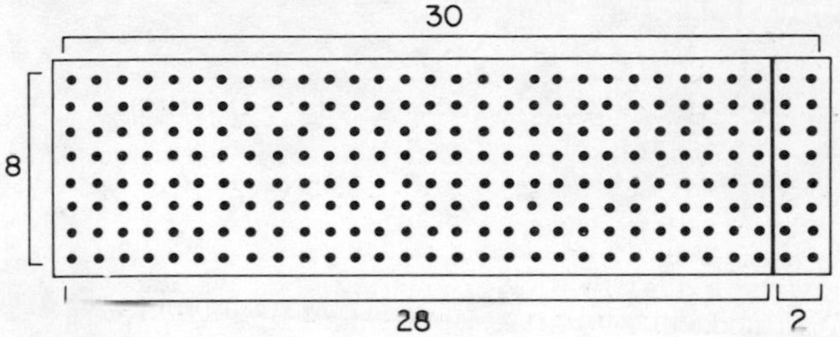

Figure 66.

Self-check

Work these out without using calculator, paper or pencil.

1   9×71
2   9×68
3   13×21
4   13×19

ANSWERS

1 $630 + 9 = 639$. **2** $630 - 18 = 612$. **3** $260 + 13 = 273$.
4 $260 - 13 = 247$.

You can write down what happens with **2** like this:

$9 \times 68 = 9 \times 70 - 9 \times 2$

or like this:

$9 \times 68 = 9(70 - 2)$

Similarly:

$7 \times 97 = 7(100 - 3) = 7 \times 100 - 7 \times 3$
$= 700 - 21 = 679$

$$4 \times 5.2 = 4(5 + 0.2)$$
$$= 4 \times 5 + 4 \times 0.2 = 20 + 0.8$$
$$= 20.8$$

In general:

- $c(a + b) = c \times a + c \times b$
- $c(a - b) = c \times a - c \times b$

where c, a and b can be **any three numbers** you choose. For instance, if $c = 7$, $a = 100$ and $b = 3$:

$$c(a - b) = 7(100 - 3)$$
$$= 7 \times 100 - 7 \times 3$$
$$= 700 - 21$$
$$= 679$$

Expanding and factorizing

Replacing expressions like $c(a + b)$ by $c \times a + c \times b$ is called **expanding** – in all the examples above I've expanded to help with the multiplying.

Going in the opposite direction is called **factorizing** and there are times when this can make things easier to work out. For instance, it's easier to work out 30×4 than to work out:

$$30 \times 187 - 30 \times 183$$

although they give the same result – try it on your calculator and see. Here $c = 30$, $a = 187$ and $b = 183$, and you **factorize**:

$$30 \times 187 - 30 \times 183 = 30(187 - 183)$$
$$= 30 \times 4$$
$$= 120$$

How could such a calculation arise? Maybe like this. I reckon to use 30 gallons of petrol a month in my car. How much do I save if I buy it at 183p a gallon rather than 187p a gallon? Answer 120p = £1.20.

Finally, just as you can omit the $\times$ sign in $c(a-b)$, so you can omit it between pairs of letters like $c \times a$, $a \times b$, etc. Thus:

- ca means the same as $c \times a$;
- ab means the same as $a \times b$.

Self-check

See if you can work these out without using a calculator or paper and pencil, but using the general result $ca - cb = c(a - b)$.

1 $7 \times 29 - 7 \times 27$

2 $40 \times 4\frac{1}{2} - 40 \times 3\frac{1}{2}$

What are the values of the following?

3 ca when $c = 6, a = 7$.

4 $ca + b$ when $c = 10, a = 6, b = 4$.

5 cab when $c = 2, a = 3, b = 4$.

6 $n(a + b)$ when $n = 6, a = 3$ and $b = 4$.

7 $na - ab$ when $n = 8, a = 3$ and $b = 5$.

8 $a(n - b)$ when $n = 8, a = 3$ and $b = 5$.

ANSWERS

1 $7 \times 29 - 7 \times 27 = 7(29 - 27) = 7 \times 2 = 14$.

2 $40(4\frac{1}{2} - 3\frac{1}{2}) = 40 \times 1 = 40$.

3 42. **4** 64. **5** 24. **6** 42. **7** 9. **8** 9.

Formulae with and without brackets

Figure 67 shows a seven-sided polygon (heptagon).

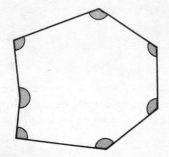

Figure 67. A heptagon

You can cut the heptagon into five triangles, showing that the seven angles at the vertices of the heptagon are made from the angles of the five triangles, and so (see Figure 68) must add up to:

$5 \times 180° = 900°$

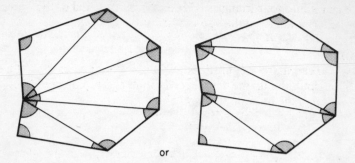

Figure 68. The seven angles at the vertices of a heptagon are made from the angles of five triangles

Another way of finding the sum of the angles of the heptagon is based on Figure 69. Here the seven vertices are joined to a point P somewhere inside the heptagon to give seven triangles. The angles of all these triangles add up to:

$180° \times 7 = 1260°$

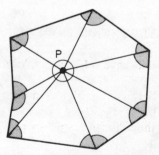

Figure 69. An alternative method of showing that the angles at the vertices of a heptagon add up to 900°

However, the angles at P add up to 360°, so the angles at the seven vertices of the heptagon will add up to:

$1260° - 360° = 900°$

the same result as before. You can use either of these two approaches for polygons. For instance, if you choose a six-sided polygon (hexagon) you can *either*:

- cut it into four triangles (Figure 68), so the total of the inside or **interior** angles at the vertices is:

    $180° \times 4 = 720°$

or

- you can mark a point P somewhere inside the hexagon (Figure 69) and join up the vertices to P, making six triangles – then the total of the interior angles will be:

    $180° \times 6 - 360° = 1080° - 360°$
    $- 720°$

In general, for a polygon with n sides and with s standing for 'the sum of the interior angles in degrees', you can use the formula:

$s = 180 (n - 2)$

or:

$s = 180n - 360$

I've shown you how these two formulae are based on two different ways of cutting up polygons into triangles, but I'm sure you'll also have noticed that if you expand $180 (n - 2)$ you obtain:

$180n - 180 \times 2 = 180n - 360$

Self-check

1 An octagon has eight sides. What do its interior angles add up to?
2 A pentagon has five sides. What do its interior angles add up to?
3 A regular decagon has all its ten interior angles the same size. How big are they?
4 Complete the following table for polygons with up to ten sides.

n	s
3	180
4	
5	
6	
7	900
8	
9	
10	

ANSWERS

1 $180° \times 6 = 1080°$.   **2** $180° \times 3 = 540°$.
3 $180° \times 8 = 1440°$, so each angle is $1440° \div 10 = 144°$.
4 Values of s are 180, 360, 540, 720, 900, 1080, 1260, 1440.

Formulae in reverse – equations

Suppose you know what the interior angles of a polygon add up to, but don't know the number of sides. Let's suppose the angles add up to 3060°, so:

$$180(n - 2) = 3060$$

You can **solve this equation**, i.e. find the particular value of the letter, in various ways. For instance. you could:

- extend the table in question **4** in the self-check above until you reach 3060 in the s column;
- use the same table to plot a graph of n and s, as you did in Chapter 2, and extend the graph until the value of s is 3060;
- use your calculator to check a guess at the value of n, then repeat your guessing till you find the value of n which fits;
- 'work backwards' from the equation until you find n.

I'll explain what I mean by the last method.

Working backwards

You start with $180 (n - 2) = 3060$ as before, that is, if you multiply $n - 2$ by 180 you obtain 3060.

The equation is saying '$180 \times$ something $= 3060$', or in other words 'how many 180s make 3060?' You can solve this directly by calculating $3060 \div 180$. Do it now, and check that you obtain 17 on your calculator. This shows that $n - 2 = 17$, so n must be 2 above this, i.e. $n = 19$. You can set it out like this:

$180 (n - 2) = 3060$ means that:

$$n - 2 = 3060 \div 180$$
$$= 17$$

Thus:

$$n = 17 + 2 \text{ (because } n \text{ is 2 more than } n - 2)$$
$$= 19$$

and the polygon has 19 sides.

Self-check

1 Use the method above or 'guess and check' to find:
   a the number of sides; and
   b the size of each interior angle (to the nearest degree);
   in a regular polygon whose interior angles add up to 6300°.

2 Look at the set of figures below. Some stand for the number of sides of polygons, others stand for the sum of the interior angle of different polygons.

4	1260	2520	19	15	5400
2340	32	20	9	?	3960
3240	16	360	24	4140	3060

Match up any pairs (angle sums matching number of sides) and find the missing number of sides.

ANSWERS

1a 37; **b** 170°. **2** (4,360) (9,1260) (15,2340) (16,2520) (19,3060) (20,3240) (24,3960) (32,5400) (25,4140)

Here's another example. Imagine you intend to run a disco in a local hall. You have to pay for:

hire of the DJ and his equipment   £50;
hire of the hall   £25.

You want to make a profit (to cover any damage, etc.). You cover these costs by selling tickets, so:

$$\left(\begin{matrix} \text{Number of} \\ \text{tickets sold} \\ n \end{matrix} \right) \times \left(\begin{matrix} \text{Cost of a} \\ \text{ticket in £} \\ c \end{matrix} \right) = \left(\begin{matrix} \text{Hire} \\ \text{costs} \\ 75 \end{matrix} \right) + \left(\begin{matrix} \text{Profit} \\ \text{in £} \\ p \end{matrix} \right)$$

or, in short:
$$nc = 75 + p$$
Suppose you sell 180 tickets at 75p. What profit do you make?
$$180 \times 0.75 = 75 + p$$
So:
$$135 = 75 + p$$
so p must be 60, because $135 = 75 + 60$, i.e. the profit is £60.

Self-check

Use the relation:
$$nc = 75 + p$$
in all these questions, with n, c and p as described above.
1 Find the profit if $n = 140$, $c = 0.80$.
2 If $n = 180$ and $c = 0.60$, find the profit.
3 If $p = 25$, fill in the table below to show the number of tickets which have to be sold for each price.

c	n
0.40	
0.50	
0.60	
0.70	
0.80	
1.00	

Solve the following equations, i.e. find the correct value of the letter.
4 $7n + 143 = 171$
5 $8(x - 4) = 56$
6 $210 - 2m = 180$

ANSWERS

1 £37. 2 £33. 3 250, 200, 167, 143, 125, 100.
4 $7n = 28$, so $n = 4$. 5 $x - 4 = 7$, so $x = 11$.
6 $2m = 30$, so $m = 15$.

Review

1 In the formula:
$$y = 7(x - 6)$$
find the values of y when $x = 8$ and when $x = 106$. Then find the values of x when $y = 21$ and when $y = 70$.
2 Which of the following pairs of calculations have equal values?
a $31 \times 4 - 29 \times 4$; 2×4
b $16 \times 25 + 16 \times 5$; 16×30

    c $14 \times 101 - 14 \times 99;$ 14×100

    d $a(x + y);$ $ax + ay$

    e $3c + 4;$ $3(c + 4)$

    f $10 \times x - 10y;$ $10(x - y)$

3 Evaluate

    $4^3;\ 3 \times 2^4;\ 10^{-1};\ 8^\circ;\ 2^{-3}.$

5 | Fractions and decimals

Measuring and counting – what's the difference?

- 'How long would it take you to travel to the centre of London from your house?'
- 'What is your exact height?'
- 'How high should the hem be?'

All these questions involve measurements – of length, time, etc.

Surprisingly, they can never have completely accurate answers. Ask someone to measure your height, maybe with the help of a tape measure, pencil and perhaps a book, as in Figure 70. My height is about 184 centimetres; it might be 184.4 cm. or 183.8 I'm not quite sure because the measuring tape that's used stretches a bit, so each time I'm measured the result differs slightly from previous results. Of course, at any moment an exact measurement exists (though it's probably changing by a tiny amount all the time). The problem is that it's impossible to find out exactly what that measurement is.

Figure 70. Measuring someone's height

Very accurate measuring techniques are available now, using lasers, etc., but even these cannot measure distances exactly – they'll only be 'correct to the nearest millionth of a millimetre' or some other very small unit.

SI units

Nowadays, more and more measurements are given in metric units, using the so-called **SI** (Système Internationale). For length, mass and time the basic SI units are the:

* **metre**;
* **kilogram**; and
* **second**;

with larger and smaller units derived from these.

1 Length.
* 1000 millimetres (mm)   = 1 metre (m)
* 1000 metres   = 1 kilometre (km)
* 10 millimetres   = 1 centimetre (cm)
* 100 centimetres   = 1 metre

2 Mass.
* 1000 grams (g)   = 1 kilogram (kg)
* 1000 kilograms   = 1 tonne (t)

3 Time.
* 60 seconds (s)   = 1 minute

Strictly speaking, the kilogram is a measure of **mass** (quantity of matter) in an object, whereas the object's **weight** is the force exerted on it due to gravity. An object's weight can vary depending on where you measure it (think of people on the moon, or weightless spacemen floating around inside their space capsules), whereas its mass doesn't change. However, in everyday speech people talk about their weight or the weight of a sack of potatoes rather than their masses, so I'll use both terms here. Other units, including those used to measure area, volume, speed, etc., are derived from the basic units.

See how many pairs of units listed above are connected by a factor of 1000 (1000 times bigger or 1/1000th as big).

Conversion between units

My height of 184 cm equals:

$184 \times 10 = 1840$ mm (10 mm = 1 cm)

or

$184 \div 100 = 1.84$ m (100 cm = 1 m)

See how there are **more** millimetres than centimetres because millimetres are **smaller** than centimetres, whereas there are **fewer** metres because metres are **larger** than centimetres.

My height is also:

$1.84 \div 1000 = 0.00184$ km

though people's heights aren't usually given in kilometres.

Self-check

Using your calculator if you wish, convert the following.

1 1.65 m into centimetres.
2 1.65 m into millimetres.
3 735 m into km.
4 260 g into kg.
5 3.6 t into kg.
6 18.6 m into millimetres.
7 47.31 cm into mm.
8 0.6 mm into m.

ANSWERS

1 165 cm.   **2** 1650 mm.   **3** 0.735 km.
4 0.260 kg.   **5** 3600 kg.   **6** 18600 mm.
7 473.1 mm.   **8** 0.0006 m.

Sometimes you will meet different units in the same measurement. For instance, 6 m 3 cm is the same as 6.03 m or 603 cm.

Self-check

Convert the following.
1 18 m 9 cm to centimetres.
2 18 m 9 cm to metres.
3 3 minutes 28 seconds to seconds.
4 4 kg 28 g to grams.
5 17 km 6 m to metres.
6 17 km 6 m to kilometres.

ANSWERS

1 1809 cm.   **2** 18.09 m.
3 180 + 28 = 208 seconds.   **4** 4028 g.
5 17006 m.   **6** 17.006 km.

Significant figures and accuracy

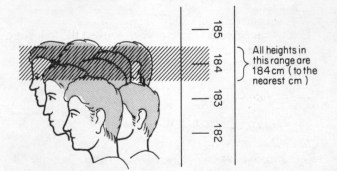

All heights in this range are 184 cm (to the nearest cm)

Figure 71.

My height again! You'll remember that it is about 184 cm. I know it's closer to 184 cm than it is to 183 cm or 185 cm, but I don't know whether it's 184.4 or 183.8 or 184.0 or 183.65 cm. My height is 184 cm **to the nearest centimetre**. This means it is somewhere between 183.5 cm and 184.5 cm (see Figure 71).

Just by using different units, I could say that my height is 1840 mm or 1.84 m or 0.00184 km or 1840000 μ. The accuracy hasn't changed – the 184 is still there, surrounded by quite a few 0s in some cases. In each case, my height is given **correct to 3 significant figures**. This means that each number has three important or **significant** figures or digits (1, 8 and 4), apart from any 0s whose job is just to show where the decimal point is.

Here are some more examples.

- Imagine that the distance from your front door to the post box is about 760 m (to the nearest 10 metres). Then 760 m is **correct to 2 significant figures**. This is because you're counting in blocks of 10 metres, i.e. 1, 2, 3... up to 76 10s = 760 m. You could also write the distance as 0.76 km or 76000 cm or 760000 mm – all **correct to 2 significant figures**, and in each case with two digits (7 and 6), apart from spacing 0s.

- Last year I put on about 4 kg in weight (or strictly speaking mass), i.e. my increase was somewhere between 3.5 kg and 4.5 kg. The 4 kg is not exact – just think how your weight varies from day to day – it's accurate to **1 significant figure** only. You could also write this increase as 4000 g or 0.004 t – both are correct to **1 significant figure** – there's just one digit (4), apart from the spacing 0s.

You'll remember the ≃ sign from Chapter 1, meaning approximately equal to. I can say that my height ≃ 184 cm or 1.84 m or 0.00184 km (correct to 3 significant figures), or the distance to the post box ≃ 760 m (2 s.f.), and so on.

Sometimes measurements which are too accurate can be misleading. For instance, which would you find easier to remember from this pair of statements?

- 'I used exactly 19.48 g of sugar in this recipe' *or*
- 'I used about 20 g of sugar in this recipe.'

It makes sense to use the 1 s.f. approximation of 20 g. Even if you could measure sugar as accurately as shown, it is unlikely that the next time you made that cake all the other features, like quality of flour, etc., would be exactly the same; next time round, you might need only 17g of sugar.

Re-writing numbers to a given accuracy can provide problems. If you are approximating 25.2kg, for example, to one significant figure (1 s.f.) you only need one digit or figure in your answer, apart from spacing 0s. So here you're seeing whether 25.2 is closest to 20, 30, 40, etc ; 25.2 is a little **over** halfway from 20 to 30, so it's closer to 30 than to 20 (or to 40 for that matter) and you can write:

$25.2 \simeq 30$ (1 s.f.)

Of course, if you were working to an accuracy of two significant figures, you would be seeing which of 22, 23, 24, 25, 26, etc., is closest to 25.2, so you would write:

$25.2 \simeq 25$ (2 s.f.)

In practice, it all depends on whether the first digit which disappears when you round your starting number is 5 or more, e.g.:

- $25.71 \simeq 26$ (2 s.f.) because of the **7**;
- $25.56 \simeq 26$ (2 s.f.) because of the **5**.

However:

- $25.49 \simeq 25$ (2 s.f.) because of the **4**;
- $0.02549 \simeq 0.025$ (2 s.f.) for the same reason.

Changing fractions into decimals

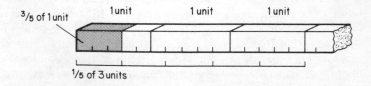

Figure 72.

Figure 72 shows:
 the fraction $\frac{3}{5}$ of 1 unit, or $\frac{1}{5}$ of 3 units, or $3 \div 5$.

You can see that they are the same. After all, $\frac{1}{5}$ of 3 units will be 3 times as much as $\frac{1}{5}$ of 1 unit, i.e. the same as $\frac{3}{5}$ of 1 unit.

Try these on your calculator now:

$\boxed{1}\ \boxed{\div}\ \boxed{5}\ \boxed{\times}\ \boxed{3}\ \boxed{=}$ ($\frac{3}{5}$s of 1 unit);

$\boxed{3}\ \boxed{\div}\ \boxed{5}\ \boxed{=}$ ($\frac{1}{5}$ of 3 units).

Did you find both answers were 0.6?

Figure 73 shows a 'fifths' scale beside a 'tenths' (decimal) scale. You can see how $\frac{3}{5}$ is at the same place on the lines as 0.6. In the same way, you can calculate the decimal equivalent of $\frac{7}{20}$ by finding $1 \div 20 \times 7$, or $7 \div 20$. Both give 0.35. Do you agree?

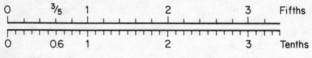

Figure 73.

Self-check

1 Convert these fractions into decimals:
$\frac{7}{25}; \frac{3}{8}; \frac{7}{20}; \frac{13}{40}; \frac{5}{16}; \frac{17}{50}.$

2 Now re-write the set of fractions in **1** in order, from smallest to largest.

ANSWERS

1 0.28; 0.375; 0.35; 0.325; 0.3125; 0.34.
2 $\frac{7}{25}; \frac{5}{16}; \frac{13}{40}; \frac{17}{50}; \frac{7}{20}; \frac{3}{8}.$

Recurring decimals and rounding

You will remember the diagrams of $\frac{1}{3}$s on page 22, and you will remember that $\frac{1}{3}$ is larger than 0.3 but smaller than 0.4. Change this to a decimal now, using your calculator. You'll obtain:

$1 \div 3 = 0.3333333$

filling the display with 3s. The 3s don't stop there though. This decimal is not exactly the same as $\frac{1}{3}$, as you can see by calculating 0.3333333×3. You'll obtain 0.9999999 – nearly 1 but not quite.

In fact:

$\frac{1}{3}$ = 0.3333333... continuing for ever

The more 3s you have, the closer the decimal is to $\frac{1}{3}$, but the decimal **never ends**.

You say that 0.3333333... is a **recurring** decimal. The pattern of 3s **recurs**. In the same way:

- $\frac{4}{11}$ = 0.3636363..., recurring every 2 figures;
- $\frac{4}{7}$ = 0.571428571428 , recurring every 6 figures.

You won't be able to see all these figures on your calculator, so you need to use other methods to investigate recurring decimals more fully. I'll return to this later. Often it is sufficient to give any decimal version of a fraction correct to 3 or 4 significant figures. So:

$\frac{4}{11}$ ≃ 0.3636   (4 s.f.)

or

$\frac{4}{11}$ ≃ 0.364   (3 s.f.)

See how I have chosen 0.364 rather than 0.363 for the 3 significant figure version. Look back to page 117 if you're not sure why.

Self-check

1 Convert these fractions to decimals using your calculator. Write down all the figures in your calculator display each time:

$\frac{3}{11}$; $\frac{5}{9}$; $\frac{4}{15}$; $\frac{7}{12}$; $\frac{9}{12}$; $\frac{3}{7}$; $\frac{13}{32}$; $\frac{10}{7}$; $\frac{130}{7}$; $\frac{196}{25}$.

2 Decimals which do not continue for ever are said to **terminate**. Which of the fractions in **1** are you sure give terminating decimals?

3 Give all your answers to **1** correct to 3 significant figures.

ANSWERS

These are the results from my calculator. Yours may give longer or shorter displays.

1 0.2727272;   0.5555555;   0.2666666;   0.5833333;   0.75;
  0.4285714; 0.40625; 1.4285714; 18.571429; 7.84.

2 $\frac{9}{12}$; $\frac{13}{32}$; $\frac{196}{25}$.

3 0.273; 0.556; 0.267; 0.583; 0.75; 0.429; 0.406; 1.43; 18.6; 7.84.

Numerator and denominator

These are two words which you use to describe the 'top' and 'bottom' numbers in a fraction.

- The **denominator** (bottom number) tells you **what sort** of fraction you have (sevenths, fifteenths, halves, etc.).
- The **numerator** (top number) tells you **how many** of that fraction you have.

For example, in the fraction $\frac{4}{7}$, 7 is the denominator (sevenths) and 4 is the numerator (4 of them).

Mixed numbers

In the last self-check there were some fractions with a larger numerator than denominator.

| *Activity*
|
| Which were they? Look back and write them down now.
| Did you find three of them?

Let's look at one of them now and its matching decimal:
$\frac{10}{7} \simeq 1.43$ (3 s.f.)
You could make up $\frac{10}{7}$ from 7 sevenths and 3 more sevenths (see Figure 74). This shows how:
$\frac{10}{7} = \frac{7}{7} + \frac{3}{7}$
The seven sevenths is the same as 1 unit, so:
$\frac{10}{7} = 1 + \frac{3}{7}$ or $1\frac{3}{7}$

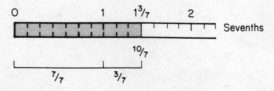

Figure 74.

Work out $\frac{3}{7}$ on your calculator now. You'll find it's 0.4285714, so:

$1\frac{3}{7} = 1 + 0.4285714 = 1.4285714$

as you obtained before when you worked out $\frac{10}{7}$. $1\frac{3}{7}$ is called a **mixed number** because it contains a whole number and a fraction. You can use this idea to change more awkward fractions into mixed numbers. For example, you've already found that:

$\frac{130}{7} = 18.571$

This means that $\frac{130}{7} = 18$ units + some extra sevenths. As there are 7 sevenths in each unit, in 18 units there will be $18 \times 7 = 126$ sevenths. So $\frac{130}{7}$ includes 4 extra sevenths and $\frac{130}{7} = 18\frac{4}{7}$. You can check this by just calculating $4 \div 7 = 0.571...$ as you'd expect.

Changing decimals to fractions

You'll remember from Chapter 1 that 74.86 stands for 74 units, 8 tenths and 6 hundredths. Let's look at the part after the decimal point, i.e. the 0.86. Figure 75 shows the decimal number line between 74 and 75. You can see the tenths marked in at 74.1, 74.2, 74.3, etc. So 74.86 is between 74.8 and 74.9 (or $74\frac{8}{10}$ and $74\frac{9}{10}$). Each of the 'tenth' spaces is split up into 10 smaller spaces, so that altogether the line between 74 and 75 is split into 100 smaller spaces. This means that each of these smaller spaces is 1 hundredth ($\frac{1}{100}$) of the distance from 74 to 75, and 74.86 is 6 hundredths beyond 74.8 or 86 hundredths beyond 74.

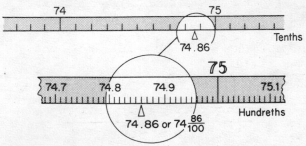

Figure 75. Part of the decimal number line between 74 and 75

This means that you can re-write 74.86 as:

74 and $\frac{86}{100} = 74\frac{86}{100}$

You can easily check this by finding $86 \div 100 = 0.86$, on your calculator. In the same way:

- $74.35 = 74\frac{35}{100}$;
- $31.08 = 31\frac{8}{100}$;
- $26.09 = 26\frac{9}{100}$;

and, extending into thousandths:

- $74.857 = 74\frac{857}{1000}$;
- $8.049 = 8\frac{49}{1000}$;
- $17.006 = 17\frac{6}{1000}$.

Self-check

Re-write these decimals as mixed numbers:
1 8.45.　　**2** 31.04.　　**3** 1.634.　　**4** 17.042.　　**5** 12.60.

ANSWERS

1 $8\frac{45}{100}$. **2** $31\frac{4}{100}$. **3** $1\frac{634}{1000}$. **4** $17\frac{42}{1000}$. **5** $12\frac{60}{100}$ or $12\frac{6}{10}$.

Some common fractions and decimals

Activity

Use your calculator to work out the missing decimals below, then make a note of all these results, so you can refer to them when you need to.

- Half　　　　$\frac{1}{2} = 0.5$
- Thirds　　　$\frac{1}{3} = 0.333...$
  　　　　　　$\frac{2}{3} = 0.666...$
- Quarters　　$\frac{1}{4} = 0.25$
  　　　　　　$\frac{2}{4} =$ 　　　　　
  　　　　　　$\frac{3}{4} =$ 　　　　　
- Fifths　　　$\frac{1}{5} = 0.2$
  　　　　　　$\frac{2}{5} =$ 　　　　　
  　　　　　　$\frac{3}{5} =$ 　　　　　
  　　　　　　$\frac{4}{5} =$

- Eighths $\frac{1}{8} = 0.125$

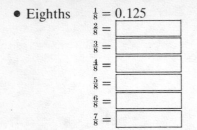

Of course, you'll remember that $\frac{1}{10} = 0.1$, $\frac{2}{10} = 0.2$, etc.

Activity

Trace the number line in Figure 76 and mark in the position of the fractions above. You may wish to calculate and mark in the positions of some other fractions of your choice.

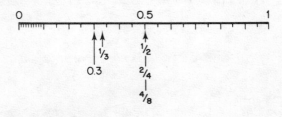

Figure 76. Fractions on number line

Finding fractions of fractions

Imagine you're serving minestrone soup for a lunch party of 40 people. The people are sitting five to a table, so that's eight tables altogether.

- To be fair, each person should receive $\frac{1}{40}$ of the soup.
- You could also put $\frac{1}{8}$ of the soup into a smaller serving bowl for each table, and let people serve themselves. Each person should then take $\frac{1}{5}$ of their own table's soup.

I've shown these two serving methods in Figure 77. Of course, whichever method you use, people should get the same amount of soup. You can see now that:

$\frac{1}{5}$ of $\frac{1}{8}$ (that is $\frac{1}{5} \times \frac{1}{8}$) equals $\frac{1}{40}$

I'm sure you can imagine different-sized tables with different numbers of people, so you can see how:

- $\frac{1}{5} \times \frac{1}{6}$ ($\frac{1}{5}$ of $\frac{1}{6}$) $= \frac{1}{30}$
- $\frac{1}{4} \times \frac{1}{7}$ ($\frac{1}{4}$ of $\frac{1}{7}$) $= \frac{1}{28}$

Each bowl holds 1/40 of the soup

Each bowl holds 1/5 of the soup for the table

Each serving bowl holds 1/8 of the soup, enough for one table

Figure 77. Two ways of dividing soup between 40 people

Self-check

Copy these calculations, filling in the boxes as you go.

1 $\frac{1}{4} \times \frac{1}{3} = \square$

2 $\frac{1}{6}$ of $\frac{1}{4}$ $= \square$

3 $\frac{1}{5}$ of $\frac{1}{3}$ $= \square$

4 $\frac{1}{12}$ of $\frac{1}{3} = \square$

5 $\frac{1}{3}$ of $\square = \frac{1}{18}$

6 $\frac{1}{4} \times \square = \frac{1}{36}$

ANSWERS

1 $\frac{1}{12}$. **2** $\frac{1}{24}$. **3** $\frac{1}{15}$. **4** $\frac{1}{36}$. **5** $\frac{1}{6}$. **6** $\frac{1}{9}$.

Returning to the soup example with forty people, imagine that at one table there's a family of three. Two of them cannot stand minestrone soup, so the third member (who's something of a glutton) has their shares as well. He will have had $\frac{3}{40}$ of all the soup (three lots of $\frac{1}{40} = 3 \times \frac{1}{40}$). He will also have had $\frac{3}{5}$s of his table's soup (remember, five on each table) and the table of five people was allowed $\frac{1}{8}$ of all the soup. They're just different ways of thinking about the same amount of soup. So you can see how:

$\frac{3}{5}$ of $\frac{1}{8} = \frac{3}{5} \times \frac{1}{8} = \frac{3}{40}$

and you can extend this approach further, so:

$\frac{4}{5}$ of $\frac{1}{8} = \frac{4}{5} \times \frac{1}{8} = \frac{4}{40}$ (another glutton)

and finally:

$\frac{4}{5}$ of $\frac{7}{8}$ is 7 times as much as $\frac{4}{5}$ of $\frac{1}{8}$

so:

$\frac{4}{5}$ of $\frac{7}{8} = \frac{4}{5} \times \frac{7}{8} = \frac{28}{40}$

Figure 78 will help make this clear. It shows a seating plan for part of a grandstand at an athletics meeting; $\frac{7}{8}$ of the seats can be booked in advance (these are shown shaded lightly) and of these $\frac{4}{5}$ have been sold already (shown shaded darkly). In the diagram there are 40 seats altogether, so 28 seats have been sold, i.e. 28 out of 40, again showing how:

$\frac{4}{5} \times \frac{7}{8} = \frac{28}{40}$

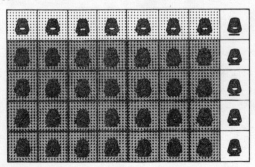

Figure 78. Seating plan for part of a grandstand, showing how $\frac{4}{5} \times \frac{7}{8} = \frac{28}{40}$

Self-check

Use the same fractions of $\frac{7}{8}$ and $\frac{4}{5}$ for the seating as above in questions **1–4**.

1 Another stand of 40 is used. How many seats in the two stands are now sold?

2 If there are 4000 seats at the match altogether, how many are already sold?

3 How many seats are unsold out of the 4000?

ANSWERS

1 56. **2** 2800. **3** 1200.

Review

1 Convert each of these measurements to metres, giving your answers correct to 2 significant figures.
a 34.614 m. **b** 18.26 km. **c** 47.8 cm.
d 21430 mm. **e** 4 m 7 cm.

2 A lorry is weighed before and after loading. The readings are 4.413 t and 11.069 t. What is the weight of the load in kilograms?

3 a Convert these fractions to decimals (correct to 3 s.f.):
$\frac{7}{13}$; $\frac{8}{14}$; $\frac{9}{15}$; $\frac{10}{16}$.
b Using your answers, make a guess for the value of $\frac{11}{17}$ then check with your calculator.

4 Convert these mixed numbers to fractions:
$3\frac{1}{5}$; $17\frac{4}{11}$.

5 Convert these fractions to mixed numbers:
$\frac{84}{10}$; $\frac{98}{15}$; $\frac{1427}{31}$.

6 Complete the following.

a $\frac{1}{7} \times \frac{1}{3} = \frac{1}{\square}$

b $\frac{2}{3} \times \frac{4}{5} = \square$

c $\frac{4}{3} \times \frac{2}{\square} = \frac{8}{21}$.

7 On a train of eight coaches, two are first class, five are second class and the remaining coach is a buffet car which is closed. $\frac{7}{8}$ of the 72 seats in each second-class coach and $\frac{1}{5}$ of the 55 seats in each first-class coach are occupied. There are no standing passengers.
a How many passengers are there on the train?
b After a breakdown the same passengers have to change to another train with seven coaches – four second class and three first class. How many passengers have no seats?

c The guard allows the passengers without seats to sit in the first-class coaches. What fraction of the first-class seats are now occupied? Give this answer as a decimal correct to 2 s.f.

Equivalent fractions

Look back to page 125 and the questions about the grandstands. Twenty-eight out of every 40 seats were sold in advance, i.e. $\frac{28}{40}$ of the seats. Increasing the number of blocks of 40 seats, you found 56 out of every 80 seats, 2800 out of every 4000 seats and so on, so 28 out of every 40 = 56 out of every 80 = 2800 out of every 4000, etc., or:

$$\frac{28}{40} = \frac{56}{80} = \frac{2800}{4000} = \ldots$$

These fractions are **equivalent** to each other, as is $\frac{14}{20}$. Can you see how 14 out of every 20 is **equivalent** to 28 out of every 40? Think of the stand of 40 being in two 20-seat sections, so that 14 seats sold in every 20 is the same as 28 in every 40.

Now look back to the list of common fractions and decimals you made (see page 122). You can see how $\frac{1}{2}$, $\frac{2}{4}$, $\frac{4}{8}$ and 0.5 ($=\frac{5}{10}$) are all the same. Again, these fractions are equivalent to each other. In other words, they look different but have the same value as each other. Here's another set of equivalent fractions:

$$\frac{3}{5}, \frac{6}{10}, \frac{9}{15}, \frac{12}{20} \ldots$$

You'll see these illustrated in Figure 79.

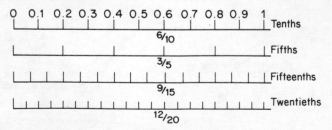

Figure 79. Fractions equivalent to $\frac{3}{5}$

Maybe you've already noticed how multiplying both the numerator and denominator (top and bottom) of the simplest fraction by the **same amount** brings you to another equivalent fraction (see Figure 80).

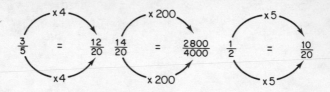

Figure 80. Multiplying numerator and denominator by the same amount gives equivalent fractions

Using the same idea but in reverse, you can often **simplify** fractions by dividing both numerator and denominator by the same amount (see Figure 81). Notice how you have to choose your dividing number so that you can divide both numerator and denominator **exactly**. When you cannot find such a number (that is, when there is no **common factor** of numerator and denominator) you will have simplified the fraction as far as possible.

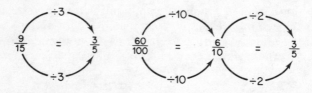

Figure 81. Dividing the numerator and denominator by the same amount simplifies fractions

Self-check

1 Fill in the missing numbers in the following.

$\frac{3}{5} = \frac{\square}{30}$;

$\frac{7}{8} = \frac{21}{\square}$

$\frac{\square}{6} = \frac{15}{18}$

$\frac{1}{10} = \frac{\square}{1000}$.

2 Simplify the following as far as possible.

$\frac{8}{20}, \frac{9}{81}, \frac{26}{52}, \frac{800}{1000}, \frac{625}{1000}$.

ANSWERS

1 $\frac{18}{30}$; $\frac{21}{24}$; $\frac{5}{6}$; $\frac{100}{1000}$. **2** $\frac{2}{5}$; $\frac{1}{9}$; $\frac{1}{2}$; $\frac{4}{5}$; $\frac{5}{8}$.

Simplifying in more detail

Let's break down the steps in simplifying a fraction like $\frac{625}{1000}$. You'll remember that, as a decimal: $\frac{625}{1000} = 0.625$. I'm really asking you to convert 0.625 to the simplest fraction you can. The key is to find a whole number (**any** whole number apart from 1) which you can divide both numerator and denominator by. You may find your calculator a help here. For a start, 2 divides into 1000 exactly:

$1000 \div 2 = 500$

but 2 does *not* divide into 625 exactly:

$625 \div 2 = 312.5$

So although it's correct to say that:

$\frac{625}{1000} = \frac{312.5}{500}$

the fraction has been made more complicated, if anything. So dividing by 2 is not a help.

Try dividing 625 and 1000 by 3, 4, 5... You'll find that:

$625 \div 5 = 125$ and $1000 \div 5 = 200$

so 5 is a **common factor** of 625 and 1000:

$\frac{625}{1000} = \frac{125}{200}$

You've made a start. Try dividing by 5 again. It works!

$\frac{125}{200} = \frac{25}{40}$

And again. It works again:

$\frac{25}{40} = \frac{5}{8}$

Thus $\frac{625}{1000}$ has been simplified to $\frac{5}{8}$.

Here's the process again in brief with another two fractions.

- $\frac{24}{84}$ $\qquad = \frac{12}{42}$ $\qquad = \frac{6}{21}$ $\qquad = \frac{2}{7}$

  $\qquad\qquad$ ($\div$ by 2) ($\div$ by 2) ($\div$ by 3)
- $\frac{210}{525}$ $\qquad = \frac{70}{175}$ $\qquad = \frac{14}{35}$ $\qquad = \frac{2}{5}$

  $\qquad\qquad$ ($\div$ 3) ($\div$ 5) ($\div$ 7)

It's a good idea to check using your calculator. Just change the starting and finishing fractions into decimals and check that they are the same. For example:

$\frac{24}{84} \simeq 0.285$ and $\frac{2}{7} \simeq 0.285$

so that fractions *are* equivalent.

Self-check

1 Simplify these fractions:
$$\frac{375}{1000}; \frac{64}{80}; \frac{96}{128}; \frac{3125}{10000}.$$

2 Check your answers by converting into decimals.

ANSWERS

1 $\frac{3}{8}; \frac{4}{5}; \frac{3}{4}; \frac{5}{16}$.

2 0.375; 0.8; 0.75; 0.3125.

Equivalent fractions in measuring

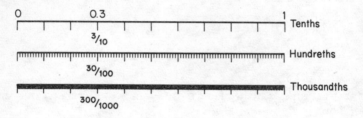

Figure 82.

You have seen how sets of equivalent fractions like:
$$\frac{3}{10}, \frac{30}{100}, \frac{300}{1000}$$
crop up when you are working in decimals (see Figure 82). You will also come across fractions where the denominator is a power of 2. Does that sound complicated? Let's see what I mean by that. Powers of 2 (see Chapter 4) include numbers like:

- $8 = 2 \times 2 \times 2$ or 2^3
- $32 = 2 \times 2 \times 2 \times 2 \times 2$ or 2^5
- $64 = 2 \times 2 \times 2 \times 2 \times 2 \times 2$ or 2^6

The 3, 5 and 6 are **powers** or **indices** telling you how many 2s have been multiplied. The fractions I'm talking about include:
$$\frac{1}{8}, \frac{5}{32}, \frac{11}{64}, \frac{7}{8}, \frac{28}{64}, \text{etc.}$$

If you have an inch ruler to hand, look at the inch markings. Besides the decimal ($\frac{1}{10}$th of an inch) markings, you may find markings as in Figure 83. Instead of being split into 10, 100,

1000 equal parts like decimals, the inches are split into 2, 4, 8, 16... equal parts to give $\frac{1}{2}$s, $\frac{1}{4}$s, $\frac{1}{8}$s, $\frac{1}{16}$s of an inch. In Figure 83:

- A is at $\frac{2}{4}$ or $\frac{1}{2}$ – they're equivalent, but you generally choose $\frac{1}{2}$ as it's simpler;
- C is at $2\frac{3}{4}$ (or $2\frac{6}{8}$);
- D is at $3\frac{3}{8}$, which cannot be simplified.

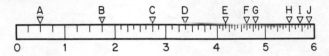

Figure 83. The first 2 inches of this ruler are marked in quarters of an inch. Over the next 2 inches each quarter inch is divided into two to give eighths of an inch. Over the next 2 inches each eighth of an inch is divided into two to give sixteenths of an inch

Self-check

1 Make a list of the simplest fractions for positions A to J in Figure 83.

2 Some of the following are the same. Match them up.
$2\frac{3}{8}$; $1\frac{2}{4}$; $3\frac{7}{8}$; $1\frac{4}{16}$; $1\frac{1}{2}$; $2\frac{6}{16}$; $1\frac{16}{32}$; $2\frac{5}{16}$; $2\frac{7}{8}$; $1\frac{2}{8}$.

ANSWERS

1 A $\frac{1}{2}$in.   B $1\frac{3}{4}$in.   C $2\frac{3}{4}$in.   D $3\frac{3}{8}$in.
  E $4\frac{3}{16}$in.   F $4\frac{5}{8}$in.   G $4\frac{13}{16}$in.   H $5\frac{1}{2}$in.
  I $5\frac{23}{32}$in.   J $5\frac{29}{32}$in.

2 $\{1\frac{2}{4}, 1\frac{1}{2}, 1\frac{16}{32}\}$; $\{2\frac{3}{8}; 2\frac{6}{16}\}$; $\{1\frac{4}{16}, 1\frac{2}{8}\}$.

Equivalent fractions – what happens in general

Look back to page 128. You can also set out the first pairs of fractions like this:

- $\frac{3}{5} = \frac{4 \times 3}{4 \times 5} = \frac{12}{20}$
- $\frac{14}{20} = \frac{200 \times 14}{200 \times 20} = \frac{2800}{4000}$
- $\frac{1}{2} = \frac{1 \times 5}{2 \times 5} = \frac{5}{10}$

Instead of explaining what's happening with words, you can use letters instead of numbers as a shorthand to show the general pattern like this:

● $\frac{a}{b} = \frac{k \times a}{k \times b} = \frac{ka}{kb}$: the **equivalent fractions** rule.

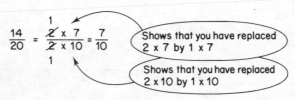

Figure 84.

Let's have another look at how you can set out the simplifying, using $\frac{14}{20}$ as an example (see Figure 84). This shows that you have divided numerator and denominator by 2. In general:

$$\frac{\overset{1}{\cancel{k}} a}{\underset{1}{\cancel{k}} b} = \frac{a}{b}$$

shows you have divided numerator and denominator by k.

‖ *Self-check*

Simplify these fractions as far as you can.

1 $\frac{8 \times 17}{15 \times 17}$

2 $\frac{4 \times 2 \times 3 \times 31}{5 \times 2 \times 3 \times 49}$

3 $\frac{m\,c}{m\,d}$

ANSWERS

1 $\frac{8}{15}$. **2** $\frac{4 \times 31}{5 \times 49} = \frac{124}{245}$. **3** $\frac{c}{d}$.

Multiplying fractions – what happens in general

Look back to pages 122 to 124.

● $\frac{1}{4} \times \frac{1}{3} = \frac{1}{12}$
● $\frac{1}{5} \times \frac{1}{3} = \frac{1}{15}$
● $\frac{1}{4} \times \frac{1}{9} = \frac{1}{36}$

You can show the general pattern of what is happening, using letters again. In general:

- $\frac{1}{b} \times \frac{1}{d} = \frac{1}{b \times d} = \frac{1}{bd}$

Examples like:

$\frac{4}{5} \times \frac{7}{8} = \frac{28}{40}$

lead to the general pattern:

- $\frac{a}{b} \times \frac{c}{d} = \frac{a \times c}{b \times d} = \frac{ac}{bd}$

This is the **multiplying fractions** rule. If a and c both have the value 1, the multiplying fractions rule becomes the simpler rule above. If $b = 1$, the multiplying fractions rule becomes:

- $\frac{a}{1} \times \frac{c}{d} = \frac{a \times c}{1 \times d} = \frac{ac}{d}$

- $\frac{a}{1}$ means a units, so you can replace $\frac{a}{1}$ by a. For example, if $a=3$, $c=4$ and $d=5$:

$\frac{a}{1} \times \frac{c}{d}$ becomes $\frac{3}{1} \times \frac{4}{5} = \frac{12}{5}$

that is, 3 lots of $\frac{4}{5} = \frac{12}{5}$ altogether. You can write this rule as:

- $a \times \frac{c}{d} = \frac{ac}{d}$

If $b = c$, the general rule becomes:

- $\frac{a}{b} \times \frac{b}{d} = \frac{a \times \overset{1}{\cancel{b}}}{\underset{1}{\cancel{b}} \times d} = \frac{a}{d}$

illustrating the **equivalent fractions** rule. As an example of this, imagine that $a = 4$, $b = 5$ and $d = 11$. Then:

$\frac{4}{5} \times \frac{5}{11} = \frac{4 \times \overset{1}{\cancel{5}}}{\underset{1}{\cancel{5}} \times 11} = \frac{4}{11}$

dividing through by 5 and showing how $\frac{20}{55} = \frac{4}{11}$.

Self-check

Multiply and, if possible, simplify the following.

1 $\frac{2}{5} \times \frac{5}{11}$ **5** $\frac{3}{4} \times \frac{8}{15}$

2 $\frac{3}{7} \times \frac{7}{8}$ **6** $\frac{2}{3} \times \frac{3}{10}$

3 $6 \times \frac{5}{3}$ **7** $\frac{1}{5} \times \frac{20}{25}$

4 $8 \times \frac{3}{5}$ **8** $\frac{1}{3} \times \frac{9}{10}$

ANSWERS

1 $\frac{2 \times 5}{5 \times 11} = \frac{2}{11}$. **2** $\frac{3}{8}$. **3** $\frac{30}{3} = 10$.

4 $\frac{24}{5} = 4\frac{4}{5}$. **5** $\frac{2}{5}$. **6** $\frac{1}{5}$. **7** $\frac{4}{25}$. **8** $\frac{3}{10}$.

Multiplying and dividing

Just as adding and subtracting are tied together, so multiplying and dividing are closely connected. Often you'll find yourself **multiplying** to check that a **division** is correct. Here is an example to explain what I mean.

- You share the cost of petrol for a car journey with three passengers by **dividing** the petrol cost by 3. You **check** by **multiplying** each passenger's cost by 3 (or by adding the three passengers' amounts together, which comes to the same thing).

> *Activity*
>
> Try these on your calculator.
> **1** $12.51 \div 3 \times 3 =$
> **2** $5.610 \div 5 \times 5 =$
> In each case you'll arrive back at or very close to your starting number (12.51, 5.610, etc.). Try some more examples of your own, where you divide and multiply by the same number. See what happens.

For example:

- $7 \div 0.6 \times 0.6 = 7$
- $7 \div 0.19 \times 0.19 = 7$

In general:

- $n \div a \times a = n$

or:

- $n \times a \div a = n$

Suppose you start with 32 (so $n = 32$), then multiply by 1.6 (so $a = 1.6$), then **divide** by 1.6. You're back at 32, as you'd expect.
Now try:

  $32 \times 1.6 \times 0.625 =$

Again you're back at 32, so **multiplying by 0.625** has the same effect as **dividing by 1.6**.

Self-check

Use your calculator (with repeated guesses) to find the missing numbers in the following.

1 $20 \times 2.5 \times$ [   ] $= 20$

2 $20 \times 0.3125 \times$ [   ] $= 20$

3 $30 \times 1.5 \times$ [   ] $= 20$

4 $20 \times 0.8 \times$ [   ] $= 20$

ANSWERS

1 0.4. **2** 3.2. **3** 0.666666... **4** 1.25.

Activity

Now see what happens when you convert all these decimals into fractions.

- 2.5 becomes $2\frac{1}{2}$ or $\frac{5}{2}$
- 0.4 becomes $\frac{4}{10}$ or $\frac{2}{5}$

Try the other three pairs yourself and see what happens. Remember that $0.666666... = \frac{2}{3}$.

Did you find:

- $\frac{4}{5}$ and $\frac{5}{4}$;
- $\frac{5}{16}$ and $\frac{16}{5}$;
- $\frac{3}{2}$ and $\frac{2}{3}$?

Thus:

- $20 \times \frac{5}{2} \times \frac{2}{5} = 20$ just as $20 \times \frac{5}{2} \div \frac{5}{2} = 20$
- $20 \times \frac{4}{5} \times \frac{5}{4} = 20$ just as $20 \times \frac{4}{5} \div \frac{4}{5} = 20$
- $20 \times \frac{5}{16} \times \frac{4}{5} = 20$ just as $20 \times \frac{5}{16} \div \frac{5}{16} = 20$
- $20 \times \frac{3}{2} \times \frac{2}{3} = 20$ just as $20 \times \frac{3}{2} \div \frac{3}{2} = 20$

And the pattern on page 134, which becomes:

$$n \times \frac{c}{d} \div \frac{d}{c} = n$$

when you use $\frac{c}{d}$ to stand for the fraction, changes to:

$$n \times \tfrac{c}{d} \times \tfrac{d}{c} = n$$

showing how you can **replace**:

$$\div \tfrac{c}{d} \text{ by } \times \tfrac{d}{c}$$

This is not so surprising, as:

$$\tfrac{c}{d} \times \tfrac{d}{c}$$

is really a special case of the **multiplying fractions rule** and:

$$\tfrac{c}{d} \times \tfrac{d}{c} = \tfrac{cd}{dc} = 1$$

so:

$$n \times \tfrac{c}{d} \times \tfrac{d}{c} \text{ is simply } n \times 1$$

which is just n as before. If you still need convincing, look at this example:

$$31 \times \tfrac{9}{7} \div \tfrac{9}{7} = 31$$

(as you saw in the previous section) but:

$$31 \times \tfrac{9}{7} \times \tfrac{7}{9} = 31 \times \tfrac{63}{63} = 31 \times 1 = 31$$

using $n = 31, c = 9, d = 7$, so:

$$\times \tfrac{7}{9} \text{ has the same effect as } \div \tfrac{9}{7}$$

Dividing by a fraction

From what you've seen, you can carry out calculations like:

$$\tfrac{10}{11} \div \tfrac{3}{7}$$

more simply by writing:

$$\tfrac{10}{11} \div \tfrac{3}{7} = \tfrac{10}{11} \times \tfrac{7}{3} = \tfrac{70}{33} = 2\tfrac{4}{33}$$

The calculation is asking you to find how many $\tfrac{3}{7}$ths make $\tfrac{10}{11}$ths. $\tfrac{3}{7}$ths is a little less than a half, while $\tfrac{10}{11}$ is just below 1, so you'd expect an answer of about 2 (two $\tfrac{1}{2}$s = 1), which is what you found. You can do the whole thing on your calculator, if a decimal is all right as the result, but it takes a little thought before you start.

$$\tfrac{10}{11} \div \tfrac{3}{7} =$$

becomes:

$$\boxed{(}\;\boxed{10}\;\boxed{\div}\;\boxed{11}\;\boxed{)}\;\boxed{\div}\;\boxed{(}\;\boxed{3}\;\boxed{\div}\;\boxed{7}\;\boxed{)}\;\boxed{=}$$

If you try this without the brackets to tell you where to start, you find that:

$$\boxed{10}\;\boxed{\div}\;\boxed{11}\;\boxed{\div}\;\boxed{3}\;\boxed{\div}\;\boxed{7}\;\boxed{=}$$

gives 0.04329 – clearly much too small, as the answer is approximately 2. You have to press:

$$\boxed{3} \;\boxed{\div}\; \boxed{7} \;\boxed{=}$$

first to find $\frac{3}{7}$, then store it in the memory. Do it now. You'll have stored 0.4285. Now press:

$$\boxed{10} \;\boxed{\div}\; \boxed{11} \;\boxed{=}$$

to give $\frac{10}{11}$ and continue with:

$$\boxed{\div} \;\boxed{\text{memory recall}}\; \boxed{=}$$

to divide by $\frac{3}{7}$. You'll obtain 2.121212..., the decimal version of:
$$\frac{70}{33} = 2\frac{4}{33}$$
which you found before.

Self-check

Look at questions **1–4** below. Without making any detailed calculations, say whether the result of each is:
a above 5;
b between 2 and 5;
c between 1 and 2;
d between $\frac{1}{2}$ and 1;
e between $\frac{1}{5}$ and $\frac{1}{2}$;
f below $\frac{1}{5}$.

1 $\frac{3}{4} \div \frac{3}{100} =$
2 $\frac{3}{4} \div \frac{3}{5} =$
3 $\frac{3}{4} \div \frac{2}{7} =$
4 $\frac{3}{4} \div \frac{7}{8} =$

5–8 Now find the simplest exact fractions as answers to **1–4**.

9–12 Change each of your answers in **5–8** into a decimal.

13–16 Now answer each of **1–4** on your calculator as a decimal, but using the calculator method above.

ANSWERS

1 a There are over 30 $\frac{3}{100}$ths in a unit, so there will be over 20 in $\frac{3}{4}$s.

2 c $\frac{3}{5}$ is less than $\frac{3}{4}$, but two lots of $\frac{3}{5}$ is a little more than 1, so the answer will be between 1 and 2 $\frac{3}{5}$ths in $\frac{3}{4}$.

3 b Two lots of $\frac{2}{7}$ is $\frac{4}{7}$ – a little over $\frac{1}{2}$ and less than $\frac{3}{4}$.

4 d $\frac{7}{8}$ is a little more than $\frac{3}{4}$, so the result will be a little less than 1.

5 25. **6** $\frac{5}{4} = 1\frac{1}{4}$. **7** $\frac{21}{8} = 2\frac{5}{8}$.
8 $\frac{6}{7}$. **9, 13** 25. **10, 14** 1.25.
11, 15 2.625. **12, 16** 0.8571.

Solving equations with fractions or decimals

With a calculator you can solve just about any equation by
'guess and check' methods, though often there are techniques
you can use to speed up the process and 'home in' on an exact
answer straightaway. Here's an example using the two
approaches. Solve the equation:
$$7x + 5 = 13.6$$

'Guess and check'

Try $x = 1$. Then:
$$7x + 5 = 7 \times 1 + 5 = 12$$
Try $x = 2$. Then:
$$7x + 5 = 7 \times 2 + 5 = 19$$
Try $x = 1.25$. Then:
$$7x + 5 = 13.75$$
Try $x = 1.23$. Then:
$$7x + 5 = 13.61$$
I've used each result to make an improved guess, trying to get
the left-hand side as close as I can to 13.6. By now, I know that
x is somewhere close to 1.23.

> *Activity*
>
> Carry on and see how close you can get to 13.6, using this
> method.

'Working backwards'

$$7x + 5 = 13.6$$
Thus:
$$7x = 8.6$$
because $8.6 + 5 = 13.6$. Therefore:
$$x = \tfrac{1}{7} \text{ of } 8.6$$
$$= \tfrac{1}{7} \times 8.6$$

$$= 8.6 \div 7$$
$$= 1.2285714$$

or, in fractions:

$$= \tfrac{8.6}{7} = \tfrac{86}{70}$$
$$= \tfrac{43}{35}$$
$$= 1\tfrac{8}{35}$$

See how the 'working backwards' approach can save time. Whatever method you use, though, you should always check – even if it's just in your head – that the solution you end up with is correct. Do this by using your solution to find the values of the left-hand side and right-hand side of your equation and checking they are the same.

Self-check

1 Here are some equations and solutions. Not all of the solutions are correct. Say which solutions are correct and which are wrong, by checking.

   a $4x - 3 = 12, x = 5$

   b $2(x - 3) = 4, x = 3.5$

   c $4x = 15, x = 60$

   d $\tfrac{x}{3} = 8, x = 24$

   e $\tfrac{4}{9} = \tfrac{x}{18}, x = 2$

   f $\tfrac{2}{5} \times \tfrac{x}{3} = \tfrac{8}{15}, x = 4$

2 Solve these equations giving solutions correct to 3 significant figures.

   a $\tfrac{x}{7} = \tfrac{5}{9}$

   b $x \times \tfrac{3}{8} = 4$

   c $\tfrac{4}{5}y = \tfrac{2}{3}$

Carry out a check for each of the equations.

ANSWERS

1 **a** Wrong: $4 \times 5 - 3 = 17$, not 12.

   b Wrong: $2(3.5 - 3) = 2 \times 0.5 = 1$, not 4.

   c Wrong: $4 \times 60 = 240$, not 15.

   d Correct: $\tfrac{24}{3} = 24 \div 3 = 8$.

   e Wrong: $\tfrac{2}{18} = \tfrac{1}{9}$, not $\tfrac{4}{9}$.

   f Correct: $\tfrac{2}{5} \times \tfrac{4}{3} = \tfrac{8}{15}$.

2 In these solutions, I've started by changing fractions to decimals using my calculator.

a $x \div 7 = 0.55555$, so $x = 7 \times 0.555555... = 3.8888 \simeq 3.89$.

b $x \times 0.375 = 4$, so $x = 4 \div 0.375 = 10.666 \simeq 10.7$.

c $0.8y = 0.6666$, so $y = 0.6666 \div 0.8 = 0.8333... \simeq 0.833$.

Checking:

a $3.89 \div 7 = 0.5557$; $\frac{5}{9} = 0.5556$.

b $10.66 \times 0.375 = 3.9975 \simeq 4$.

c $4 \times 0.833 \div 5 = 0.6664 \simeq \frac{2}{3}$.

You'll find another approach to solving equations like these in the next section.

Solving equations without changing fractions to decimals

Here are the equations in question 2 of the self-check above, solved by using fractions only. I've used the 'equivalent fractions' and 'multiply fractions' rules to help me, but don't think there is only one way to solve such equations. You may like to use other approaches – the important thing is to **check your solution** at the end.

a $\frac{x}{7} = \frac{5}{9}$

$\frac{x}{7}$ means $x \div 7$, so x must be 7 times as big as $\frac{5}{9}$

$\qquad x = 7 \times \frac{5}{9}$

means 'implies that' or 'which means that'

$\qquad\quad = \frac{35}{9}$

$\qquad\quad = 3\frac{8}{9}$

and I've converted the fractions to a mixed number.

Check:

$\frac{35}{9} \div 7 = \frac{35}{9} \times \frac{1}{7} = \frac{5}{9}$

$x \times \frac{3}{8} = 4$

$\Rightarrow x = 4 \div \frac{3}{8}$

$\Rightarrow x = 4 \times \frac{8}{3}$

$\qquad = \frac{32}{3}$

$\qquad = 10\frac{2}{3}$

Check:

$\frac{32}{3} \times \frac{3}{8} = \frac{32}{8} = 4$

Do the fractions confuse you? Suppose you'd started with $x \times 3 = 4$, then x would have been $\frac{1}{3}$ of 4 or $4 \div 3$. Use the:
$\frac{a}{b} \div \frac{c}{d} = \frac{a}{b} \times \frac{d}{c}$ rule.

c $\quad \frac{4}{5}y = \frac{2}{3}$
$\quad =>y = \frac{2}{3} \div \frac{4}{5}$
$\qquad = \frac{2}{3} \times \frac{5}{4}$
$\qquad = \frac{10}{12}$
$\qquad = \frac{5}{6}$

Check:
$\quad \frac{4}{5} \times \frac{5}{6} = \frac{4}{6} = \frac{2}{3}$

You can probably work out your own steps here. They're much like the steps used in **b** above.

Self-check

Now try these. In each case, try to find the exact solution as a fraction or mixed number. If you find some of them hard, use the 'guess and check' method to find an approximate solution (correct to 3 s.f.).

1 $\frac{x}{3} = 5$
2 $\frac{y}{5} = \frac{1}{3}$
3 $2x = 7$
4 $7x = 31$
5 $4x + 5 = 2$
6 $\frac{x}{3} = \frac{3}{4}$
7 $\frac{y}{4} = \frac{7}{9}$
8 $\frac{2}{3}z = \frac{3}{5}$
9 $\frac{x}{5} + 1 = 3\frac{3}{4}$

ANSWERS

1 $x = 15$
2 $y = 1\frac{2}{3}$ or 1.67
3 $x = 3\frac{1}{2}$
4 $x = 4\frac{3}{7}$ or 4.43
5 $x = ^{-}\frac{3}{4}$ or $^{-}0.75$
$\qquad 4x = ^{-}3$, i.e. 5 below 2
$\qquad x = ^{-}3 \div 4 = ^{-}\frac{3}{4}$
6 $x = 2\frac{1}{4}$ or 2.25
$\qquad x \div 3 = \frac{3}{4}$
$\qquad x = 3 \times \frac{3}{4} = \frac{9}{4} = 2\frac{1}{4}$

7 $y = 3\frac{1}{9}$ or 3.11

8 $z = \frac{9}{10}$ or 0.9

9 $x = 13\frac{3}{4}$ or 13.75

$\frac{x}{5} = 2\frac{3}{4}$

$x = 5 \times 2\frac{3}{4} = 5 \times 2 + 5 \times \frac{3}{4} = 10 + \frac{15}{4} = 13\frac{3}{4}$

Review

1 Write down the simplest fraction you can find equivalent to:

$\frac{4}{8}, \frac{27}{30}, \frac{16}{20}, \frac{49}{56}, \frac{84}{98}, \frac{0.6}{0.9}$.

2 Copy these statements, then insert letters or numbers to make them true in general.

$\frac{a}{b} \times \square = \frac{ap}{bq}$

$\frac{h}{k} = \frac{mh}{\square}$

$\frac{a}{b} \div \square = \frac{ap}{bq}$

3 Solve the following equations, giving your answers as exact fractions.

$4x = \frac{5}{9}$

$\frac{y}{3} = \frac{1}{4}$

$\frac{2}{3}z = \frac{1}{10}$

$\frac{2w}{3} = \frac{7}{8}$

4 Calculate the following, giving your answers as: decimals correct to 3 s.f., and exact fractions.

$\frac{2}{3} \times \frac{7}{8}$

$\frac{2}{3} \div \frac{7}{8}$

$\frac{7}{8} \div \frac{2}{3}$

6 | Percentages, ratio and more fractions

You will need a calculator for parts of this chapter. If you find percentages hard to deal with, you'll probably find your calculator helps, even if it doesn't have a % key.

Topics covered

- What percentages mean.
- Finding percentages on your calculator.
- Fractions and percentages.
- Comparing with percentages.
- Finding percentages of amounts.
- Borrowing money, etc.
- Adding and subtracting percentages.
- Ratio.
- Adding and subtracting fractions.
- Fraction patterns.

What percentages mean

Per cent means **'out of a hundred'** or 'per hundred' (think of 100 **cents** = 1 dollar). The sign % is short for 'per cent' (as distinct from ° which means degrees).

Imagine you carried out a survey on local bus services. You asked people in the street 'Have you travelled on a bus during the past week?' In your first 20 answers, 13 out of 20 people said 'Yes'. If you carried on asking more groups of 20 people, and in each group 13 out of 20 said 'Yes', you would have obtained:

- 26 'yes' out of 40;
- 39 'yes' out of 60;
- 52 'yes' out of 80;
- 65 'yes' out of 100.

So the 13 out of 20 is the same fraction as 65 out of 100, or 65%, i.e.:

   13 out of 20 = 65%

   Self-check

   1 How many people out of 20 said 'No'?
   2 What is this as a % of the people asked?

ANSWERS

1 7. **2** 35%.

If you'd gone on to ask 200 people altogether, and you continued to get 13 'yes' answers in every 20, then 130 out of 200 would have said 'yes'. Thus 130 out of 200 is the same as 65 out of 100 or 65%.

   Self-check

   1 In another survey 18 out of 25 said 'yes'. What percentage said 'yes'? What percentage didn't say 'yes'?
   2 What is 16 out of 50 as a %?
   3 What is £36 out of £300 as a %?
   4 What is £4 out of £5 as a %?

ANSWERS

1 72%, 28%. **2** 32%. **3** 12%. **4** 80%.

Finding percentages on your calculator

13 out of 20 is $\frac{13}{20}$ths of the people asked in the survey, just as 65 out of 100 is the same as $\frac{65}{100}$ths. So a percentage just tells you 'how many hundredths'. You'll remember from Chapter 5 how:
   $\frac{13}{20}$ is equivalent to $\frac{65}{100}$
Using your calculator, what is 18 out of 25 as a percentage?

$$\boxed{1}\,\boxed{8}\,\boxed{\div}\,\boxed{2}\,\boxed{5}\,\boxed{=}\,\boxed{0}\,\boxed{.}\,\boxed{7}\,\boxed{2}$$

that is 72 hundredths, so 18 out of 25 = 72%. In the same way:
$36 \div 300 = 0.12$

that is 12 hundredths or 12%.

$4 \div 5 = 0.8 = \frac{8}{10} = \frac{8.0}{100}$ or 80%

You'll find your calculator very useful when dealing with more awkward percentages. For example, imagine the rent for your flat (or your weekly mortgage payment) going up from £28 to £33. What is this rise **as a percentage**? The rise is £5, but this is not a % as it's a change of £5 compared with £28, not compared with £100. Using equivalent fractions:

$\frac{5}{28} = \frac{10}{56} = \frac{15}{84} = \frac{20}{112}$

so 5 out of 28 is the same as 15 out of 84 or 20 out of 112, etc. This is about 18 out of 100, so 5 out of 28 is approximately 18%.

Now work out:

$$\boxed{5}\,\boxed{\div}\,\boxed{2}\,\boxed{8}\,\boxed{=}$$

on your calculator. You'll obtain 0.178571, i.e. 17.8571 hundredths, which is 17.8571%. Thus:

$\frac{5}{28} \simeq 17.9\%$

You can check this, if you feel unsure about the position of the decimal point, by calculating $17.8571 \div 100$, that is 17.8571 out of 100. You'll arrive back at 0.178571.

Self-check

Use your calculator to change these into percentages. Round off answers to 2 decimal places (that is, two places after the decimal point).

1 27 out of 67

2 146 out of 635

3 $\frac{15}{67}$

4 2.3 out of 19.6

ANSWERS

1 40.30%. **2** 22.99%. **3** 22.39%. **4** 11.73%.

Using percentages to compare

In a magazine survey into shopping habits (based on a survey carried out by IPC on behalf of their magazines *Family Circle*, *Living* and *Woman's Realm*), 1022 parents were asked 'When you go shopping, who usually goes with you?' Their replies were as in the table below.

| | Age | | | |
Answer	21–30	31–35	36–45	All ages
I go alone	75	177	218	470
Only my partner	51	66	73	190
Only my children	83	77	33	193
Partner and children	59	76	34	169
Total	268	396	358	1022

The results are hard to compare because the column totals are different. It would be much easier if every column showed the same total number of replies. You can do this by finding what each number is as a % of the column total – as if each column total was 100. For instance:

- 470 out of 1022 = 45.988 or about 46%
-   75 out of   268 = 27.985 or about 28%
- 177 out of   396 = 44.696 or about 45%

> ### Self-check
>
> 1 Use your calculator to change each number in the table into a percentage of the column totals, to the nearest whole number.
> 2 Fill in your results in a table like the one above.
> 3 Total each column in your table. What do you obtain?
> 4 What % of people questioned were aged 36 or over?

ANSWERS
1–3

Answer	Age			
	21–30	*31–35*	*36–45*	*All ages*
I go alone	28	45	61	46
Only my partner	19	17	20	19
Only my children	31	19	9	19
Partner and children	22	19	9	17
Total	100	100	99	101

The columns don't all total to exactly 100 because the figures in the columns are not exact.

4 $358 \div 1022 \simeq 35\%$

Finding percentages of amounts

Per cent (%) means 'out of 100', so 3% means '3 out of 100' or $\frac{3}{100}$ths. Thus 3% of £86 means $\frac{3}{100}$ths of £86 or $86 \times \frac{3}{100}$. You can probably work this out in your head as:

$\frac{258}{100} = £2.58$

If you're doubtful, use your calculator to find:

$$\boxed{8}\,\boxed{6}\,\boxed{\times}\,\boxed{3}\,\boxed{\div}\,\boxed{1}\,\boxed{0}\,\boxed{0}\,\boxed{=}$$

giving £2.58 as before.

> *Self-check*
>
> Calculate these, giving answers to the nearest penny.
> **1** 7% of £86
> **2** 36.5% of £86
> **3** 10.4% of £608
> **4** 68% of £72.49
> **5** Which is a bigger cash reduction, 21% off a price of £86 or 19% off a price of £98?

ANSWERS

1 £6.02. **2** £31.39. **3** £63.23.
4 £49.29. **5** 19% of £98 = £18.62 (21% of £86 = £18.06).

Adding and subtracting percentages

If you eat out, or pay for any service, you often find that your bill includes extras such as VAT at 15%, service charge 10%, and so on. The percentages will be based on the basic bill. Price reductions or discounts are also quoted in percentages – $12\frac{1}{2}\%$ off, 5% discount, etc.

Thus, for example, if your basic bill was £18.34 at a restaurant, the VAT would be 15% of £18.34 so the total bill would be:

£18.34 + 15% of £18.34

= £18.34 + 0.15 × 18.34

= £18.34 + 1.83

= £20.17

A 5% discount on a price of £15.32 means that the price is reduced to:

$£(15.32 - \frac{5}{100} \times 15.32) = £15.32 - £0.77$
$= £14.55$

You'll often find that slightly odd-looking percentages (like $12\frac{1}{2}\%$, $33\frac{1}{3}\%$, etc.) are the result of changing fairly simple fractions into percentages, thus:

- $12\frac{1}{2}\% = \frac{12\frac{1}{2}}{100} = \frac{25}{200} = \frac{5}{40} = \frac{1}{8}$
- $33\frac{1}{3}\% = \frac{33\frac{1}{3}}{100} = \frac{100}{300} = \frac{1}{3}$

and you've already noticed that:

- $10\% = \frac{10}{100} = \frac{1}{10}$

It's tempting to think that if 10% is $\frac{1}{10}$, then 5% is $\frac{1}{5}$, but you can easily see that this is not correct. In fact:

- $5\% = \frac{5}{100} = \frac{1}{20}$

while:

- $\frac{1}{5} = \frac{20}{100} = 20\%$

so '$\frac{1}{5}$th off' is much better value than '5% off', and 20% off is much better value than $\frac{1}{20}$th off.

Self-check

1 In a sale prices are reduced by 25%. Calculate the new prices of items if the original prices were:

£18; £26.50; £14.84; £7.63.
2 At a closing down sale prices are first reduced by 12½%. These prices are then reduced by a further 40%. What are the final prices of items which were originally £20, £32 and £58?

ANSWERS

1 £13.50; £19.88; £11.13; £5.72.
2 After 12% reduction, prices are £17.50, £28 and £50.75. Final prices are £10.50, £16.80, £30.45.

Savings – simple and compound interest

Suppose you save £500 in a bank or building society, and they pay interest at, say, 8% pa (per annum or per year). Then each year your £500 would earn 8% of 500 = £40. Over two years, your £500 would earn you 2 × £40 = £80, and so on.

If you just left the starting amount of £500 (the **principal**) in the bank your £500 would be earning **simple interest** of £40 per year. Of course, in practice you might choose to leave the interest in the bank each year, so that your principal increased year by year as well. Your savings would then be earning **compound interest**.

In this case, in the second year, your principal would be £540 and the corresponding interest would be 8% of £540 = £43.20. So the total interest over two years = 40 + 43.20 = £83.20.

Ratio

You'll find this word used whenever you are **comparing** measurements or quantities, **sharing out** amounts or **enlarging** different measurements. For instance, you have a recipe where you need 30g of sugar for every 40g of flour, or you have to share out food between two groups of people according to the number of people in the groups, or you measure a distance between two places on a map and enlarge the measurement to find the true distance between the places. The idea of **ratio** is involved in all these situations. You'll notice that they are closely connected with fractions, multiplying and dividing.

Using ratio to compare

In the example above you need 30g of sugar for every 40g of flour. You could just as well have been measuring the parts in ounces – 30 ounces of sugar could require 40 ounces of flour – or in kilograms even – 30kg of sugar compared with 40kg of flour. What is important is that you are measuring both ingredients in the same unit – both grams or both ounces or both in kg.

In every case, you require 30 parts of sugar for every 40 parts of flour; in short, the **ratio** of sugar to flour is 30 to 40 (often written 30:40). The ratio tells you how the amount of sugar **compares with** the amount of flour. In the example, 60g of sugar could need 80g of flour, but the ratio of sugar to flour is still the same, i.e.:

60:80 = 30:40

Scaling down the quantities, 15g of sugar need only 20g of sugar, so:

15:20 = 30:40

Scaling down further gives:

15:20 = 3:4

You can check this by thinking of the sugar and flour in 10g measures, so that 3 measures (30g) of sugar required 4 measures (40g) of flour, so that is:

30:40 = 3:4

3:4 is the simplest version of this ratio, as scaling it down any further involves you in fractions or decimals.

The ratios 30:40, 15:20, 60:80 and 3:4 are **equivalent** to each other – they are just different ways of describing the same comparison. You can probably see how you can find more equivalent ratios simply by multiplying or dividing both numbers by the same amount, very much in the same way as you could extend sets of equivalent fractions.

Self-check

Find the missing numbers in these sets of equivalent ratios.

1 30:40; 3:4; 300:☐; 90:☐; ☐:160; ☐:2.
2 50:60; ☐:6; ☐:18; 100:☐; $2\frac{1}{2}$:☐.

ANSWERS

1 30:40; 3:4; 300:400; 90:120; 120:160; $1\frac{1}{2}$:2.
2 50:60; 5:6; 15:18; 100:120; $2\frac{1}{2}$:3.

Notice how, once you've simplified a ratio as far as you can, you can use this simplest version to find other equivalent ratios by multiplying or dividing both numbers by the same amount, e.g.:

3:4 = 300:400 (×100)
3:4 = 90:120 (×30)
3:4 = $1\frac{1}{2}$:2 (÷ 2 or × 0.5)

Using ratio to share

You can make concrete using a mix of 1 bucket of cement to 2 buckets of sand to 4 buckets of gravel, making 7 bucketfuls of mixture, i.e. the ratio of cement to sand to gravel is:

1:2:4

You can scale it up or down as before, so 70 bucketfuls of dry concrete mix will need 10 bucketfuls of cement, 20 of sand and 40 of gravel, and 1 bucketful of concrete mix will need $\frac{1}{7}$th of a bucketful of cement, $\frac{2}{7}$ of sand and $\frac{4}{7}$ of gravel.

In the first example, I used a **scale factor** of 10 to give me 10 times the quantities, and then used a scale factor of $\frac{1}{7}$ to give me $\frac{1}{7}$th of the original quantities. (The amount of water you need depends on the dampness of the sand so I haven't included it here.)

Using ratio to describe an enlargement

Refer to Chapter 11 to see how ratios are used.

Self-check

1 Three dyes, A, B and C, are mixed in the ratio:
A:B:C = 4:8:11
You have just 80 g of B. How much of A and C should you mix with it (to the nearest gram)?

2 The ratio of cars to lorries on a motorway is said to be 7:2. How many lorries would you expect for every 10000 cars (answer to nearest 100)?

3 In a factory the ratio of women:men is 8:11. If there are 600 women employed, how many men are there?

ANSWERS

1 Quantity of A $= \frac{1}{8} \times 80 = 40$ g.
Quantity of C is $\frac{11}{8}$ of $80 = 110$ g.

2 Two lorries for every seven cars, so $\frac{2}{7}$ths of a lorry for every car, so:
$\frac{2}{7} \times 10\,000 \simeq 2900$ lorries.

3 No. of men $= \frac{11}{8} \times$ No. of women
$= \frac{11}{8} \times 600 = 825$ men

Review

1 The replies to the question 'How easy do you find it to manage on the amount you set aside for house-keeping?', posed in a survey, are in the following table.

		Age		
Answer	*21–30*	*31–35*	*36–45*	*Total*
Reasonably easy	92	162	148	402
Rather difficult	154	194	188	536
Very difficult	22	40	22	84
Totals	268	396	358	1022

In a copy of the table, change each number into a % of the column total.

2 A contractor charges £1600 for a job taking 3 weeks. It costs him £300 per week in labour and £400 for materials. What is his profit? What is this as a percentage of his costs?

3 You have to charge VAT of 15% on a bill of £36.24. What is the total bill?

4 An identical computer is included in the sales of three different shops. In shop A the original price is £166, with a sale reduction of 10%. In shop B the original price is £178, with a sale reduction of 20%, while in shop C the price is £175, with £15 off during the sale. Which is the cheapest?

Adding and subtracting fractions

In Chapter 5 you found a simple rule for multiplying fractions.
An example of this is:

$\frac{9}{10} \times \frac{4}{5} = \frac{9 \times 4}{10 \times 5} = \frac{36}{50}$

and in general:

$\frac{a}{b} \times \frac{c}{d} = \frac{ac}{bd}$

How then do you add fractions?

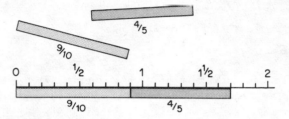

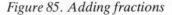

Figure 85. Adding fractions

As in other situations, it helps to answer this question with a
diagram (See Figure 85). One length is $\frac{9}{10}$ of a unit and the other
is $\frac{4}{5}$ of a unit, so placing these lengths end to end should give a
length equal to $\frac{9}{10} + \frac{4}{5}$. You can see that the result is over $1\frac{1}{2}$.
Using the decimal scale you can read off the total of $\frac{9}{10} + \frac{4}{5}$ as $1\frac{7}{10}$
(or $\frac{17}{10}$).

From the diagram, or by using the idea of **equivalent frac-
tions**, you can see that $\frac{4}{5} = \frac{8}{10}$. Now you can add the top numbers
(**numerators**) of the two fractions, because you're adding two
fractions of the same type (both tenths), so:

$\frac{9}{10} + \frac{4}{5} = \frac{9}{10} + \frac{8}{10} = \frac{17}{10} = 1\frac{7}{10}$

In a similar way:

$\frac{9}{10} - \frac{4}{5} = \frac{9}{10} - \frac{8}{10} = \frac{1}{10}$

as you can see from Figure 86.

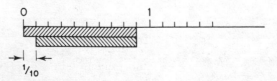

Figure 86. Subtracting fractions

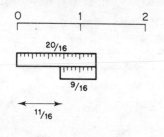

$$1\tfrac{1}{4} - {}^{9}/_{16} = {}^{20}/_{16} - {}^{9}/_{16} = {}^{11}/_{16}$$

Figure 87.

Here are more examples (see also Figure 87) to show the addition and subtraction of fractions.

1 $\frac{3}{7} + \frac{5}{7} = \frac{8}{7} = 1\frac{1}{7}$

2 $2.6 + 1.5 = 4.1$

$2\frac{6}{10} + 1\frac{5}{10} = 3\frac{11}{10}$ or $4\frac{1}{10}$

3 $\frac{1}{2} + \frac{3}{8} = \frac{4}{8} + \frac{3}{8} = \frac{7}{8}$

4 $1\frac{1}{4} - \frac{9}{16} = 1\frac{4}{16} - \frac{9}{16} = \frac{20}{16} - \frac{9}{16} = \frac{11}{16}$

As you can see, the key step is to make sure that the fractions you're adding or subtracting have the same denominator.

> *Self-check*
>
> Add or subtract these fractions, giving your answer as a fraction (or mixed number if greater than 1 unit).
>
> **1** $\frac{5}{16} + \frac{1}{16}$
>
> **2** $\frac{3}{10} + \frac{7}{100}$
>
> **3** $\frac{3}{8} - \frac{1}{32}$
>
> **4** $1 - \frac{2}{7}$
>
> **5** $\frac{3}{5} - \frac{3}{20}$
>
> **6** Draw a diagram to show how $\frac{1}{6} + \frac{2}{3}$ does *not* equal $\frac{3}{9}$.

ANSWERS

1 $\frac{6}{16} = \frac{3}{8}$. **2** $\frac{37}{100}$. **3** $\frac{12}{32} - \frac{1}{32} = \frac{11}{32}$.
4 $\frac{7}{7} - \frac{2}{7} = \frac{5}{7}$. **5** $\frac{12}{20} - \frac{3}{20} = \frac{9}{20}$. **6** See Figure 88.

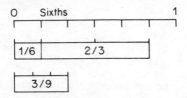

Figure 88.

Finding the correct denominator

With many pairs of fractions, one denominator is a multiple of the other, e.g. 10 is a multiple of 5, 100 is a multiple of 10, 16 is a multiple of 8, etc. It is therefore straightforward to convert one fraction to another equivalent fraction to make adding and subtracting possible.

However, dealing with calculations like:

$\frac{7}{8} + \frac{4}{5}$ or $\frac{3}{4} - \frac{1}{5}$

is more awkward. The object is to replace these pairs of fractions with equivalent fractions which each have the same denominator, for example:

- $\frac{7}{8} = \frac{7 \times 3}{8 \times 3}$ or $\frac{7 \times 8}{8 \times 8}$ or $\mathbf{\frac{7 \times 5}{8 \times 5}}$ or $\frac{7 \times 2}{8 \times 2}$, etc.

- $\frac{4}{5} = \frac{4 \times 3}{5 \times 3}$ or $\frac{4 \times 8}{5 \times 8}$ or $\mathbf{\frac{4 \times 5}{5 \times 5}}$ or $\frac{4 \times 2}{5 \times 2}$, etc.

Of these the two fractions in **bold** type have the **same denominator** (40), so you can replace:

$\frac{7}{8} + \frac{4}{5}$ by $\frac{7 \times 5}{8 \times 5} + \frac{4 \times 8}{5 \times 8} = \frac{35}{40}$ + $\frac{32}{40}$

$= \frac{67}{40} = 1\frac{27}{40}$

In the same way, you can replace:

$\frac{3}{4} - \frac{1}{5}$ by $\frac{3 \times 5}{4 \times 5} - \frac{1 \times 4}{5 \times 4} = \frac{15}{20} - \frac{4}{20} = \frac{11}{20}$

Self-check

Add or subtract these fractions.

1 $\frac{1}{4} + \frac{3}{5}$

2 $\frac{1}{5} + \frac{1}{3}$

3 $\frac{2}{3} + \frac{3}{4}$

4 $\frac{4}{5} - \frac{1}{3}$

5 $\frac{2}{3} - \frac{3}{5}$

ANSWERS

1 $\frac{5}{20} + \frac{12}{20} = \frac{17}{20}$.   **2** $\frac{8}{15}$.   **3** $\frac{17}{12} = 1\frac{5}{12}$.
4 $\frac{7}{15}$.   **5** $\frac{1}{15}$.

General rules for adding or subtracting fractions

If you've managed the questions in the last self-check correctly, you will probably have noticed the general pattern in the way the numbers combine when you add or subtract two fractions.

As before, you can show this clearly by using letters to stand for numbers. In general, for **adding**:

● $\frac{a}{b} + \frac{c}{d} = \frac{ad}{bd} + \frac{bc}{bd} = \frac{ad + bc}{bd}$

Using question **1** of the last self-check as an example, when $a = 1$, $b = 4$, $c = 3$, $d = 5$, then:

$\frac{a}{b} + \frac{c}{d}$

becomes:

$\frac{1}{4} + \frac{3}{5}$

and:

$\frac{ad + bc}{bd}$

becomes:

$\frac{1 \times 5 + 3 \times 4}{3 \times 5} = \frac{17}{20}$

For **subtracting**:

● $\frac{a}{b} - \frac{c}{d} = \frac{ad}{bd} - \frac{bc}{bd} = \frac{ad - bc}{bd}$

So, for example $\frac{4}{5} - \frac{2}{3} = \frac{4 \times 3 - 5 \times 2}{5 \times 3} = \frac{2}{15}$

> *Self-check*
>
> See if you can fill in the gaps in these versions of the adding/subtracting fractions rule.
>
> **1** $\frac{p}{q} + \frac{r}{s} = \frac{\boxed{} + qr}{qs}$
>
> **2** $\frac{w}{v} - \frac{h}{k} = \frac{wk - \boxed{}}{\boxed{}}$
>
> You will find the word 'difference' used to mean how much greater one number is than another, e.g. the difference between 5 and 8 is 3.
>
> **3** What is the difference between $\frac{1}{4}$ and $\frac{1}{3}$?
> **4** What is the difference between $\frac{1}{9}$ and $\frac{1}{10}$?

ANSWERS

1 $\frac{ps + qr}{qs}$.   **2** $\frac{wk - hv}{vk}$.   **3** $\frac{4 - 3}{12} = \frac{1}{12}$.   **4** $\frac{1}{90}$.

Fraction patterns

Figure 89 shows one way by which you can compare fractions. You can imagine it being extended as far down as you wish. Lay your ruler on the diagram and use it to pick out sets of equivalent fractions. For example, if you line it up with the arrows A and B, you will find it is at the end of $\frac{2}{3}$, $\frac{4}{6}$, $\frac{6}{9}$ and $\frac{8}{12}$.

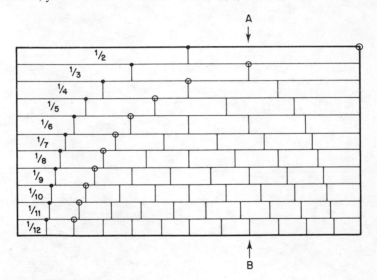

Figure 89. Comparing fractions

Review

1 Lengths of wood are to be cut into $\frac{1}{4}$ m pieces. Unfortunately they are cut into $\frac{1}{3}$ m pieces instead. What fraction of a metre should be cut off each piece to make it the correct length?

2 A farm has an area of 120 hectares. Two-thirds of the farm is planted with wheat and the remainder with sugar beet. Next year the beet crop has to be reduced to

$\frac{4}{5}$ of what it was, while 30 hectares are planted with barley. What fractions of the farm area will be used for each crop?

3 Look at the following calculations:

$\frac{1}{2} + \frac{2}{5}$ $\frac{2}{3} + 1\frac{1}{5}$ $\frac{1}{8} - \frac{1}{10}$

$\frac{5}{8} - \frac{1}{10}$ $0.8 \div 0.5$ $0.8 + 0.05$

0.8×0.5

Here are the answers:

$\frac{17}{20}$ $\frac{13}{12}$ $1\frac{3}{5}$

$\frac{1}{40}$ 0.9 0.525

$\frac{4}{10}$

Match up each question with its correct answer and put right the one answer that is wrong.

7 | Another look at formulae and equations

Topics covered

- Variables, constants and expressions.
- Illustrating formulae with graphs.
- Using formulae in everyday situations.
- Making up formulae.
- Evaluating and simplifying expressions.
- Rearranging formulae.
- Multiplying negative numbers.
- Dividing negative numbers.
- Solving equations by simplifying and rearranging.

In this chapter I expand on the ideas set out in Chapters 2 and 4 concerning formulae and equations, and I'll use graphs to help.

As before, the second half of the chapter contains more involved ideas than the first. In particular it covers methods for multiplying two negative numbers. Some courses do not include negative numbers, so this might be a good time to check up on your own course syllabus.

Variables, constants and expressions

Here is a **formula** linking two **variables** a and b:

$a = 2b + 3$

What is the value of a when $b = 5$? Answer:

$a = 13$, since $13 = 2 \times 5 + 3$

$\uparrow\uparrow$

ab

In reverse, what is the value of b when a is 17?

$b = 7$, since $17 = 2 \times 7 + 3$

$\uparrow\uparrow$

ab

If $a = 8.6$ then $2b + 3 = 8.6$
$\quad b = \frac{1}{2}$ of $5.6 = 2.8$
and so on.

Let's look at the formula again. It includes two **variables**, a and b; these can take many different values. Some parts of the formula don't change, though. The b value is **always** multiplied by 2 and 3 is **always** added on. Because of this, 2 and 3 are called **constants**.

On the right-hand side of the = sign, there are two **terms**, $2b$ and 3. The 3 is a constant term, while the $2b$ is a variable term and these two terms are combined to form the **expression** $2b + 3$. On the left there's just one term.

Illustrating formulae with graphs

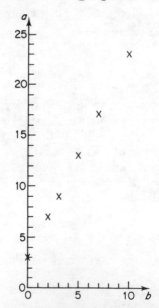

Figure 90. (b, a) values for the formula of $a = 2b + 3$

The table below shows some b-values and the matching values of a.

b	a
0	3
2	7
3	9
5	13
7	17
10	23

Plotting them on a graph (see Figure 90) with the b-axis to the right and the a-axis upwards, you will see how all the points lie in a line. In fact, whatever other pairs of (b, a) values you choose, you will find that the matching points always lie on the same line, extended if necessary. That's why you can join up the points with a line, as in Figure 91.

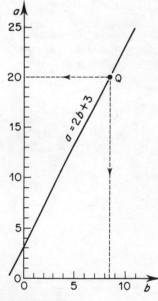

Figure 91. The graph of $a = 2b + 3$

You can use the graph line to find other pairs of (b, a) values, though their accuracy will depend on how you have drawn the graph. For instance, point Q has an *a*-value of 20 and a matching *b*-value of about 8.5, telling you that $a = 20$ when $b = 8.5$. You can see that this fits the formula, since:

$$20 = 2 \times 8.5 + 3$$

Self-check

1 Copy and complete this table from:
   $$y = 10 - 2x$$

x	y
0	
2	
4	
5	

2 Use your table from **1** to plot a graph of:
   $$y = 10 - 2x$$
   y-axis upwards, *x*-axis to the right.

3 Use your graph line to find the value of *x* which matches $y = 4.8$, then see how accurate your answer is by checking in the formula.

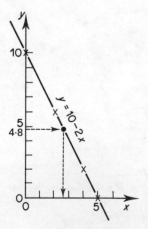

Figure 92.

ANSWERS

1

x	y
0	10
2	6
4	2
5	0

2 See Figure 92. **3** $x = 2.6$.

Using formulae

Here are two everyday formulae. In each case I've given an example to show how they work. You have a chance to see if you can use them in the following self-check.

Formula 1: $W = VA$

This formula gives power (in watts) compared with current (in amps) and voltage drop (in volts) where W = power in watts, V = voltage drop in volts, A = current in amps. For example, if $V = 250$ and $A = 8$:

$W = 250 \times 8 = 2000$

So power of 2000 watts uses 8 amps at 250 volts.

Formula 2: $t = \frac{d}{s}$

This formula gives the time (in hours) for a journey of known distance (in miles) at a known speed (in mph), where t = time in hours, d = distance in miles, s = speed in miles per hour. For example, if $d = 120$ and $s = 50$

$t = 120 \div 50 = 2.4$

So time = 2.4 hours (2 hours 24 minutes, since 6 minutes = 0.1 hours).

> *Self-check*
>
> Use formula 1 to find:
> **1** W when $V = 250$ and $A = 15$;
> **2** W when $V = 12$ and $A = 3$.
> Use formula 2 to find:

3 t when $d = 120$ and $s = 55$;
4 t when $d = 105$ and $s = 50$.

ANSWERS

1 $W = 3750$. **2** $W = 36$. **3** 2 hours 11 minutes. **4** 2 hours 6 minutes.

Making up formulae

Suppose you have to make up a formula to give the total cost (c pence) of petrol and oil bought at a garage if a litre of petrol costs 40p and a litre of oil costs 90p.

First you choose letters to stand for the number of litres of petrol and oil:

- let x = number of litres of petrol sold;
- let y = number of litres of oil sold.

To convert numbers of litres into cost in pence, you see that each litre of petrol costs 40p, so 2 litres costs 40×2p, 3 litres costs 40×3 and so on, so x litres costs $40 \times x$ or $40x$ pence. In the same way y litres of oil costs $90y$ pence. Thus the total cost is:

$40x + 90y$ pence

and the formula is:

$c = 40x + 90y$

Self-check

1 How would you alter the formula above if a litre of petrol now costs 40.5p and a litre of oil costs 95p?
2 Now alter your formula from **1** to give the cost of the petrol and oil in pounds, not pence. Use P to stand for the total cost in £.
3 Use your formula to find P when $x = 38$ and $y = 3$.
4 The total time for a journey is j minutes. The journey consists of a 10-minute walk, a wait at the bus stop of b minutes, then a bus ride of d miles, where each mile takes 3.5 minutes. So, for example, a journey including a 4-mile bus ride with 3 minutes' wait at the bus stop would take:

10 + 3 + 4 × 3.5 = 27 minutes
The table shows other journeys.

b	d	j
3	4	27
2	5	29.5
7	3	27.5
3	8	
2		22.5
	6	38

Complete the table.
5 Write down a formula for *j* in terms of *b* and *d*.

ANSWERS

1 *c* = 40.5*x* + 95*y*.
2 $P = \frac{1}{100}(40.5x+95y)$ or $P = (40.5x + 95y) \div 100$.
3 *P* = 18.24.
4 Missing values are *j* = 41, *d* = 3, *b* = 7.
5 *j* = 10 + *b* + 3.5*d*.

Evaluating more complicated expressions

Here are some examples to clarify the meanings of some expressions. **Powers** only apply for the number, letter or bracket **immediately in front** of them. For instance:

- $3r^2$ means $3 \times r \times r$
  e.g. if *r* = 6:
  $3r^2 = 3 \times 36 = 108$

- an^3 means $a \times n \times n \times n$
  e.g. if *a* = 5, *n* = 3, then:
  $an^3 = 5 \times 27 = 135$

- $4a^2 + 5b^2$ means $4 \times a \times a + 5 \times b \times b$

- $(4a + 5b)^2$ means $(4a + 5b) \times (4a + 5b)$
  e.g. if *a* = 9, *b* = 10;
  $4a^2 + 5b^2 = 4 \times 81 + 5 \times 100 = 824$
  while:
  $(4a + 5b)^2 = (36 + 50)^2 = 86^2 = 7396$

Fractions can be replaced by division. For instance:

- $\frac{1}{2}ma$ means $(m \times a) \div 2$
  e.g. if $m = 5$, $a = 7$:
  $\frac{1}{2}ma = 35 \div 2 = 17.5$

- $\frac{3}{4}t^2 = \frac{3t^2}{4} = (3 \times t \times t) \div 4$

  e.g. if $t = 5$:
  $\frac{3}{4}t^2 = 75 \div 4 = 18.75$

- $\frac{1}{av}$ means $\frac{1}{a \times v}$ or $1 \div (a \times v)$
  e.g. if $a = 4$, $v = 5$:
  $\frac{1}{av} = \frac{1}{4 \times 5} = \frac{1}{20}$ or 0.05

> ## Self-check
>
> Evaluate each of the following expressions, where $a = 4$, $b = 5$, $c = 6$. Give your answer correct to 3 s.f. where it is not an exact number.
> 1 $4b^2$
> 2 $4(b + c)^2$
> 3 $\dfrac{1}{ab} - \dfrac{1}{bc}$
> 4 $\frac{1}{2}(b^2 + c^2 - a^2)$

ANSWERS

1 64. **2** 484. **3** 0.0167. **4** 22.5.

Using more formulae

Example 1

Simple interest:
$$I = \frac{Prt}{100}$$
where I = interest in £, P = principal in £, r = rate of interest as a %, t = no. of years. For example, when principal = £600, rate of interest is 7% and number of years = 3:

$$I = \frac{600 \times 7 \times 3}{100} = 126$$

and interest = £126.

Example 2

$t = Fx$

where t is the turning effect on a bolt exerted by a force of F units applied to a spanner x units long. For example, if $F = 16$, $x = 5$, then $t = 80$.

> ### Self-check
>
> Using the formulae above find the values of the following.
> 1 I when $P = 530$, $r = 7.5$ and $t = 8$.
> 2 t when $F = 14.5$, $x = 6.3$.

ANSWERS

1 318.
2 91.35.

Simplifying expressions

Often you can simplify expressions by using some of the rules you met on pages 102–4, so that they become easier to evaluate. For instance, it is easier to work out $7a$ than $4.6a + 2.4a$, but they are equivalent:

$4.6a + 2.4a = a \times 4.6 + a \times 2.4$
$= a(4.6 + 2.4)$ (as a is a common factor)
$= 7a$

You can check this by choosing a value for a (6, say) and making sure that $7a = 4.6a + 2.4a$, when $a = 6$:

$7a = 7 \times 6 = 42$
$4.6a + 2.4a = 4.6 \times 6 + 2.4 \times 6 = 27.6 + 14.4 = 42$

Both expressions have the same value. In the same way:

- $3ah - 2.5ah = ah(3 - 2.5) = 0.5ah$
- $\frac{6a}{3} = 2a$
- $\frac{2x \times 8x}{5} = \frac{10x}{5} = 2x$

Here is a check to make sure that:

$$\frac{2x + 8x}{5} = 2x$$

when $x = 3$:

$$\frac{2x + 8x}{5} = \frac{6 + 24}{5} = \frac{30}{5} = 6$$

and $2x = 2 \times 3 = 6$.

See how this can help in this example: does $4x + 7$ equal $11x$?
Let $x = 3$, say, then:

$$4x + 7 = 12 + 7 = 19$$
$$11x = 11 \times 3 = 33$$

Because 19 is not the same as 33, $4x + 7$ does *not* equal 11.

Self-check

Simplify each of the following expressions as much as possible and write out a check to make sure you are correct. You can use any values for the variables apart from 1 or 0, but possible values of variables are given which match the check answers below.

1 $101x - 99x$ (check: $x = 2$).
2 $px + 2px$ ($p = 3, x = 5$).
3 $6x^2 + 4x^2 - 5$ ($x = 3$).
4 $x - 2(x + y) + 2y$ ($x = 2, y = 3$).
5 $\frac{2x}{3} + \frac{7x}{3}$ ($x = 4$).
6 $\frac{x}{3} + \frac{2x}{4}$ ($x = 2$).
7 $\frac{6mx}{3x}$ ($m = 2, x = 3$).
8 $\frac{3v^2}{v}$ ($v = 4$).

ANSWERS

1 $2x$ (check 4). **2** $3px$ (check 45). **3** $10x^2 - 5$ (check 85).
4 $x - 2(x + y) + 2y = x - 2x - 2y + 2y$
$$= {}^-x \text{ (check } {}^-2).$$
5 $\frac{9x}{3} = 3x$ (check 12).
6 $\frac{x}{3} + \frac{x}{2} = \frac{5x}{6}$ (check $1\frac{2}{3}$). **7** $2m$ (check 4).
8 $3v$ (check 12).

Rearranging simple formulae

Look at the table of values below for a formula connecting x and y, with matching graph in figure 93.

Point	x	y
A	1	1
B	2	3
C	3	5
D	4	7
E	5	9
F	0	$^-1$
G	$^-1$	$^-3$
H	$1\frac{1}{2}$	2
I	$^-1\frac{1}{2}$	$^-4$

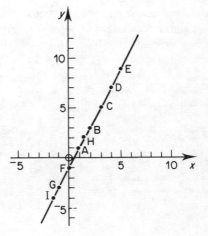

Figure 93.

The matching graph in Figure 93 is extended to the left and below the origin to show negative values of x and y.

There are many ways you can describe the connection between every matching (x, y) pair. Here are three.

- $y = 2x - 1$
  A: $1 = 2 - 1$
  B: $3 = 4 - 1$
  C: $5 = 6 - 1$
  D: $7 = 8 - 1$

or:
- $y - x = x - 1$
  C: $5 - 3 = 3 - 1$
  D: $7 - 4 = 4 - 1$
  etc.

or:
- $2x = y + 1$
  B: $4 = 3 + 1$
  C: $6 = 5 + 1$
  etc.

You may have spotted others.

All these ways of describing the connection between x and y are correct. If you alter the expression on one side of the equals sign, you have to alter the expression on the other side **in the same way**, so that the expressions, though changed, still remain equal to each other.

See how you can use this idea to derive all the different connections above, starting from $y = 2x - 1$ (see Figure 94).

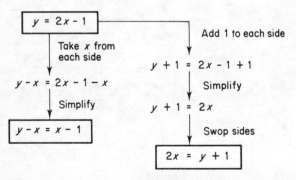

Figure 94

Here is the same process for the formula $x + 2y = 10$, with a table of values below.

- $x + 2y = 10$
  Take $2y$ from each side:
      $\Rightarrow x + 2y - 2y = 10 - 2y$
  Simplify:

$$=>x = 10 - 2y$$
- $x + 2y = 10$
  Take x from each side:
    $$=>x + 2y - x = 10 - x$$
  Simplify:
    $$=>2y = 10 - x$$
  Or swop sides:
    $$=>10 - x = 2y$$
- Or starting from:
    $$2y = 10 - x$$
  Halve each side:
    $$=>\tfrac{1}{2} \times 2y = \tfrac{1}{2}(10 - x)$$
  Simplify:
    $$=>y = \tfrac{1}{2}(10 - x)$$

x	y
0	5
1	$4\tfrac{1}{2}$
2	4
6	2
8	1

You can check that these altered versions of $x + 2y = 10$ are correct by using pairs of values from the table.

Self-check

Copy and fill in what has happened at each step.

1 $y = 2x + 4$

   ....:
      $$=>y - 4 = 2x + 4 - 4$$
   ....:
      $$=>y - 4 = 2x$$

2 $y = 2x + 4$

   ....:
      $$=>y - 2x = 2x + 4 - 2x$$
   ....:
      $$=>y - 2x = 4$$

ANSWERS

The complete layouts are as follows.

1 $y = 2x + 4$
Take 4 from each side:
   $y - 4 = 2x + 4 - 4$
Simplify:
   $y - 4 = 2x$

2 $y = 2x + 4$
Take $2x$ from each side:
   $y - 2x = 2x + 4 - 2x$
Simplify:
   $y - 2x = 4$

You can use this 'do the same to both sides' approach to solve equations too. Here I've used it to solve the equation
   $2(x + 4) - 3 = 39$
Add 3:
   $2(x + 4) - 3 + 3 = 39 + 3$
Simplify:
   $2(x + 4) = 42$
Halve:
   $\frac{1}{2} \times 2(x + 4) = \frac{1}{2} \times 42$
Simplify:
   $x + 4 = 21$
Take away 4:
   $x + 4 - 4 = 21 - 4$
Simplify:
   $x = 17$

See how the steps you have taken are the reverse of the original instructions:
   $x = 17$
Add 4:
   $x + 4 = 21$
Double:
   $2(x + 4) = 42$
Take away 3:
   $2(x + 4) - 3 = 39$

Self-check

Copy and complete the steps used in solving the equations below (the 'simplify' stages have been omitted).

1 $\frac{1}{2}(x - 3) = 6$

.................:

$\Rightarrow x - 3 = 12$

.................:

$\Rightarrow x = 15$

2 $2(x + 7) - 40 = 16$

.................:

$\Rightarrow 2(x + 7) = 56$

.................:

$\Rightarrow x + 7 = 28$

.................:

$\Rightarrow x = 21$

ANSWERS

1 Double.
  Add 3.
2 Add 40.
  Divide by 2 (halve).
  Take away 7.

As always **checking** is important. For instance, is $x = 21$ the correct solution for **2**? If $x = 21$, then:

$$2(x + 7) - 40 = 2 \times 28 - 40$$
$$= 56 - 40$$
$$= 16$$

so the left-hand side = right-hand side, and the solution is correct.

In solving equations, you are aiming to end up with the unknown letter on its own on one side of the = sign. Often, you can see which steps to take, but are not sure which to take first. It's a case of experience often. Whatever you do, remember to:

- do the same to both sides of an equation or formula;
- check that your solution or values fit afterwards.

Self-check

Now try solving some equations, setting them out as I did on page 17. Even if you can spot the answer, still write down the steps. It's good practice, and you will learn which steps to take in harder questions – and don't forget to check your answers.

1 $2x - 10 = 18$
2 $6(x + 3) = 30$
3 $5(2x - 1) = 35$

Here the first steps are given.

4 $24 - x = 2x$ (add x)
5 $\frac{1}{3}(2x + 5) = 11$ (multiply by 3)

Some slightly harder ones – answers could be negative or fractions.

6 $4x - 3 = 10$
7 $3(x - 1) = 17$
8 $23 - x = 2x$
9 $\frac{1}{2}(x - 5) = 20$
10 $5 + 4x = 9 - x$

ANSWERS

1 $x = 14$. **2** $x = 2$. **3** $x = 4$. **4** $x = 8$. **5** $x = 14$. **6** $x = 3\frac{1}{4}$. **7** $x = 6\frac{2}{3}$. **8** $x = 7\frac{2}{3}$. **9** $x = 45$. **10** $5 + 5x = 9 \Rightarrow x = \frac{4}{5}$

Rearranging more formulae

It is worth seeing how you can rearrange some of the other formulae you've met in the book, to avoid the 'guess and check' methods (which can be time-consuming). Here are two examples.

Example 1

A pentagon has angles a, b, c, d and e adding to 540°. Angles b, c and d are equal to each other, a is $\frac{1}{4}$ of b and e is $2 \times b$. Find the size of each angle.

Start with the fact that the angles add to 540°:

$a + b + c + d + e = 540$

Now replace b, c and d by $3b$, a by $\frac{1}{4}b$ and e by $2b$:
$$\tfrac{1}{4}b + 3b + 2b = 540$$
Simplify the left-hand side:
$$5\tfrac{1}{4}b = 540$$
Divide **both sides** by $5\frac{1}{4}$ to leave b on its own:
$$b = 540 \div 5\tfrac{1}{4}$$
If a decimal answer is good enough:
$$b = 540 \div 5.25 \simeq 102.9$$
and the angle $b = 102.9°$. If you require an exact answer:
$$b = 540 \div \tfrac{21}{4}$$
$$= 540 \times \tfrac{4}{21}$$
$$= \tfrac{2160}{21}$$
$$= \tfrac{720}{7}$$
$$= 102\tfrac{6}{7}$$
So the angle sides are $25\frac{5}{7}°$, $102\frac{6}{7}°$, $102\frac{6}{7}°$, $102\frac{6}{7}°$ and $205\frac{5}{7}°$. As a check:
$$25\tfrac{5}{7} + 102\tfrac{6}{7} + 102\tfrac{6}{7} + 102\tfrac{6}{7} + 205\tfrac{5}{7} + = 540$$

Example 2

The simple interest on £430 at 9% is £650. How long has the money been invested?

Start with the simple interest formula:
$$I = \tfrac{Prt}{100}$$
At this stage it's probably easier to replace any variables you know with their values:
$$\frac{430 \times 9 \times t}{100}$$
$$650 = \frac{430 \times 9 \times t}{100}$$
$$= 38.7t$$
and simplify if you can:
$$\frac{650}{38.7} = t$$
Divide both sides by 38.7, so:
$$t \simeq 16.8 \text{ years}$$

Self-check

Find the following.
1 The value of P if $I = 80$, $t = 4$ and $r = 6$, and $I = Prt/100$.
2 The value of w if $t = 1\frac{3}{4}$, and $t = \frac{1}{3}(1 + w)$.
3 The value of a if $m = 52$, $b = 60$ and $c = 30$, and $m = (2a + b + c)/4$.

ANSWERS

1 333.33. **2** 4.25. **3** 59.

Multiplying two negative numbers

Showing multiplication on a graph

Look at Figure 95. Line 1 shows the formula $y = 2x$, with a selection of points on the line as in the table below.

x	y
4	8
3	6
0	0
⁻3	⁻6
⁻4	⁻8

In every case the y value is double the x value, so when $x = {}^-3$:
$$y = 2 \times {}^-3 = {}^-6$$
Line 2 shows the formula $y = 3x$, passing through $(1, 3)$, $(2, 6)$, etc., and extending backwards through $({}^-1, {}^-3)$, $({}^-2, {}^-6)$, etc. Line 3 shows the formula $y = x$, and line 4 shows the formula $y = \frac{1}{2}x$.

You'll see that as the number multiplying (that is, the **coefficient** of x) gets smaller, so the matching line rotates clockwise.

Line 5 shows the formula $y = 0$. It coincides with the x-axis.

In the formula $y = {}^-2x$, you can find y values for positive x values, as I've shown in the following table.

x	y
4	⁻8
3	⁻6
0	0
⁻3	?
⁻4	?

For example, when $x = 3$:
$$y = {}^-2 \times 3$$
$$= 3 \times {}^-2$$
$$= {}^-6$$
and when $x = 4$:

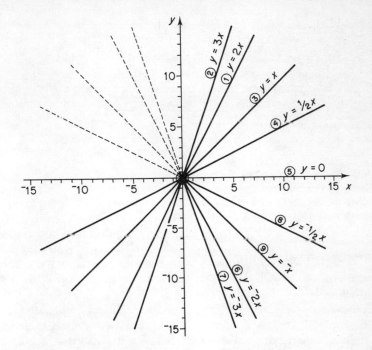

Figure 95.

$$y = {}^-2 \times 4$$
$$= 4 \times {}^-2$$
$$= {}^-8$$

Line 6 shows the formula $y = {}^-2x$, and line 7 shows the formula $y = {}^-3x$, passing through $(3, {}^-9)$, $(2, {}^-6)$, etc.

Look at the way the lines fit into an overall pattern, along with line 8 $(y = {}^-\frac{1}{2}x)$ and line 9 $(y = {}^-x)$. It seems reasonable to extend these lines into the top left-hand arc of the graph (as shown dotted), just as the other lines 1–5 extended through the origin for negative values of x and y. This means that ${}^-2 \times {}^-3 = 6$, ${}^-2 \times {}^-4 = 8$, etc. A similar argument applies to the other dotted lines suggesting that, for example, ${}^-3 \times {}^-1 = 3$, ${}^-3 \times {}^-2 = 6$, ${}^-\frac{1}{2} \times {}^-3 = 1\frac{1}{2}$.

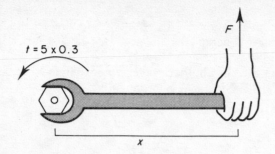

Figure 96. F = 5, x = 0.3

You have met formulae like these already. For example, on page 167 the formula $t = Fx$ referred to the twisting effect, t, exerted on a bolt by a force of F units applied to a spanner x units long (see Figure 96). As shown, the tendency is to turn the bolt anti-clockwise. Think of using the longest spanner you can and pulling up as hard as you can to undo a nut or bolt that is stuck.

Now, suppose you put the spanner on the left-hand side (see Figure 97) so that x is now negative. To produce the same twisting effect, you have to pull downwards, also in a negative direction, so a force of, say, 5 units upwards exerted on the spanner 0.3 metres to the right of the screw has the same effect as a force of 5 units downwards (⁻5 units) exerted on the spanner 0.3 metres to the left (⁻0.3), i.e.:

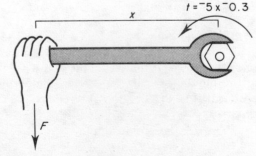

Figure 97. F = ⁻5, x = ⁻0.3

$5 \times 0.3 = {}^-5 \times {}^-0.3$

Again, this example suggests that, when you multiply two negative numbers together, you obtain a positive result. You can confirm this by seeing how this result fits the distributive rule:

$c(a + b) = ca + cb$

which you used in Chapter 4 when you expanded and factorized expressions. For instance, you can replace:

${}^-5 \times 7 = {}^-35$

by:

${}^-5 (10 + {}^-3) = {}^-35$

because:

$7 = 10 + {}^-3$

Expanding the brackets gives:

${}^-5 \times 10 + {}^-5 \times {}^-3 = {}^-35$

so:

${}^-50 + {}^-5 \times {}^-3 = {}^-35$

As ${}^-35$ is 15 units above ${}^-50$ on the number line (see Figure 98) ${}^-5 \times {}^-3$ must equal 15. Again:

```
20─┤
10─┤
 0─┤
⁻10─┤
⁻20─┤
⁻30─┤
⁻40─┤
⁻50─┤
```

Figure 98. Number line from 20 to ⁻50

Negative number × negative number = positive number
By altering the numbers in the example above you can show that this result is true in general.

To summarize for all multiplication involving negative numbers:

1 ${}^-a \times b = {}^-(ab)$
2 $a \times {}^-b = {}^-(ab)$ } See page 59

3 $^-a \times {}^-b = ab$

whatever the value of a or b. Here are some examples of these rules in use:

- $0.6 \times {}^-3 = {}^-1.8$ (rule **2**)
- $^-8.1 \times 0.1 = {}^-0.81$ (rule **1**)
- $^-2 \times {}^-51 = 102$ (rule **3**)
- $^-4 \times {}^-0.2 = 0.8$ (rule **3**)

Self-check

Use rules **1**, **2** and **3** to find the values of the following.

1 $^-3 \times {}^-7$	**2** $^-2 \times {}^-6.4$
3 $2 \times {}^-8$	**4** $^-5 \times {}^-0.3$
5 $^-2 \times 3.6$	**6** 7×5.1
7 $3.4 \times {}^-0.1$	**8** $^-2.1 \times {}^-100$

ANSWERS

1 21. **2** 12.8. **3** $^-16.$ **4** 1.5.
5 $^-7.2.$ **6** 35.5. **7** $^-0.34.$ **8** 210.

Using your calculator

If your calculator has a $^+/_-$ key, you should be able to use it for calculations like these. On my calculator question **2** above becomes:

2	$^+/_-$	+	6	.	4	$^+/_-$	=

giving 12.8 as before.

Division with negative numbers

You can build on the idea that division 'undoes' multiplication to extend these results to division by negative numbers. In general if:

$a \times b = c$

then:

$c \div b = a$

So you can extend results **1**, **2** and **3** above to give the following general results, using c to stand for ab:

4 $^-c \div b = {}^-(c \div b)$ or $\frac{^-c}{b} = {}^-(\frac{c}{b})$
5 $^-c \div {}^-b = {}^-(c \div b)$ or $\frac{c}{b} = {}^-(\frac{c}{b})$
6 $^-c \div {}^-b = c \div b$ or $\frac{^-c}{^-b} = \frac{c}{b}$

This shows that similar **signs rules** apply to dividing as to multiplying, i.e. a negative number divided by another negative number gives a positive result, as in **6** above.

Self-check

Find the value of the following in the simplest form you can.
1 $^-8 \div 4$.   **2** $^-8 \times {}^-4$.   **3** $^-15 \div {}^-3$.
4 $\frac{^-7}{^-8}$.   **5** $\frac{4}{^-5}$.   **6** $^-\frac{36}{72}$

ANSWERS

1 $^-2$. **2** 2. **3** 5. **4** $\frac{7}{8}$.
5 $^-\frac{4}{5}$. **6** $\frac{1}{2}$.

As a reminder, here are the other rules concerning negative numbers which you met in Chapter 2.
9 $a + {}^-b = a - b$
10 $a - {}^-b = a + b$
with some examples of their use:

- $14 + {}^-3 = 14 - 3 = 11$
- $^-2 + {}^-3 = {}^-2 - 3 = {}^-5$
- $14 - {}^-3 = 14 + 3 = 17$
- $^-2 - {}^-3 = {}^-2 + 3 = 1$

Incorporating brackets:

- $4 - (2 - 5) = 4 - {}^-3 = 4 + 3 = 7$
- $(^-2 - 5) - 8 = {}^-7 - 8 = {}^-15$
- $(2 - 5) - (10 - 12) = {}^-3 - {}^-2 = {}^-3 + 2 = {}^-1$

Self-check

Find the values of
1 $17 + {}^-9$ **2** $^-4 + {}^-6$
3 $^-4 - {}^-6$ **4** $^-4 - (6 - 3)$
5 $^-4 - (6 - 8)$ **6** $(^-4 - 6) - 8$
7 $(^-4 - {}^-3) - (^-2 - {}^-1)$
8 $13 - 14 + 18 - {}^-2$

ANSWERS

1 8. **2** ⁻10. **3** 2.
4 ⁻4 − 3 = ⁻7. **5** ⁻2. **6** ⁻18.
7 ⁻1 − ⁻1 = 0. **8** 19.

Simplifying expressions again

Think of solving:
1 $5(2x − 3) − 7x = 19$
Now compare it with:
2 $3x − 15 = 19$
Equation **2** is much simpler, but in fact both give the same value for x because you can simplify $5(2x − 3) − 7$ to produce $3x − 15$.

Let's see how you can simplify $5(2x − 3) − 7x$. By the distributive rules and by expanding brackets (page 104):

$$5(2x − 3) − 7x = 5 \times 2x − 5 \times 3 − 7x$$
$$= 10x − 15 − 7x$$
$$= 3x − 15$$

So the equation $5(2x − 3) − 7x = 19$ becomes:
$3x − 15 = 19$
which you can solve to give:
$x = 11\frac{1}{3}$

> *Self-check*
>
> Re-write these expressions by expanding the brackets first then simplifying the result as far as you can. Don't forget to check in each case that your final expression is equivalent to your starting expression.
> **1** $2(x + 3) + 3x$
> **2** $4(2x − 5) − 9$
> **3** $8 − 2(x + 3) + 2x$
> **4** $12x − 3(4x + 2) + 9$

ANSWERS

1 $2x + 6 + 3x = 5x + 6$. **2.** $8x − 20 − 9 = 8x − 29$.
3 $8 − 2x − 6 + 2x = 2$. **4** $12x − 12x − 6 + 9 = 3$.

When you have to simplify expressions which include a lot of minus signs, it can sometimes help if you interchange − with + ⁻, as in this example.

- **Simplify** $4(x - 3) - 5(x - 4)$:
  Replace − 5 by + ⁻5 and − 4 by + ⁻4:
    $4(x - 3) + {}^-5(x + {}^-4)$
  Expand brackets:
  $= 4x - 12 + {}^-5x + {}^-5 \times {}^-4$
  Replace ⁻5 × ⁻4 by 20:
  $= 4x - 12 + {}^-5x + 20$
  Replace + ⁻5 by − 5:
  $= 4x - 12 - 5x + 20$
  Rearrange order:
  $= 20 - 12 + 4x - 5x$
  $= 8 - x$

Check by letting $x = 6$, say, in which case:
    $4 \times 3 - 5 \times 2 = 12 - 10$
    $\qquad\qquad\qquad = 2$
and:
    $8 - x = 8 - 6$
    $\qquad\quad = 2$

Self-check

Simplify the following expressions. Don't forget to check that your results are correct, as above.

1 $4(x - 3) - 3(x - 1)$
2 $6(x + 1) - 6(x - 1)$
3 $4(2x + 3) - 4(2x - 3)$

ANSWERS

1 $x - 9$. 2 12. 3 24.

Solving equations by simplifying and rearranging

I'll start with equations using the methods you used in the previous section. In each case, your first step should be to expand the brackets.

Self-check

1 $12x - 3(4x - 1) = x$
2 $12x - 5(2x - 3) = 9$
3 $12x - 3(3x - 2) = 7(x + 1)$

ANSWERS

1 $x = 3$. **2** $2x + 15 = 9$ so $x = {}^-3$.
3 $6 + 3x = 7x + 7 \Rightarrow x = {}^-\frac{1}{4}$.

Equations with fractions

You can use the rules for adding fractions and for simplifying fractions to help you solve equations which include fractions.

There are several different approaches you can use – in the example below I've started by using equivalent fractions to re-write the equations so that all the fractions have the same denominator.

● **Solve** the equation:
$\frac{x}{2} + \frac{x}{3} = \frac{3}{4}$
12 is a multiple of 2, 3 and 4 so you can write all these fractions as $\frac{1}{12}$ths.
$\frac{6x}{12} + \frac{4x}{12} = \frac{9}{12}$
Because there must be the same number of 12ths on each side of the = sign:

$6x + 4x = 9$
$10x = 9$
$x = \frac{9}{10}$

Check:
$\frac{1}{2} \times \frac{9}{10} + \frac{1}{3} \times \frac{9}{10} = \frac{9}{20} + \frac{9}{30} = \frac{27}{60} + \frac{18}{60}$
$= \frac{45}{60}$
$= \frac{3}{4}$

Self-check

1 $\frac{2x}{3} = \frac{1}{3}$
2 $\frac{2a}{3} - 5 = \frac{a}{2}$

ANSWERS

1 $\frac{4x}{6} + \frac{3x}{7} = \frac{2}{6} \Rightarrow x = \frac{2}{7}$.

2 $a = 30$

Simplifying expressions with fractions

Look at these examples, then try the self-check below.

Combining fractions with the same denominator

- $\frac{4}{x} - \frac{y}{x} = \frac{4-y}{x}$

Simplifying

- $\frac{3a}{6} = \frac{a}{2}$
- $\frac{2ab}{5b} = \frac{2a}{5}$

Combining with different denominators

- $\frac{a}{4} + \frac{2a}{3} = \frac{3a}{12} + \frac{4 \times 2a}{12}$
  $$= \frac{11a}{12}$$

Self-check

Simplify the following.

1 $\frac{3x}{12}$

2 $\frac{16a^2}{24a}$

3 $\frac{28m^2}{35m}$

Combine the following to form single fractions.

4 $\frac{x}{5} - \frac{2y}{5}$

5 $\frac{2}{5} + \frac{1}{3}$

6 $\frac{a}{b} + \frac{1}{c}$

7 $\frac{2}{a} + \frac{1}{b}$

ANSWERS

1 $\frac{x}{4}$ **2** $\frac{2a}{3}$ **3** $\frac{4}{5}m$ **4** $\frac{x-2y}{5}$ **5** $\frac{11}{15}$
6 $\frac{ac+b}{bc}$ **7** $\frac{2b-a}{ab}$.

Checking when you have simplified

Combining two fractions as you did in the last self-check is difficult and you can easily make mistakes which are not obvious. As before, it's best to check your results by substituting simple values for each of the variables (letters) and then making sure that the starting and finishing expressions are equal. Your calculator will help here, in particular by replacing awkward fractions by decimals. For instance, if you take $a = 2$, $b = 3$ and $c = 5$, then, referring to the previous self-check (questions 6 and 7):

$$\frac{a}{b} + \frac{1}{c} = \frac{2}{3} + \frac{1}{5} = 0.6666... + 0.2 = 0.8666...$$

while:

$$\frac{ac+b}{bc} = \frac{10+3}{15} = \frac{13}{15} = 0.8666...$$

So expressions can be the same.

> *Self-check*
>
> Look at these pairs of expressions. In each case use a check to see which pairs of expressions are *not* equal to each other.
>
> **1** $\frac{2}{x} + 3, \frac{5}{x}$
> **2** $\frac{2}{x} + \frac{x}{3}, \frac{2+x}{x+3}$.
> **3** $\frac{x}{2} - \frac{x}{3}, \frac{x}{6}$

ANSWERS

(Using $x = 4$, $y = 5$, $a = 6$, $c = 7$, but you can choose your own values for the variables.)

1 $\frac{1}{2} + 3 = 3\frac{1}{2}, \frac{5}{2} = 2\frac{1}{2}$, so expressions not equal.

2 $\frac{2}{x} + \frac{x}{3} = \frac{2}{4} + \frac{4}{3} = 0.5 + 1.33 = 1.83$ } so expressions not
$\frac{2+4}{4+3} = \frac{6}{3} = 0.85...$ } equal.

3 $\frac{x}{2} - \frac{x}{3} = 2 - 1.333... = 0.666..., \frac{4}{6} = 0.666...$

Using tables to solve equations

You can solve equations with the unknown letter appearing in several places (like those in the self-check on page 184) by making tables of values and then drawing graphs if you wish. After all, in solving an equation you are trying to find the value(s) of any unknown letter which makes the left-hand side equal the right-hand side, and you can do this by 'guess and check' or graph plotting, however complicated the equation is.

Consider $12x - 3(4x - 1) = 4(x + 1)$. The left-hand side is $12x - 3(4x - 1)$ and the right-hand side is $4(x + 1)$. I'll call the left-hand side a and the right-hand side b. Then I'll choose several values for x and see how close a is to b for each value. I'll carry on until a and b are equal (or at least close enough). To start with, I'll choose the x values at random:

x	a	b
1	$12 - 3(4 - 1) = 12 - 9 = 3$	$4 \times 2 = 8$
3	$36 - 3(12 - 1) = 36 - 33 = 3$	$4 \times 4 = 16$
5	$60 - 3(20 - 1) = 60 - 57 = 3$	$4 \times 6 = 24$

You can see that although a always equals 3, b is more and increases as x increases, so it's worth choosing lower values of x to give values of b closer to 3:

x	b
0	$4 \times 1 = 4$
$^-1$	$4 \times 0 = 0$
$^-2$	$4 \times {}^-1 = {}^-4$

Now I'll look at x values between 0 and $^-1$:

x	b	
$^-0.5$	$4 \times {}^-0.5 = 2$	Too small
$^-0.3$	$4 \times 0.7 = 2.8$	Too small
$^-0.2$	$4 \times 0.8 = 3.2$	Too large
$^-0.25$	$4 \times 0.75 = 3$	Correct

Finally I'll check that a still equals 3 when $x = {}^-0.25$:
$$a = 12 \times {}^-0.25 - 3(4 = {}^-0.25 - 1) = {}^-3 - 3({}^-1 \times - 1)$$
$$= {}^-3 - 3 \times {}^-2$$
$$= {}^-3 - {}^-6$$
$$= 3$$

So solution is $x = {}^-0.25$.

Review

1 There are eight calculations below and a selection of answers. Choose the correct answer for each calculation (the same answer may be correct for more than one calculation).

 a $6 \times {}^-3$ **c** ${}^-3 \times {}^-3$ **e** ${}^-12 - {}^-3$ **g** $9 - 27$
 b $18 \div {}^-2$ **d** ${}^-36 \div {}^-2$ **f** $3 + {}^-12$ **h** $27 - 9$

 Choose from these answers:
 ${}^-36 \; {}^-18 \; {}^-12 \; {}^-9 \; 0 \; 9 \; 12 \; 18 \; 36$

2 Simplify these fractions as far as you can.
 a ${}^-\frac{8}{16}$ **b** $\frac{24}{18}$ **c** $\frac{3c}{cd}$ **d** $\frac{x}{3xy}$

3 Find the values of the following when $y = 3$.
 a $6(y + 3)$ **c** $18 - 2(y - 4)$
 b $12 - 6y$ **d** $2(y + 1) - 3(y - 1)$

4 Simplify the expressions in **3c** and **3d** as far as you can.

5 Solve the equations:
 a $2(x + 3) = 3(x - 1)$
 b $4(2 - x) + 6x = 5 + x$

8 | Area and volume

Measuring area

All measuring is a matter of **comparing**; for instance, you measure a **length** of material by **comparing** it with the marks on a tape measure.

In practice areas are measured by finding out how many squares of a given size can fit inside them. In Figure 99 the shaded area is **1 square centimetre** (written $1\,cm^2$ for short), so the total area of the shape is $6\,cm^2$.

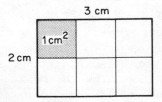

Figure 99.

Figure 100 shows the floor plan of a large room in a house. Here each square stands for 1 square metre ($1\,m^2$):

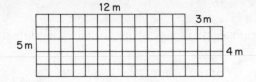

Figure 100. Floor plan of a room

I calculated the area of this shape by thinking of it as two rectangles, 12 by 5 metres and 3 by 4 metres. In the larger rectangle there are five rows each of 12 metre squares, giving:

$12 \times 5 = 60\,\text{m}^2$

altogether, and the smaller rectangle added a further four rows each of three squares giving:

$3 \times 4 = 12\,\text{m}^2$

So the total floor area is $12 \times 5 + 3 \times 4 = 72\text{m}^2$.

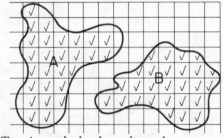

Figure 101. Two irregularly-shaped ponds

Sometimes you can only find an approximate value for the area of a shape. In Figure 101 ponds A and B have awkward curved edges, so squares won't fit nicely inside them. As an approximate method you can **count** any square that is more than half inside the shape (these squares are ticked) and ignore all the remaining squares. In the diagram, each square stands for 1m^2, so the area of pond A $\simeq 27\text{m}^2$ and the area of B $\simeq 27\text{m}^2$. The shapes are different, but they have about the same area.

Area and perimeter

- The **area** of a shape is the space inside it.
- The **perimeter** of a shape is the distance round its edge – quite a different idea.

The perimeter of the rectangle in Figure 99 is:
  3 + 2 + 3 + 2 = 10 cm
while the perimeter of the room in Figure 100 is:
  12 + 1 + 3 + 4 + 15 + 5 = 40 m

You would need to know the area of the floor if you were buying carpet, and the perimeter of the floor to find the number of strips of wallpaper required to re-paper the room. Oddly enough you can change the area of a shape while keeping its perimeter fixed, and vice versa. You can even reduce the area of a shape whilst increasing its perimeter. Imagine removing the middle square on the top row of the shape in Figure 99. The area reduces to 5 cm^2 whilst the perimeter increases to 12 cm. Figure 102 shows shapes with the same area but different perimeters, whilst Figure 103 shows shapes with the same perimeter but different areas.

To find perimeters of shapes like those in Figure 101 you may have to resort to laying a thread or string along the edge of the shape, then measuring the length of the thread with a rule.

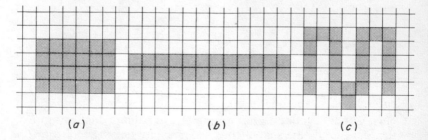

Figure 102. Shapes with the same area but different perimeters.
(a) *area = 24, perimeter = 20.* (b) *Area = 24, perimeter = 28.*
(c) *Area = 24, perimeter = 50.*

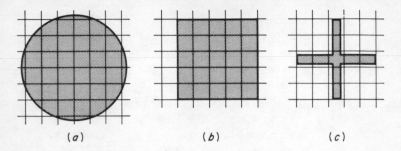

Figure 103. Shapes with the same perimeter but different areas.
(a) *Area = 32, perimeter = 20.* (b) *Area = 25, perimeter = 20.*
(c) *Area = $4\frac{3}{4}$, perimeter = 20.*

Shapes made from rectangles

Many of the more complicated shapes whose areas you need to find can be split into rectangles (as in Figure 104) or can be made by subtracting small rectangles from a larger one (as in Figure 105). In Figure 104:

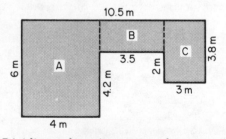

Figure 104. Dividing a shape into rectangles

- area A = 6 × 4 = 24 m²;
- area B = 3.5 × 1.8 = 6.3 m²;
- area C = 3 × 3.8 = 11.4 m²;

so the total area of the shape is:

- A + B + C = 41.7 m²

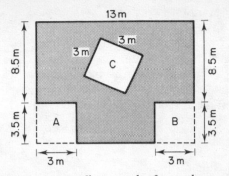

Figure 105. Subtracting small rectangles from a larger one

In Figure 105:
 Shaded area = Area of large rectangle − (Areas of A, B and C)
      = 13 × 12 − (3 × 3.5 + 3 × 3.5 + 3 × 3)
      = 156 − 30
      = 126 m²

Area formulae

With many shapes, you can use **formulae** to save time when you need to calculate areas.

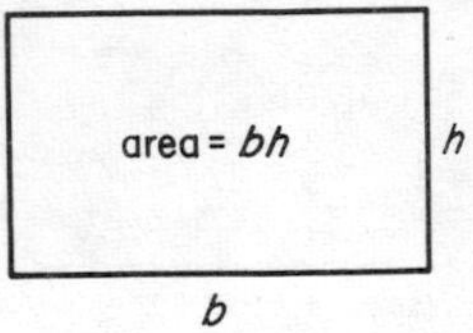

area = *bh* *h*

b

Figure 106. Area of rectangle = bh

Rectangle

For a **rectangle** (Figure 106):

- Area = Base length × Height
- $A = bh$ (remember bh means $b \times h$)

where b stands for base length, h stands for height and A stands for area. This just puts into words the method used on page 190 – the number of squares in a *b* by *h* rectangle is *h* rows each of *b* squares, i.e. $b \times h$ squares altogether.

Notice that all the measurements must be in the same family of units, e.g. if *b* is in metres, *h* must be in metres also, and the area will be *bh* square metres. If *b* and *h* are in centimetres, *A* will be in square centimetres, etc.

Square

For a **square** (Figure 107):

• $A = b^2$ (that is, $b \times b$)

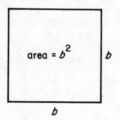

Figure 107. Area of square = b^2

Parallelogram

For a **parallelogram** (Figure 108):

• $A = bh$ again

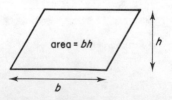

Figure 108. Area of parallelogram = bh

You can see why from Figure 109. Imagine cutting off the shaded triangle and placing it on the right, as shown; you would then have made a rectangle out of the parallelogram.

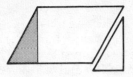

Figure 109.

Notice that:

- b is the base length measured along the edge, *not* the total length of the parallelogram;
- h is the height **measured at right angles** to the base, *not* the length of the other side.

Triangle

For a **triangle** (Figure 110):

- $A = \frac{1}{2}bh$ or $\dfrac{bh}{2}$

If you place two identical triangles together, as in Figure 111, you produce a parallelogram of area bh, which explains why the area of one of the triangles is $\frac{bh}{2}$.

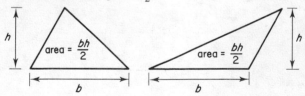

Figure 110. Area of triangle $= \frac{bh}{2}$

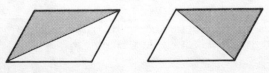

Figure 111.

Trapezium

For a **trapezium** (Figure 112):

- $A = \frac{h(a + b)}{2}$

You can make up a trapezium from two triangles, as in Figure 113. The trapezium area, A, is given by:

$$A = \frac{ah}{2} + \frac{bh}{2}$$
$$= \frac{ah + bh}{2}$$
$$= \frac{h(a + b)}{2}$$

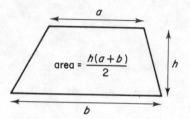

Figure 112. Area of trapezium $= \frac{h(a + b)}{2}$ *or* $\frac{ah}{2} + \frac{bh}{2}$

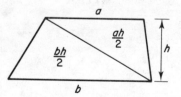

Figure 113.

More complicated shapes

As before, more complicated shapes can be split up into simpler shapes, as in Figure 114, so that the area can be found more easily. Here, shape A is a trapezium with $a = 8\,$cm, $b = 6\,$cm and $h = 3\,$cm, so:

$$\text{area A} = \frac{3(8 + 6)}{2} = \frac{3 \times 14}{2} = 21\,\text{cm}^2$$

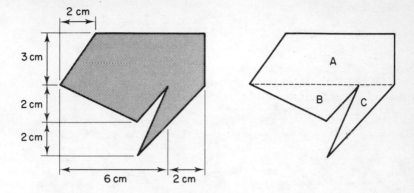

Figure 114.

Shapes B and C are triangles, with b = 6cm, h =2cm, and b = 2cm, h =4cm, so:

area B = $\frac{6 \times 2}{2}$ = 6cm^2

area C = $\frac{2 \times 4}{2}$ = 4cm^2

Total area = 21 + 6 + 4 = 31cm^2

Don't forget the subtraction method you met before (see Figure 115). Here:

Shaded area = Triangle − Rectangle

$\qquad = \frac{32 \times 24}{2} - 8 \times 12$

$\qquad = 384 - 96$

$\qquad = 288\,\text{cm}^2$

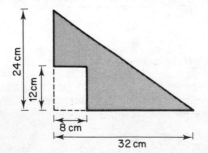

Figure 115.

Self-check

1–7 Find the shaded areas of the shapes in Figure 116.

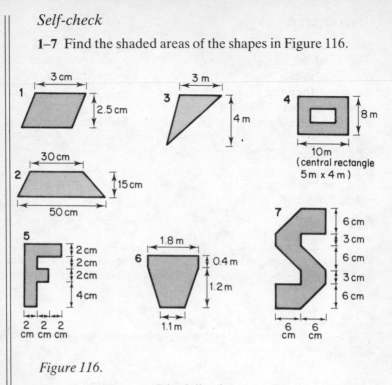

Figure 116.

Calculate the area of the following.
  8 A triangle 7 m long and 6 m high.
  9 A parallelogram 9 m long and 6.34 m high.
  10 A trapezium with parallel sides of 6 m and 7.6 m, 2.4 m apart.

ANSWERS

1 $7.5 \, \text{cm}^2$. **2** $600 \, \text{cm}^2$. **3** $6 \, \text{m}^2$. **4** $60 \, \text{m}^2$.
5 $32 \, \text{cm}^2$. **6** $2.46 \, \text{m}^2$. **7** $180 \, \text{cm}^2$. **8** $21 \, \text{m}^2$.
9 $57.06 \, \text{m}^2$. **10** $16.32 \, \text{m}^2$.

Units of area

Before you calculate any area, all the length measurements you need must be in the same units. The area will then be in the matching 'square' units: for instance, if all length measurements are in cm, then the area is in cm^2; if the lengths are all in metres then the area will be in m^2; and so on.

For length measure, $100 cm = 1 m$, but for area measure, a metre square can be split into 100 rows 1 cm wide, each holding 100 cm squares, so:

- $1 m^2 = 100 \times 100 = 10000 cm^2$

In the same way:

- $1 cm^2 = 10 \times 10 = 100 mm^2$
- $1 km^2 = 1000 \times 1000 = 1000000 m^2$

You may also come across another unit of area, the **hectare** (ha for short). It is an area of a square measuring 100 m by 100 m, so:

- $1 ha = 100 \times 100 = 10000 m^2$

You may have to convert from one set of units to another and these tables will help you.

Length measure	Conversion	
millimetre (mm)		
centimetre (cm)	1 cm	= 10 mm
metre (m)	1 m	= 1000 mm
		100 cm
kilometre (km)	1 km	= 1000 m

Area measure	Conversion	
square millimetre (mm^2)		
square centimetre (cm^2)	$1 cm^2$	$= 100 mm^2$
square metre (m^2)	$1 m^2$	$= 1000000 mm^2$
		$= 10000 cm^2$
hectare (ha)	$1 ha$	$= 10000 m^2$
square kilometre (km^2)	$1 km^2$	$= 1000000 m^2$
		$= 100 ha$

Thus to convert from mm^2 to cm^2 you divide by 100 (not 10) and to convert from m^2 to cm^2 you multiply by 10000 (not 100).

Self-check

1 Convert these lengths to metres:
   243 cm; 145 mm; 1.5 km; 2.8 cm.
2 Convert these areas to cm^2:
   46 mm^2; 0.8 m^2.
3 Convert these areas to mm^2:
   2.6 cm^2; 6.9 cm^2.
4 Convert these areas to m^2:
   2 km^2; 6741 cm^2.
5 Convert these areas to mm^2:
   8.3 cm^2; 45 cm^2.

ANSWERS

1 2.43 m; 0.145 m; 1500 m; 0.028 m.
2 0.46 cm^2; 8000 cm^2. 3 260 mm^2; 690 mm^2.
4 2 000 000 m^2; 0.6741 m^2. 5 830 mm^2; 4500 mm^2.

Self-check

Find the area of the following rectangles. In each case give your answer in square metres (m^2), correct to one decimal place.
1 5 m long by 50 cm wide.
2 3.7 m long by 124 cm wide.
3 0.1 km long by 75 m wide.
4 Area of 18 ha.
5 125 cm by 70 cm.
6 $\frac{1}{10}$ km by $\frac{1}{20}$ km.

ANSWERS

1 2.5 m^2. 2 $3.7 \times 1.24 = 4.588 \simeq 4.6$ m^2.
3 7500 m^2. 4 180 000 m^2.
5 $1.25 \times 0.7 = 0.875 \simeq 0.9$ m^2.
6 $100 \times 50 = 5000$ m^2.

Introducing volumes

Just as you use units based on **squares** with all area measurements, so with volume measurement you use units based on **cubes** (like sugar lumps, dice, etc.). In finding the volume or a capacity of a container, you are finding the amount of space inside hollow objects such as those in Figure 117.

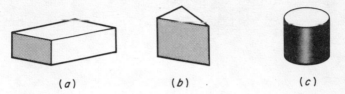

(a)   *(b)*   *(c)*

Figure 117. (a) *Cuboid.* (b) *Triangular prism.* (c) *Cylinder*

The volume of a cuboid

You can put 24 metre cubes together to give a solid with a volume of 24 cubic metres, or $24 \, m^3$ for short (see Figure 118).

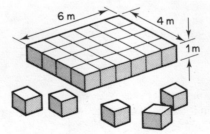

Figure 118.

Putting two more layers of $24 \, m^3$ on top, giving three layers altogether (see Figure 119), gives a solid with a volume of:

$3 \times 24 = 72 \, m^3$

This type of solid, with six rectangular faces, is called a **cuboid**. You can calculate its volume in m^3 by multiplying its base area ($24 \, m^2$) by the height ($3 \, m$), giving a volume of $72 \, m^3$. In short, you can say that for a cuboid (Figure 120):

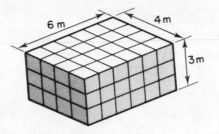

Figure 119.

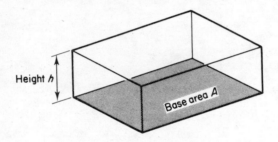

Figure 120. Volume of a cuboid = Ah

- $V = A \times h$
  $= Ah$

where V = volume, A = base area and h = height. Since you can find the base area A by multiplying the length by width, you can also say that (Figure 121):

- $V = lwh$

where l = base length, w = base width and h height.

Self-check

Find these volumes correct to 4 s.f.
1 Cuboid 13 m by 4 m by 2 m.
2 Cuboid with base area 145 cm^2 and height 9.3 cm.

ANSWERS

1 104 m³.
2 1349 cm³.

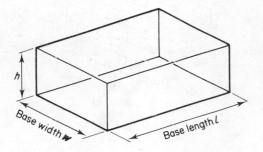

Figure 121. Volume of cuboid – lwh

Cuboids and prisms

Cuboids form a subset of a larger set of solids called **prisms**.

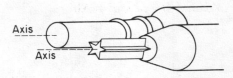

Figure 122.

Imagine you have, say, a large toothpaste tube or cake icing gun (see Figure 122). Squeeze the tube and you obtain an even strip of toothpaste or icing. The toothpaste or icing forms a **prism**, and the **axis** of the prism is through the middle of the nozzle as shown. All prisms have at least one axis. If you cut through a prism at right angles to its axis, the shape you see is called a **cross-section**. Prisms have constant cross sections, i.e. wherever you cut across the axis the cross-section you find is the same shape and size (see Figure 123).

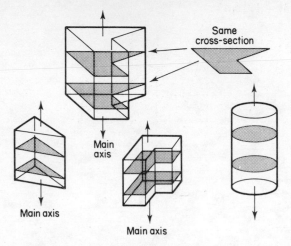

Figure 123. Some prisms, showing main axes and cross-sections

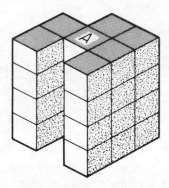

Figure 124.

Look at Figure 124. Imagine making it out of centimetre cube blocks. The shaded cross-section area A of this prism is $7\,\text{cm}^2$, and there are four layers of cubes, so you need four layers of 7 = 28 cubes to make this prism. The volume is thus:

$4 \times 7 = 28\,\text{cm}^3$

Now look at Figure 125. To make this prism you need five layers each with $3\frac{1}{2}$ cubes = $17\frac{1}{2}$ cubes. The volume is thus:

$5 \times 3\frac{1}{2} = 17\frac{1}{2} \text{cm}^3$

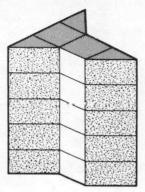

Figure 125.

Self-check

Find the volumes of the two prisms shown in Figure 126 (all built from centimetre cubes).

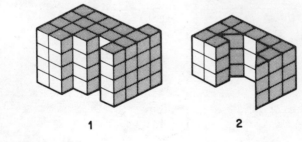

1   **2**

Figure 126.

ANSWERS

1 $17 \times 4 = 68 \text{cm}^3$. **2** $10.5 \times 3 = 31.5 \text{cm}^3$.

Prisms with complex cross-sections

You can use a similar approach to find the volumes of prisms with more awkward cross-sections. Look at Figure 127, showing a prism with cross-section approximately equal to 12 cm² and height of 6 cm. Just as you could find the approximate area of irregular shapes (as in Figure 101), so you can calculate the prism's volume by replacing it with another prism of the same total volume, made of layers of 1 cm cubes. One layer of this 'cube' prism has a volume of 12 cm³, so the total volume of the prism is approximately:

$$12 \times 6 = 72 \,\text{cm}^3$$

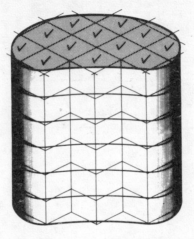

Figure 127.

From these examples you can see that, just as for calculating the volume of a cuboid, the **volume of any prism** is given by:

Volume = Cross-section area × Height
$$V = Ah$$

Self-check

Now calculate the volume of these prisms.
1–3 See Figure 128.
4 Cross-section area 32 cm², height 16 m.
5 Cross-section area 5.9 mm², height 60 cm.

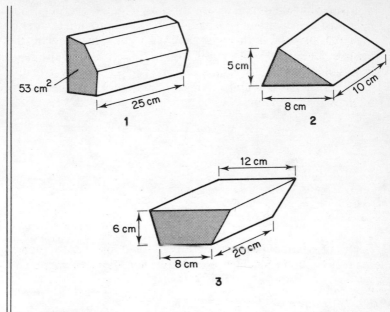

Figure 128.

ANSWERS

1 1325 cm³. **2** 20 × 10 = 200 cm³.

3 $\frac{6(12 + 8)}{2}$ × 20 = 1200 cm³.

4 Work in cm-based units, where height = 1600 cm, so volume = 51 200 cm³; *or* in m-based units, so volume = 32 ÷ 10 000 × 16 = 0.0512 m³.

5 5.9 × 600 = 3540 mm³ or 0.059 × 60 = 3.54 cm³.

Units of volume

Though you've used mm³, cm³ and metre³ for measuring volumes so far, there are two other very commonly used units of volume – the **litre** (*l*) and the **millilitre** (ml):

● 1 litre = 1000 millilitres

and, as a cubic centimetre is the same as a millilitre:

- 1 litre = 1000 cm³ (see Figure 129)

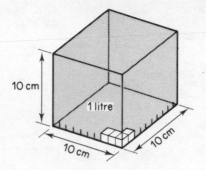

Figure 129. 1 litre = 1000 cm³ = 1000 ml

Think of 100 of those 10 cm cubes arranged in a square, then 10 layers like this producing a cubic metre, and you can see how:

- 1 m³ = 1000 litres

Similarly, 1 cm³ or 1 ml = 1000 mm³. Thus all the commonly used units of volume are connected by a factor of 1000.

Volume measure	Conversion		
Cubic millimetre (mm³)			
Cubic centimetre (cm³) ⎫		= 1000 mm³	
Millilitre (ml) ⎭		= 1 cm³	
		= 1 ml	
Litre (*l*)	1 *l*	= 1000 ml	
Cubic metre (m³)	1 m³	= 1000 *l*	

Self-check

1–5 Convert all the answers to the previous self-check into litres or millilitres (whichever you think more sensible).

ANSWERS

1 1.325 *l*. **2** 200 ml. **3** 1.2 *l*. **4** 51.2 *l*. **5** 3.54 ml.

Pyramids

You'll probably have a clear idea of the shape of a pyramid from seeing pictures of the pyramids of Egypt. Many pyramids have square bases, though pyramids, like prisms, can have bases of any polygonal shape. Instead of having edges parallel to a main axis, like a prism, the sloping edges of a pyramid meet at a single point (the **vertex**). Cutting through the pyramid parallel to its base gives cross-sections of the same shape as the base, but smaller and smaller as you approach the vertex (see Figure 130).

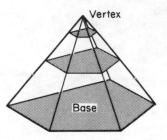

Figure 130. A pyramid

You can cut a cube (see Figure 131) into three pyramids:

- AHGCD (shown shaded)
- ABFGC
- AEFGH

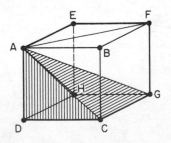

Figure 131. A cube can be divided into three pyramids

each with a square base. As all three pyramids are the same as each other, the volume of each is $\frac{1}{3}$ of the volume of the cube. This is a special use of the general result that:

- Pyramid volume = $\frac{1}{3}$ × Enclosing prism volume
  $= \frac{1}{3}$ (Base area × Height)
  $= \frac{1}{3} Ah$ or $\frac{Ah}{3}$

So the pyramid in Figure 132 has a volume of:
$\frac{1}{3} \times 8 \times 6 \text{cm}^3 = 16 \text{cm}^3$
$\qquad\qquad\quad = 16 \text{ml}$

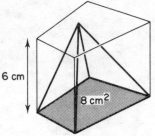

Figure 132. A pyramid and its enclosing prism

Self-check

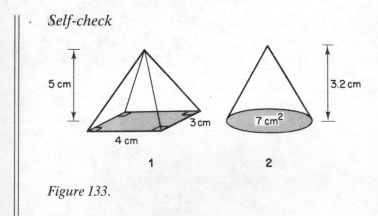

Figure 133.

1–2 Calculate the volumes of the pyramids in Figure 133, giving your answers in ml.

3 A pyramid has a base area of $7.5\,m^2$ and a height of $3\,m$. What is its volume?

4 A pyramid has a base area of $120\,cm^2$ and a height of $15\,cm$. What is its volume in litres?

ANSWERS

1 $\frac{12 \times 5}{3} = 20\,cm^3 = 20\,ml.$

2 $\frac{7 \times 3.2}{3} \simeq 7.47\,cm^3 = 7.47\,ml.$

3 $7.5\,m^3$. **4** Vol. $= \frac{120 \times 15}{3} = 600\,cm^3 = 0.6l.$

I hope you've found this first part of the chapter fairly straightforward. I have deliberately avoided more complicated questions at this stage; you'll find plenty in the second part. You may also have wondered about the absence of any problems involving circles, cones, cylinders, etc. You'll find these in Chapter 10.

Review

Calculate the following, correct to 3 s.f.

1 Rectangle, length $8\,m$, width $60\,cm$. Find area in m^2.

2 Triangle, length $4.6\,cm$, height $31\,mm$. Find area in cm^2.

3 Triangle, length $0.65\,m$, width $21\,cm$. Find area in cm^2.

4 Convert to cm^2:
   $2\,m^2$; $160\,mm^2$; $0.65\,m^2$.

5 A concrete beam has a cross-section and length as shown in Figure 134. Find the volume in m^3.

6 A pyramidical container is $80\,cm$ high and has a square base of side $40\,cm$. What is its volume in litres?

7 Convert the following to ml:
   $148\,cm^3$; $14\,mm^3$; $1.4l$.

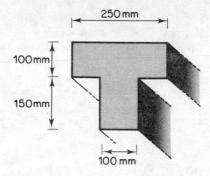

Figure 134. (a) *Dimensions in mm; length of beam 8 m.*

Problems in reverse

Often with problems involving areas or volumes, you already know an area or volume and you have to work back to find, say, an unknown height or length. Here is an example.

You drain 4 litres of oil from your car sump into a cuboid container as shown in Figure 135. What will the depth of oil be in the container?

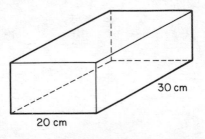

Figure 135.

Solution

First I convert the 4 litres of oil into 4 × 1000 = 4000 ml or 4000 cm³ so that all the units are in the same family. Here I know that each 1 cm increase in depth corresponds to:

$20 \times 30 \times 1 = 600\,\text{cm}^3$

so it is a matter of finding how many $600\,\text{cm}^3$ make $4000\,\text{cm}^3$.

I can answer this by 'guess and check' or directly by calculating $4000 \times 600 = 6.66\ldots \simeq 7\,\text{cm}$, so the depth will be a little less than $7\,\text{cm}$.

See how the calculation involves division. I calculated the volume of oil ÷ container area to give 6.666... cm – the depth of oil. You can see how this works for cuboids in general:

Volume (V) = Area (A) × height (h)

I rearranged $V = A \times h$ to give:

$\frac{V}{A} = h$

Dividing both sides of the formula by A makes h the subject. Similarly, dividing by h gives:

$\frac{V}{h} = A$

Self-check

1 Find the heights of these cuboids.
   a Volume $216\,\text{cm}^3$, base area $72\,\text{cm}^2$.
   b Volume $1047\,\text{cm}^3$, base area $270\,\text{cm}^2$.
   c Volume $7.34\,\text{m}^3$, base area $9.3\,\text{m}^2$.

2 $2.5\,\text{m}^3$ of concrete is poured into a foundation pit shown in Figure 136. What is the depth of concrete (to the nearest cm)?

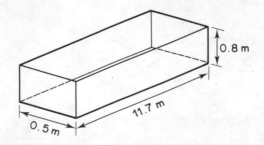

Figure 136.

ANSWERS

1 $3\,\text{cm}$; $3.88\,\text{cm}$; $0.79\,\text{m}$.
2 $43\,\text{cm}$ (or $0.43\,\text{m}$).

Rearranging volume formulae

Rearranging the cuboid formula

You have seen that you can rearrange the cuboid formula $V = Ah$ to give:

- $h = V/A$
- $A = V/h$

In a similar way, you can rearrange the cuboid formula $V = lwh$ to make l the subject:

- $l = \frac{V}{wh}$

If this confuses you, just think for a moment what you would do to calculate l if you knew V, w and h. Starting from:

$V = lwh$

your problem would be to find a value of l so that when you multiplied it by wh you would obtain the correct value for V.

Suppose that $V = 1000 \text{m}^3$, $w = 8 \text{m}$ and $h = 9 \text{m}$. What is the length of the cuboid?

$1000 = l \times 8 \times 9$

so:

$l \times 72 = 1000$

and:

$l = \frac{1}{72} \text{ of } 1000$

or:

$1000 \div 72 = 13.9 \text{m}$

You can see that:

$l = \frac{1000}{8 \times 9} = \frac{V}{wh}$

As a check:

$l \times w \times h = 13.9 \times 8 \times 9 \simeq 1000$

Self-check

1 What is the length of a cuboid when the volume is 6000cm^3, width is 20cm and height is 6cm?

2 Rearrange the formula $V = lwh$ to make w the subject.

3 Rearrange the formula $V = lwh$ to make h the subject.

ANSWERS

1 $l = \frac{6000}{120} = 50$ cm.   **2** $w = \frac{V}{lh}$.   **3** $h = \frac{V}{lw}$.

Rearranging the prism formula

You can rearrange $V = Ah$ to give:

- $\dfrac{V}{A} = h$

or:

- $\dfrac{V}{h} = A$

just as for cuboids. Here's an example.

The prism in Figure 137 has a volume of 500 ml. The dimensions of the cross-section are as shown. What is the correct value for h?

First, the shaded cross-section is a triangle, so its area is:
$\frac{10 \times 8}{2} = 40$ cm^2

Then:
$$h = \frac{V}{A}$$
$$= \frac{500}{40} = 12.5 \text{ cm}$$

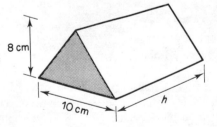

Figure 137.

Rearranging the pyramid formula

Make h the subject of:
$$V = \tfrac{1}{3}Ah$$
First:

$\frac{1}{3}Ah = V$

so Ah will be three times as much, that is:

$Ah = 3V$

then dividing by A as before:

$h = 3V \div A$

$\quad = \frac{3V}{A}$

For instance, if a pyramid had a volume of $80\,\text{cm}^3$ and its base area was $16\,\text{cm}^2$, then:

$h = \frac{3 \times 80}{16} = 15\,\text{cm}$

You can check that this is correct in the original formula:

$\frac{1}{3}Ah = \frac{1}{3} \times 16 \times 15 = \frac{1}{3} \times 240 = 80$

as you would expect.

Self-check

1 A pyramid is required to have a volume of 125 ml and a base area of $20\,\text{cm}^2$. How high should it be?

2 A pyramid has a square base. Its height is 8 cm and its volume is $216\,\text{cm}^3$. What is the area of its base? What is the side length of the base?

ANSWERS

1 18.75 cm. **2** $81\,\text{cm}^2$; 9 cm.

Using tables to solve problems

This section shows you how you can use tables to find the best solutions to some practical problems involving areas and volumes.

Suppose you have a rectangular sheet of cardboard and you want to cut and fold the corners to make a cuboid-shaped open-top box. You can see how the folds are made in Figure 138. You can make the base large, but this means that the sides will be low, or you can make the base smaller with higher sides.

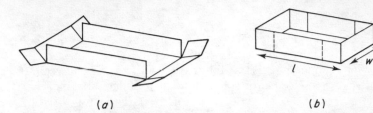

Figure 138. (a) *Cutting and folding a sheet of cardboard to make* (b) *a cuboid-shaped open-topped box*

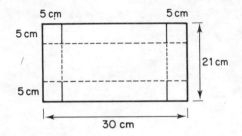

Figure 139.

I could cut and fold the sheet as in Figure 139, making four 5 cm cuts and folds. This means that the length of the box would be:

$30 - (2 \times 5) = 20$ cm

and the width would be:

$21 - (2 \times 5) = 11$ cm

The height would be 5 cm, so the volume would be:

$20 \times 11 \times 5 = 1100$ cm^3

However, I could have made 6 cm cuts, giving a box measuring:

18 cm by 9 cm by 6 cm

The base would have been smaller but the box would be deeper, giving a volume of … well, you work it out.

Activity

Can you find the length of cut which gives a box with the greatest volume? Try it now with your calculator.

ANSWER

This is a situation where using a table to store information, then plotting the information on a graph, can give you a good picture of what is happening as the dimensions of the box are altered. It will enable you to see the solution to the problem more clearly.

I've started working out the volume (V cm^3) for different lengths of cut (x cm) as in the table below.

x (cm)	Length (cm)	Width (cm)	Height (cm)	V (cm^3)
2	26	17	2	884
3				
4				
5	20	11	5	1100
6	18	9	6	
7				
8				

Activity

Copy the table and fill in the missing values.

ANSWERS

Other V values are 1080, 1144, 972, 784 and 560.

You can see that the maximum volume will be when x is close to 4 cm.

Review

1 A cuboid has a volume of 1 litre. It has a base measuring 10 cm by 8 cm. What is its height?
2 A cuboid-shaped storage tank is designed to hold 2500 litres. Its base can be no more than 1 metre deep and its height is 1.2 m. What must its length be?
3 Rearrange the formula:
   $$T = wx$$
   to make x the subject.
   What is the value of x when $T = 12$ and $w = 15$?

4 Rearrange the formula:
$$M = \frac{py}{4}$$
to make y the subject. What is the value of y when $M = 100$ and $p = 12.5$?

5 Soil is piled in a pyramid shape h metres high. The base area of the pyramid is $4h^2$ square metres. Find the approximate height of the pyramid when the volume is $5\,m^3$.

9 Conversion charts and tables, rates and proportions

Topics covered

- Conversion between units – metric/imperial.
- Charts, tables and conversion graphs.
- Gradients of graphs.
- Direct and inverse proportion and associated formulae.
- Finding constants.
- Spotting incorrect results.

Conversion between units

Our measurements are a mixture of two different systems – metric and imperial. You have already met the common metric units in this book, but there are several imperial units which are part of everyday usage as well. You probably know your height in feet and inches, your weight in stones and pounds (lb), buy milk and beer in pints, petrol in gallons, and travel miles rather than kilometres. All these units are imperial, part of a system which was used throughout Europe in the Middle Ages and earlier, before gradual introduction of the metric system over the last 150 years or so. As long as both systems are in use there will always be the need to convert from one to the other.

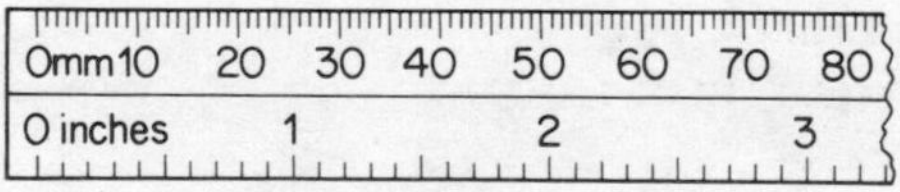

Figure 140. Millimetre and inch scales side by side

One of the easiest ways of converting is by putting two scales side by side, as in Figure 140, then reading off one scale on to the other. For example, 2.4 inches ≃ 61 mm, while 40 mm is between 1.5 and 1.6 inches, say 1.57 in. In Figure 141 you can see that petrol at 44p per litre is the same as 200p (or £2) per gallon, while petrol at 40p per litre is somewhere between 180p and 185p, say 182p, per gallon. (The diagonal stroke, /, can be used to mean 'per', e.g. pence/litre means pence per litre.)

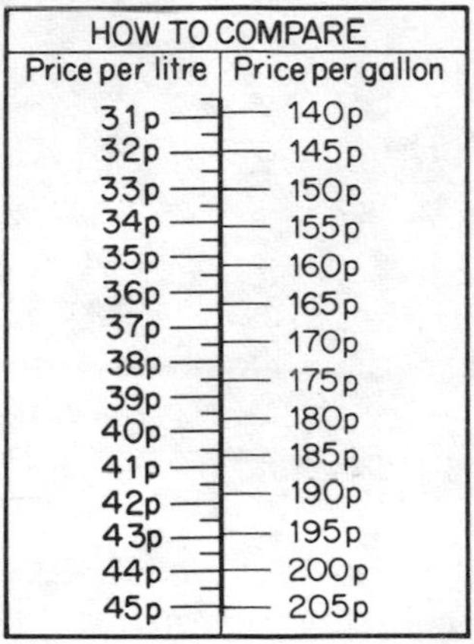

HOW TO COMPARE	
Price per litre	Price per gallon
31p	140p
32p	145p
33p	150p
34p	155p
35p	160p
36p	165p
37p	170p
38p	175p
39p	180p
40p	
41p	185p
42p	190p
43p	195p
44p	200p
45p	205p

Figure 141. Price per litre compared to price per gallon

These examples show how sometimes you have to estimate a value in between those on the scales (that is, you have to **interpolate**).

You can also use the scales to find larger or smaller amounts than those shown, by multiplying or dividing pairs of numbers by the same amounts. For example, 43 mm ≃ 1.7 in means that:

- 4.3 mm ≃ 0.17 in (÷ 10)
- 430 mm ≃ 17 in (× 10)
- 0.43 mm ≃ 0.017 in or 17 'thou'

Conversion tables

Often tables are used for conversion; as before you interpolate to find in-between values.

Conversion table for pounds and kilograms

kg		lb
0.45	1	2.20
0.91	2	4.41
1.36	3	6.61
1.81	4	8.82
2.27	5	11.02
2.72	6	13.23
3.18	7	15.43
3.63	8	17.64
4.08	9	19.84
4.54	10	22.05

You use this table by selecting a value in the middle column, then reading from the **left** to convert from pounds weight (lb) to kilograms, and from the **right** to convert from kilograms to pounds. So for instance:

- $4\,\text{lb} \simeq 1.81\,\text{kg}$
- $4\,\text{kg} \simeq 8.82\,\text{lb}$

Conversion of feet and inches to metres

Feet	0	1	2	3	4	Inches 5	6	7	8	9	10	11
0	0.00	0.03	0.05	0.08	0.10	0.13	0.15	0.18	0.20	0.23	0.25	0.28
1	0.30	0.33	0.36	0.38	0.41	0.43	0.46	0.48	0.51	0.53	0.56	0.58
2	0.61	0.64	0.66	0.69	0.71	0.74	0.76	0.79	0.81	0.84	0.86	0.89
3	0.91	0.94	0.97	0.99	1.02	1.04	1.07	1.09	1.12	1.14	1.17	1.19
4	1.22	1.24	1.27	1.30	1.32	1.35	1.37	1.40	1.42	1.45	1.47	1.50

For example:
$3\,\text{ft}\ 7\,\text{in} = 1.09\,\text{m}$
and
$0.5\,\text{m} \simeq 1\,\text{ft}\ 8\,\text{in}$

Conversion factors

Using tables means you can avoid calculations when making conversions, but a calculator makes that less of a problem anyway. Looking back at the first table, you can see how $1\,\text{lb} \simeq$

0.45 kg. More accurately, 1 lb equals 0.4536 kg or approximately 0.454 kg, so you can change a weight in pounds into kilograms by multiplying by 0.454. Similarly, you can change a weight in kilograms back to pounds by doing the opposite – dividing by 0.4536 (or multiplying by 2.205). You can make conversions of other well-known units using these results:

- 1 mile ≃ 1.609 km
- 1 foot ≃ 0.3048 m
- 1 inch ≃ 2.54 cm
- 1 gallon ≃ 4.546 litres

You can check your answers to conversions by remembering that the larger the unit, the smaller the number. For instance, a mile is **larger** than a kilometre, so there will be **fewer** miles than kilometres in a given distance.

Self-check

Using the results above, carry out the following conversions, giving your answer correct to 3 significant figures.
1 3.4 miles to kilometres.
2 9.5 gallons to litres.
3 7.4 litres to gallons.
4 What do you multiply by to convert kilometres to miles?

ANSWERS

1 5.47 km. **2** 43.2 litres. **3** 1.63 gallons.
4 1.609 km = 1 mile, so 1 km = $\frac{1}{1.609}$ = 0.622 miles, i.e. you multiply by 0.622.

You can use conversion factors to build up conversion tables of your own. For instance, using:
  1 mile = 1.609 kilometres
you can make up a table saying that:
  Distance in kilometres = 1.609 × Distance in miles

Miles	km
0	0
1	1.609
2	3.218
5	
10	16.09

Activity

Look at the table and fill in the missing figure.

Conversion charts (graphs)

You can use the table to plot a graph (see Figure 142). The graph line passes through points O, P, Q, R and S, corresponding to the numbers in the table, giving a straight graph line passing through the origin. You can use the graph to read off other conversions. For instance, arrows A show how 4 miles converts to approximately 6.4 km.

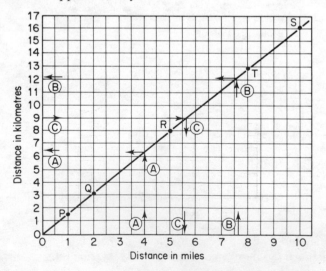

Figure 142. Conversion graph for miles to kilometres and vice versa

Self-check

1 What do the arrows B and C show?
Using the conversion chart, read off the following.
2 4.5 miles in km.
3 9.6 miles in km.
4 10.1 km to miles.
5 13.5 km to miles.
6 Correct any *wrong* conversions among these:
      3 miles = 4.8 km;
      5 km = 8 miles;
      13 km = 8.1 miles.

ANSWERS

1 Conversion of 7.6 miles to 12.2 km and of 9 km to 5.6 miles.
2 7.2 km.   **3** 15.4 km.   **4** 6.3 miles.
5 8.4 miles.   **6** 5 km = 3.1 miles.

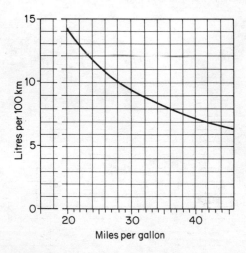

Figure 143. Conversion of petrol consumption in miles per gallon to litres per 100 km

Conversion charts are not always straight lines through the

origin. You will find an example in Figure 143, showing different ways of measuring fuel consumption for cars, and you will remember the Fahrenheit/Celsius chart from page 65.

Notice that in Figure 143 part of the graph paper is cut to show the **interrupted scale** in miles per gallon (mpg), so you could not extend the graph line very far to the left as it stands. Notice also that, as with the other conversion charts, you need to be clear how much each square is 'worth' – in this case 2 mpg going across and 1 litre/100 km upwards.

Self-check

Using Figure 143, convert the following.
1 30 mpg to litres/100 km.
2 9 litres/100 km to mpg.
3 A family go to France with their car. They reckon to cover about 1200 km and they know their car does about 36 mpg overall. How many litres of petrol do you think they'll use?

ANSWERS

1 9.4 litres/100 km.
2 31.4 mpg.
3 36 mpg ≃ 8 litres/100 km, so they'll need 8 × 12 = 96 litres.

Review

1 The scale in Figure 144 shows the conversion from °C to °F. Use it to convert the following.
  a 12 °C to °F.
  b 43 °F to °C.
  c ⁻5 °C to °F.
  d 20 °F to °C.

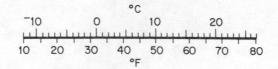

Figure 144.

2 Use your calculator, if you wish, to complete this table for converting square feet to square metres.

sq.ft	1	2	5	10	20	30
m²	0.093					

3 Convert the following.
  a 12 sq.ft to m².
  b 2 m² to sq.ft.
  c 7.2 sq.ft to m².
  d 0.65 m² to sq.ft.
4 A commercial traveller has to make a round trip from London, calling at Bristol, Leeds, Nottingham, Carlisle and Edinburgh (see Figure 145).
  a What route will give the shortest mileage?
  b What is the total mileage?

London							
105	Birmingham						
115	81	Bristol					
301	196	277	Carlisle				
378	292	373	96	Edinburgh			
189	113	194	119	202	Leeds		
122	50	145	181	262	70	Nottingham	
193	130	211	121	194	24	77	York

Figure 145. Distances between cities in miles

Formulae and gradients of graphs

Below you will find a table for the formula:
  $y = \frac{1}{2}x + 1$
The matching graph is in Figure 146.

x	y
6	4
3	$2\frac{1}{2}$
1	$1\frac{1}{2}$
0	1
$^-2$	0
$^-4$	$^-1$

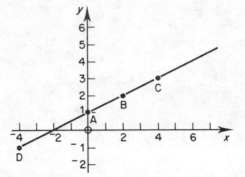

Figure 146. Graph of $y = \frac{1}{2}x + 1$

Self-check

Find y values for the formula:
$$y = \frac{1}{2}x + 1$$
which match the x values of 5, 2, $^-1$, $^-5$.

ANSWERS

$3\frac{1}{2}, 2, \frac{1}{2}, \, ^-1\frac{1}{2}.$

Look at the graph of $y = \frac{1}{2}x + 1$ again. You can see how any (x, y) pair which fits the formula will give a point which lies on the line.

You can measure the slope of the graph line by calculating its **gradient**. See how the y values increase by 1 as the x values increase by 2 all along the line, i.e. the **gradient** of the graph is $\frac{1}{2}$: 1 step up compared with 2 steps right.

As the graph line is straight, you can work out the gradient using **any** two points on the graph line:

- from A to C: $\dfrac{\text{Distance up}}{\text{Distance right}}$ $= \frac{2}{4} = \frac{1}{2}$

- from D to B: $\dfrac{\text{Distance up}}{\text{Distance right}}$ $= \frac{3}{6} = \frac{1}{2}$

- from C to D: $\dfrac{\text{Distance up}}{\text{Distance right}}$ $= \frac{-4}{-8} = \frac{1}{2}$

Self-check

Figure 147 shows the graphs of three formulae. Calculate the gradient of each graph.

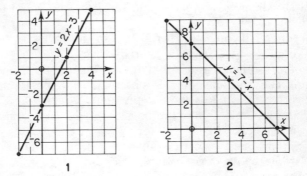

1

2

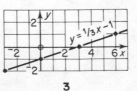

3

Figure 147.

ANSWERS

1 Using the points $(0, {}^-3)$ and $(4, 5)$, the gradient is:
   $\frac{8}{4} = 2$.
   Any other pair of points will give the same value.
2 Using the points $(0, 7)$ and $(7, 0)$, the gradient is:
   $\frac{{}^-7}{7} = {}^-1$.
3 Using the points $(0, {}^-1)$ and $(6, 1)$ the gradient $\frac{1}{3}$.

Notice how graph lines, like that of $y = 7 - x$, which slope down to the right, have negative gradients.

Graphs and direct proportion

Earlier in this chapter you met formulae like:

   Distance in kilometres $= 1.609 \times$ *Distance in miles*

   The graph you drew was a **straight line passing through the origin**. For example, each extra mile corresponds to an increase of 1.609 kilometres and you can see from the graph that the gradient is 1.609.
   In general, if you have a formula of the form:
   Variable (y) = Constant $\times$ Variable (x)
then the formula's graph will be a straight line through the origin. The constants will be the gradient of the graph if you plot variable y upwards and x to the right.
   In the example above, the constant is the **conversion factor** you met earlier on in this chapter.
   Relations like these are examples of **direct proportion**. You can always spot if two variables are in direct proportion by seeing if their graph is a straight line passing through the **origin**. Doubling one variable will result in the other doubling, e.g. double distance in miles and it will be doubled in kilometres. Similarly, trebling one variable will result in the other trebling.
   You can see that this will always happen with a pair of variables in direct proportion (see Figure 148), and this provides another way of checking if two variables *are* in direct proportion.

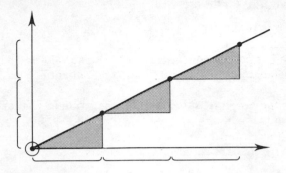

Figure 148. Graph of two variables in direct proportion

Self-check

Which of the following pairs of variables are in direct proportion?
1 Distance travelled, time taken (speed constant).
2 Speed, time taken (distance travelled constant).
3 Temperature in °F, temperature in °C (see page 65).
4 Number of litres, cost (price per litre constant).

ANSWERS

For each of these situations imagine what happens if you double or treble one variable – does the other variable double or treble?
1 Yes, so distance travelled is directly proportional to time taken.
2 No – if you double the speed you halve the time for a journey.
3 No – graph does not pass through origin.
4 Yes – double the number of litres and you double the cost.

Self-check

If $p = 3.1t$, find p when $t = 6.35$.

ANSWER

19.7.

Rearranging formulae

In the self-check above:

   $3.1t = p$

so:

   $t = p \div 3.1$
   $= p/3.1$

t is now the subject, as the formula is rearranged so that you can find t, knowing p.

> ### *Self-check*
>
> **1** If $P/3.1 = t$, find t when $p = 5.1$.
> **2** If $h = 1.609d$, re-write the formula to make d the subject.
> **3** What is the value of d when $h = 300$?

ANSWERS

1 $t = 1.65$. **2** $d = \frac{h}{1.609}$. **3** $d = 186$.

Finding the constant of proportion

Figure 149 shows a spring supported at A. When a load of L kg is hung from the spring hook, the spring extends x mm. You are told that load is proportional to extension so that:

   $L = \text{constant} \times x$

You want to find the value of the constant.

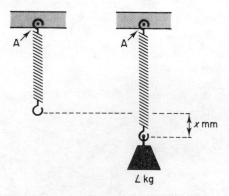

Figure 149. Extension of a spring

Imagine having a weight of 4 kg on the spring and it extends by 29 mm. Then $L = 4$ and $x = 29$, so:

   $4 = \text{constant} \times 29$

and, rearranging the formula:

   $\frac{4}{29} = \text{constant}$

As a decimal, this is about 0.138. This fixed number is called a **constant of proportion**, linking matching pairs of the two variables. You can write the formula as:

   $L = \frac{4}{29}x$

or:

   $L = 0.138x$

whichever you find more convenient. Now you can hang any other object on the spring, measure the extension, x, and use the formula to find the weight of the object.

Self-check

   1 Object A gives an extension of 10 mm. What does it weigh?

   2 What extension would you expect from a load of 8 kg?

ANSWERS

Given to 2 significant figures, as you probably cannot measure extensions more accurately.

1 1.4 kg.

2 $8/0.138 \simeq 58$ mm or double the extension for 4 kg.

Self-check

Volume of dye is proportional to the weight of cloth to be processed. $V =$ volume of dye in ml and $W =$ weight of cloth in kg; when $V = 18$, $W = 5$.

   1 Complete the formula:

   $V = \text{constant} \times \ldots$

   and find the value of the constant.

   2 Find V when $W = 7.2$.

   3 Find W when $V = 30$.

ANSWERS

1 $V = \text{constant} \times W$, so constant = 3.6.

2 $V = 3.6 \times 7.2 = 25.9$.

3 $\dfrac{30}{3.6} = 8.33$.

Inverse proportion

For **direct proportion** there is always a formula like:

$y = kx$

where x and y are variables and k is a constant. If, instead, you find that:

$y = \frac{k}{x}, = k \times \frac{1}{x}$

that is, that y is proportional to $\frac{1}{x}$, then x and y are in **inverse proportion**. You can re-write this formula by multiplying by x to give:

$xy = x \times \frac{k}{x}$

so:

$xy = k$

This shows that if two variables are in inverse proportion, their product, i.e. the result of multiplying matching pairs together, is **constant**. For instance, in this table x and y are in inverse proportion since $xy = 60$ for each pair.

x	1	2	3	4	5	6	7	8
y	60	30	20	15	12	10	8.57	7.5

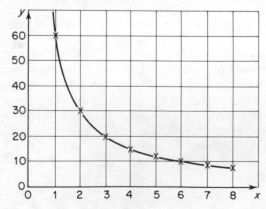

Figure 150.

What do you think the graph of *y* and *x* will look like? Have a look at Figure 150 to see if you were right.

Self-check

1 What is the value of *y* when *x* = 30?
2 What is the value of *x* when *y* = 120?
3 Describe how the graph in Figure 150 can be extended.

ANSWERS

1 *y* = 2 (2 × 30 = 60).
2 *x* = 0.5.
3 It will continue to curve, getting closer and closer to the *x* and *y* axes without ever reaching them. If you're not convinced, calculate the value of *y* when *x* = 6000 (or of *x* when *y* = 6000).

The graph in Figure 150 may remind you of another graph you met earlier in this chapter (see page 225). The table shows some pairs of values taken from the first graph, where *G* stands for miles per gallon and *L* for litres per 100 km.

G	30	38	40	20		24
L	9.4	7.4	7.0		10	

Activity

Use the graph in Figure 143 to fill in the missing numbers.

Is *L* inversely proportional to *G*? You can check by multiplying (*G*, *L*) pairs together. What do you find? You've probably seen that the product of every pair comes to a little over 280. For instance, 30 × 9.4 = 282, 38 × 7.4 = 281.2, etc. This shows that *G* and *L* are inversely proportional to each other. (The slight differences in the products are due to approximations in reading the figures from the graph.)

Self-check

1 Using *GL* = 282.5, calculate further values of *G* or *L* to complete this table.

G	26	34		
L			12	8

Check that the pairs of values correspond with points on the graph in Figure 143.

2 In a journey of 400 km you use 24 litres of petrol. How many miles per gallon has your car averaged?

ANSWERS

1 Missing figures are 10.9, 8.3, 23.5, 35.3.
2 6 litres/100 km = 47.1 mpg.

You'll notice that if you double one variable (say $G = 20$ to $G = 40$), then the other variable is halved ($L = 14$ to $L = 7$), and when you treble one variable ($L = 6$ to $L = 18$) then the other variable is divided by 3($G = 47.1$ to $G = 15.7$). This gives you another way of spotting if two variables are inversely proportional to each other. For example, if you make a journey at twice the speed, you halve the journey time, whilst at three times the speed, the journey time is only a third of what it was before, Thus it seems as though speed and time are inversely proportional to each other for journeys of constant distance.

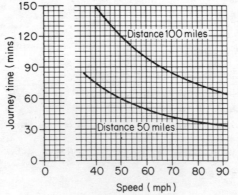

Figure 151.

You can see the graphs of two journeys like this in Figure 151. Again the graphs have the easily recognized pattern of a curve sloping down to the right, i.e. with a negative gradient, which does not meet either axis. The table below shows some pairs of values from the 50 mile graph line.

speed in mph s	40	60	80		
time in minutes t	75	50		32	96

Activity

Find the missing numbers:
1 by using the graph in Figure 151;
2 by finding the value of the constant in the formula:
  $st = $ Constant
and then using this result to calculate the missing values.

ANSWERS

Did you obtain 37.5, 94 and 31 for the three missing values? The constant is 3000 (40×75, 60×50, etc.).

Checking on direct and inverse proportion

Inverse proportion

The table below shows matching values of w and z which are in inverse proportion.

w	2	3	5	8	10	12
z	23	15.33	9.2	5.57	4.6	3.83

Activity

There is an incorrect z value; can you spot and correct it?

ANSWER

All the pairs have a product of approximately 46.0 except 8×5.57 which equals 44.56. So 5.57 is wrong. The correct z value is 5.75, as $8 \times 5.75 = 46.0$.

Direct proportion

p	2	3	5	8	10	12
q	6.6	9.9	17.5	26.4	33	39.6

This table shows matching values of p and q which are in direct proportion.

 Activity

 There is an incorrect q value. Can you spot and correct it?

ANSWER

Remember that:
  $q = \text{constant} \times p$
or:
  $\dfrac{q}{p} = \text{constant}$

Thus you can check the table by working out the values of $q \div p$ for each column – they should be the same. In fact:
  $q \div p = 3.3$
except for $17.5 \div 5$, which equals 3.5, so 17.5 is wrong – the correct q value is 16.5.

 Review

 1 Liquid velocity (v metres/second) is inversely proportional to nozzle area (A mm^2). When $A = 108$, $v = 7.5$, find:
   a A when $v = 6.5$;
   b v when $A = 75$.
 2 Breaking load (T tonnes) is directly proportional to cable cross-section area (A mm^2). When $A = 160$, $T = 3.6$. Find:
   a T when $A = 185$;
   b A when $T = 7.5$.
 3 If you plot a graph of the formula:
   $y = 2.5x + 3$
   (with x to the right and y upwards):

a what is the gradient of the graph?
b is *y* directly proportional to *x*?

10 | Circles and circular shapes

Topics covered

- Circumference and area of circles.
- Direct use of formulae for surface area and volume of cylinder, cone and sphere.
- Use of formulae for area and volume in reverse – working backwards.
- Rearranging formulae and solving equations associated with circles and circle-based solids.

Introduction

A reminder of some of the more common words used in connection with circles appears in Figure 152.

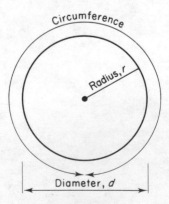

Figure 152. Terms associated with a circle

- The **diameter** (d) is the longest distance across a circle.
- The **radius** (r) is the distance from the centre of a circle to the edge.
- The **circumference** (c) is the distance all the way round the outside, i.e. the perimeter.

You can see that the diameter is twice the radius, i.e.:

$d = 2r$

You can also see that the circumference is much more than twice the diameter (or more than four times the radius) by cutting a piece of string to fit round a circular object and then comparing the length of the string with the diameter.

Figure 153 shows the start of a simple pattern you can make using ruler and compasses, together with the completed pattern of six equilateral triangles, arranged to form a regular hexagon.

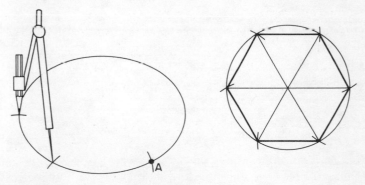

Figure 153.

Calculating the circumference

How long is the hexagon perimeter compared with the radius? You can see that it's six times as long, so the *circumference* of the circle is a little over six times the radius and three times the diameter:

$c = $ '3 and a bit' $\times d$

If you make more and more accurate measurements you will obtain better and better estimates for this number, approximately:

3.1, or 3.14, or 3.142, or 3.14159, or 3.1415927... etc.
In fact the list continues for ever as there is no exact decimal version of this number – and no exact fraction for that matter. The well-known fraction version of $3\frac{1}{7}$ is only approximate as well, though a close one. The Greek letter for P, written π and pronounced 'pie', is used to stand for the number, so:

- $\pi \simeq 3$ or 3.14 or 3.14159

and:

- $c = \pi \times d$
  $= \pi \times 2r$
  $= 2\pi r$

Note that circumference is directly proportional to diameter.

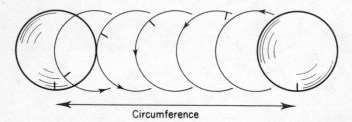

Circumference

Figure 154. Measuring the circumference of a cylindrical tin

You can check that these values of π make sense. Take an ordinary tin of food and measure its diameter in millimetres. Now make a mark on one end and place it on a flat surface. Carefully roll it along until it has turned one complete revolution (see Figure 154), then measure how far it has rolled. It will have rolled a distance equal to its circumference, so you can find π by dividing this by the diameter. In symbols:

$c = \pi d$

so:

$\dfrac{c}{d} = \pi$

Repeat the experiment several times until you have several answers very close together. You will probably find a value for π of between 3.1 and 3.2.

Self-check

Use $c = \pi d$ or $c = 2\pi r$, and take $\pi = 3.142$. Give answers to 3 significant figures.

1 Calculate the circumference of circles with radii of 6 cm, 18 cm, 5 m.

2 Calculate the circumference of circles with diameters of 8 mm, 21 mm, 12.5 cm.

3 Calculate the radii of circles with circumferences of 24 m and 13 mm.

4 A bicycle wheel is 50 cm in diameter. How far will the bicycle move if the wheel turns once?

5 A mile is about 1609 m. How many times will the bicycle wheel turn when a cyclist covers a mile?

ANSWERS

1 37.7 cm; 113 cm; 31.4 m.
2 25.1 mm; 66.0 mm; 39.3 cm.
3 3.82 m; 2.07 mm.
4 1.57 m.
5 $1609 \div 1.57 = 1025$ times.

Calculating the area

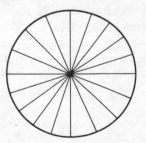

Figure 155.

Activity

Draw a circle, radius 5 cm, and then draw on lots of radii, dividing the circle into many **sectors** (see Figure 155). Cut out the circle. Its circumference is:

$2 \times \pi \times 5 = 31.4$ cm

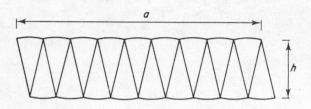

Figure 156.

Check it and see that this is correct. Now cut the circle along the radii and rearrange the sectors in an alternating pattern as in Figure 156. You'll find you have a shape very much like a parallelogram, so the area of all the sectors is approximately $a \times h$. With your circle, you'll probably find that a is about 15.7 cm, while the height h is equivalent to the circle radius of 5 cm. Thus the area of a 5 cm radius circle is roughly $15.7 \times 5 = 78.5$ cm². In general, for a circle of radius r, the area is approximately half the circumference × radius:

- Area of a circle $(A) = \pi r \times r$
  $$= \pi r^2$$

and you get closer and closer to this result as you make the sectors thinner and thinner. Using this result, a more exact value for the area of the 5 cm radius circle is 78.55 cm².

Self-check

Take $\pi \simeq 3.142$ and calculate the areas of circles with these radii. Give your answers to 3 significant figures.

1 3 cm.   **2** 2 cm.   **3** 10 cm.
4 0.4 cm.   **5** 0.2 cm.   **6** 0.3 cm.

ANSWERS

1 28.3 cm².   **2** 12.6 cm².   **3** 314 cm².
4 0.503 cm².   **5** 0.126 cm².   **6** 0.283 cm².

Check your answers carefully before you continue. If you got several wrong then it may be because you made a mistake in using the formula:

$A = \pi r^2$

Remember that this is short for $\pi \times r \times r$, so you calculate answer **1** like this:

$$\begin{aligned} \text{Area} &= \pi \times 3 \times 3 \\ &= 3.142 \times 9 \\ &\simeq 28.3 \, \text{cm}^2 \end{aligned}$$

Starting with the diameter of a circle, your first step in finding its area is to halve the diameter to obtain the radius. Then you use the formula:

$A = \pi r^2$

Thus if you had a circle of diameter 4.3 cm, then:

$$\begin{aligned} \text{circle area} &= 3.142 \times 2.15^2 \\ &= 14.523 \\ &\simeq 14.5 \, \text{cm}^2 \end{aligned}$$

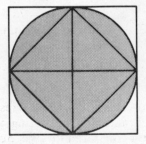

Figure 157.

As a **check** you can always compare the area of your circle with the area of a square surrounding it. You can see from Figure 157 that the circle area is about threequarters of the area of the square, so in this case the circle area should be about threequarters the area of a square of side 4.3 cm, i.e. about threequarters of 18.49 cm². You can probably see that 14 is about threequarters of 18, so your calculation of the circle area looks all right.

Area and circumference – enlarging circles

Activity

Cut out three circles, two of radius 3 cm, the third of radius 6 cm. How do their areas compare?

It's certainly *not* the case that the large one is double the area of a small circle – put the small circles on top of the large one and see how much space is left uncovered.

In fact the area of the large circle is four times the area of each smaller circle, so doubling the radius or diameter results in the area being multiplied by four, not two. Calculate the areas of the circles to see why this happens.

The questions on page 245 give further examples:

● circle 1 is 10 times the radius of circle 6, but 100 times the area;

● circle 3 is 5 times the radius of circle 2, but 25 times the area.

Fractions of circles – sectors

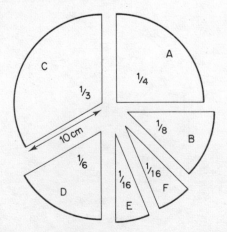

Figure 158. Sectors cut from a circle

Once you can calculate the circumference and area of circles whose radius you know, you can find ways of calculating the perimeter and area of **sectors**. Figure 158 shows several sectors cut from a circle of radius 10 cm. Sector A is $\frac{1}{4}$ of the circle, for example, so the area of sector A is:

$\frac{1}{4}$ of $\pi \times 10^2 = \frac{\pi \times 100}{4} \simeq 78.6\,\text{cm}^2$

Similarly the area of sector C is:

$\frac{1}{3}$ of $\pi \times 10^2 = \frac{\pi \times 100}{3} \simeq 104.7\,\text{cm}^2$

> *Self-check*
>
> **1** Calculate the areas of the remaining sectors.
> **2** How could adding together the answers to **1** help you to check if they were correct?

ANSWERS

1 78.6 cm²; 39.3 cm²; 104.7 cm²; 52.4 cm²; 19.6 cm²; 19.6 cm².
2 They should add to give the complete circle area of 314.2 cm².

The perimeter of each sector is made up of the curved part (the **arc** of the circle) and the two straight **edges** – both radii. Thus, for instance, the perimeter of sector C (see Figure 159) is:

$10 + 10 + \frac{1}{3}$ of $2\pi \times 10 = 10 + 10 + 20.9 = 40.9\,\text{cm}$

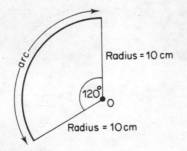

Figure 159. Sector C

Self-check

1 Calculate the perimeters of all the sectors in Figure 158.
2 How could adding together the answers to 1 help you to check if they were correct?

ANSWERS

1 35.7 cm; 27.9 cm; 40.9 cm; 30.5 cm; 23.9 cm; 23.9 cm.
2 If you add all the perimeters you should obtain the circumference + double the sector radius for each sector, i.e. 62.8 + 2 + 6 + 10 = 182.8 cm.

You can build on these methods to find the areas and perimeters of quite complicated shapes, based on circles and rectangles. In some cases you can find the area of a shape by adding two areas, in others by subtracting a small area from a larger one.

Self-check

1–3 Calculate the shaded areas of the shapes in Figure 160 to the nearest mm^2.

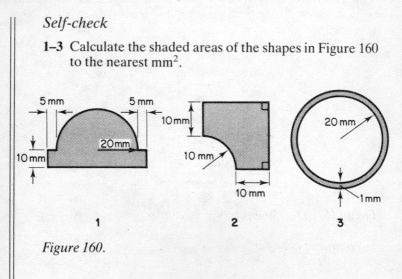

Figure 160.

4–5 Calculate the perimeter of the shapes 1 and 2 in Figure 160 to the nearest mm.

ANSWERS

1 $628 + 500 \simeq 1128\,\text{mm}^2$.
2 $400 - \frac{\pi \times 100}{4} \simeq 321\,\text{mm}^2$
3 $\pi \times 441 - \pi \times 400 = 41\pi \simeq 129\,\text{mm}^2$.
4 $5 + 10 + 50 + 10 + 5 + 62.8 \simeq 143\,\text{mm}$.
5 $10 + 20 + 20 + 10 + 15.7 \simeq 76\,\text{mm}$.

Volumes of solids

You have already met methods for calculating volumes of cuboids and prisms in Chapter 8 and you have seen how you can find the volume of a prism by calculating:
● Volume = Base area × Height

Cylinder

You can think of a cylinder as a prism with a circular cross-section, so if the base radius is r and the cylinder height is h (Figure 161), then:

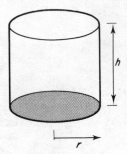

Figure 161. The dimensions of a cylinder

$$Volume\ of\ cylinder = A \times h$$
$$= \pi r^2 \times h$$
$$= \pi r^2 h$$

Cone

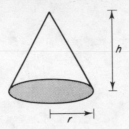

Figure 162. The dimensions of a cone

For a cone (Figure 162) the base area is a circle, radius r, and the cone height h. You can think of a cone as a special sort of pyramid with an infinite number of sloping faces, so the formula for its volume is the same as the formula for the volume of a pyramid.

Volume of cone $= \frac{1}{3} \times$ Base area $\times$ Height
$$= \frac{1}{3} \times \pi r^2 h$$
$$= \frac{\pi r^2 h}{3}$$

or one-third of the corresponding cylinder (see Figure 163).

Figure 163. A cone and its surrounding cylinder

Sphere

For a sphere (ball shape, see Figure 164) the volume is:
$$\frac{4\pi r^3}{3}$$

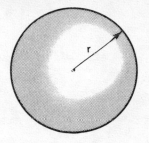

Figure 164. A sphere

At this stage it is too difficult to go into the background of why this is the case, but you can devise practical methods which will enable you to verify this, based on submerging a ball and measuring the volume of water it displaces.

Some examples

Here are three examples to help you to use these formulae correctly. In each case you start with the base radius (or radius of sphere) denoted by r, and the height (at right angles to the base) denoted by h.

- Calculate volume of cylinder where $r = 4$cm and $h = 8$cm.
  $$V = \pi r^2 h = 3.142 \times 16 \times 8 \simeq 402\,\text{cm}^3$$
- Calculate volume of pyramid where $r = 4$cm and $h = 8$cm.
  $$V = \frac{\pi r^2 h}{3} = \frac{3.142 \times 16 \times 8}{3} \simeq 134\,\text{cm}^3$$
- Calculate volume of sphere, radius 4cm.
  $$V = \frac{4\pi r^3}{3} = \frac{4 \times 3.142 \times 4^3}{3} = 268\,\text{cm}^3$$

You've probably noticed that all the solids have the same radius and same height. I chose these measurements deliberately to illustrate how the cone volume is $\frac{1}{3}$ of the cylinder volume ($\frac{1}{3}$ of 402 = 134) and the sphere volume is $\frac{2}{3}$ of the cylinder volume ($\frac{2}{3}$ of 402 = 268).

Self-check

Give answers to all these questions correct to 3 significant figures.

Calculate the volumes of cylinders with these dimensions.
1 $r = 4$ cm, $h = 10$ cm.
2 $r = 4.5$ cm, $h = 17.4$ cm.
Calculate the volume of cones with these dimensions.
3 $r = 6$ cm, $h = 13$ cm.
4 $r = 34$ mm, $h = 96$ mm.
Calculate the volume of spheres with these dimensions.
5 $r = 6$ cm. **6** $d = 4.8$ cm.

ANSWERS

1 503 cm^3. **2** 1110 cm^3. **3** 490 cm^3. **4** 116000 mm^3 = 116 cm^3.
5 905 cm^3 **6** 57.9 cm^3.

Surface areas of cylinder, sphere and cone

Cylinder

A solid cylinder has two ends (both circles) and the curved surface between them (see Figure 165).

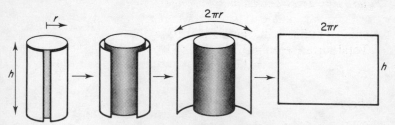

Figure 165. The curved surface area of a cylinder

- **Curved surface area** = $2\pi rh$.
As each end has an area of πr^2:
- **Total surface area** = $2\pi rh + 2\pi r^2$
$$= 2\pi r (h+r)$$

A cylinder of radius 4cm and height 9cm has:
Total surface area $= 2 \times 3.142 \times 4 \times (4 + 9)$
$$\approx 327\,\text{cm}^2$$

Cone

A cone has a circular base and the curved surface above the base.

- **Curved surface area** $= \pi r l$
where l is the slant height (see Figure 166).
- **Total surface area** $= \pi r l + \pi r^2$
$$= \pi r (l + r)$$

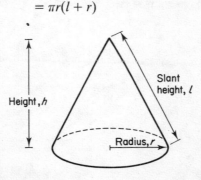

Height, h

Slant height, l

Radius, r

Figure 166. The slant height of a cone

A cone of radius 4cm, slant height 10cm, has:
Total surface area $= 3.142 \times 4 \times (10 + 4)$
$$= 176\,\text{cm}^2$$

Sphere

Surface area of a sphere $= 4\pi r^2$
A sphere of diameter 24cm has a radius of $24 \div 2 = 12$cm so:
Surface area $= 4 \times 3.142 \times 12^2$
$$\approx 1810\,\text{cm}^2$$

Self-check

For each of these shapes calculate the volume, curved surface area and total surface area. Give answers correct to 3 significant figures.

1 A cone of base radius 6cm, height 8cm and slant height 10cm.
2 A sphere of diameter 0.8m.
3 A cylinder of base radius 20m and height 18m.

ANSWERS

1 302cm³; 189cm²; 302cm².
2 0.268m³ (= 268 litres); 2.01m².
3 22600m³; 2260m²; 4780m².

Review

1 Find the area of a circle with diameter 1.6m.
2 Find the circumference of a circle diameter 10cm.
3 Calculate the perimeter and area of each of the shapes in Figure 167.

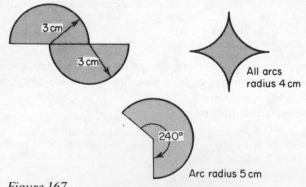

3 cm

3 cm

All arcs
radius 4 cm

240°

Arc radius 5 cm

Figure 167.

4 What is the volume of a sphere radius 3cm?
5 What is the surface area of a sphere of radius 3cm²?
6 Suppose a solid metal sphere of radius 6cm is melted down. How many spheres of radius 3cm can be made from the metal?

7 Calculate the surface area of the larger cylinder and of the small cylinders in **6**. By what has the surface area been multiplied when the large cylinder was replaced by the small cylinders?

Working backwards

Guess and check

Can you find the height of a cylinder with a base radius of 1.3 m and a volume of 20 m^3? You can always approach a problem like this by 'guess and check' methods. For example, if you guess the height to be 3 m, then:

$V = 3.142 \times 1.3^2 \times 3$

$= 15.9 \, \text{m}^3$ – too small

guess the height to be 4 m, then:

$V = 3.142 \times 1.3^2 \times 4$

$= 21.2$ – too large, but closer.

Activity

See if you can find the required height, correct to 0.01 m.

Using the formula

Alternatively, you can start with the formula $V = \pi r^2 h$ and fill in any values you know, i.e. **substitute known values**, giving:

$20 = 3.142 \times 1.3^2 \times h$

Now simplify the numbers:

$20 = 5.310 \times h$

So:

$h = 20 \div 5.310 = 3.766 \simeq 3.77 \, \text{m}$

You can see the method:

1 Start with the formula which links the given and required measurements;
2 Substitute any known values;
3 Rearrange the resulting equation to find the unknown value.
   See if you can use this approach in the following self-check. Don't forget that you can always use the 'guess and check'

method with your calculator if you feel worried rearranging the equations.

> ## Self-check
>
> **1** A cylindrical tank holds 250 litres. Convert this to ml. How high should it be if its radius is 30 cm?
> **2** An oil storage tank is a cylinder of radius 15 m and height 20 m. $100\,m^3$ of oil is pumped out. By how much does the oil level drop?

ANSWERS

1 250000 ml; 250000 = 3.142 × 900 × h, so h = 88.4 cm.
2 100 = 3.142 × 15^2 × h, so h = 0.141 m.

Rearranging formulae – two approaches

Let's look again at the last question of the self-check and see how you could also approach it by rearranging the volume formula first. I'll show both methods, so you can compare them.

Substitute, then solve an equation

Calculate h if r = 15 m and V = $100\,m^3$.
$$V = \pi r^2 h$$
So:
$$100 = 3.142 \times 15^2 \times h$$
$$= 706.95 \times h$$
Divide by 706.95:
$$h = \frac{100}{706.95}$$
$$= 0.141\,m$$

Rearranging formula, then substitute

Calculate h if r = 15 m and V = $100\,m^3$.
$$V = \pi r^2 h$$
You want to rearrange this formula to make h the subject. At

present h is **multiplied** by πr^2, so the first step is to **divide** by πr^2 to leave h on its own:

$$\frac{V}{\pi r^2} = h$$

Now substitute the values for V, π and r:

$$h = \frac{100}{3 \cdot 142 \times 15^2} = 0.141 \, \text{m as before}$$

In a similar way, you can rearrange the cone volume formula:

$$V = \frac{\pi r^2 h}{3}$$

to make h the subject. You can then use it to find the value of h directly. Here you can see that h has been multiplied by πr^2 and then divided by 3. To undo the formula to make h the subject you first have to multiply by 3 and then divide by πr^2:

Multiply by 3:

$$3V = \pi r^2 h$$

Divide by πr^2:

$$\frac{3V}{\pi r^2} = h$$

Remember, you can check that you have rearranged a formula correctly by choosing numbers which fit a starting formula and making sure that the same numbers fit the finishing formula. For example, if $r = 2$, $h = 3$ and $\pi = 3.142$, then:

$$V = \frac{3.142 \times 12}{3} = \frac{3.142 \times 4}{} = 12.568$$

Now using this value for V:

$$h = \frac{3V}{\pi r^2}$$

$$= \frac{3 \times 12.568}{3.142 \times 4}$$

$$= 3$$

bringing you back, correctly, to the value of h you chose originally.

Self-check

Rearrange the formulae below as instructed, then check your results using $r = 2$, $h = 3$, $l = 5$.

1 Rearrange $A = \pi r l$ to make l the subject.
2 Rearrange $A = \pi r l$ to make r the subject.

3 Rearrange $A = 2\pi r$ to make r the subject.

4 Rearrange $A = \dfrac{2\pi rh}{3}$ to make h the subject.

ANSWERS

1 $\dfrac{A}{\pi r} = l$, $A = 31.42$, $\dfrac{31.42}{3.142 \times 2} = 5$.

2 $\dfrac{A}{\pi l} = r$, $A = 31.42$, $\dfrac{31.42}{3.142 \times 5} = 2$.

3 $r = \dfrac{A}{2\pi}$, $A = 12.568$, $\dfrac{12.568}{2 \times 3.142} = 2$.

4 $h = \dfrac{3A}{2\pi r}$, $A = 12.568$, $\dfrac{12.568 \times 3}{2 \times 3.142 \times 2} = 3$.

Devising formulae to do with sectors

Sector area and angle

Figure 168 shows two sectors cut from a circle of radius 6 cm. The smaller (minor) sector has an angle of 150°. What is its area? Can you use this example to find a formula for the area of a sector with any angle you wish?

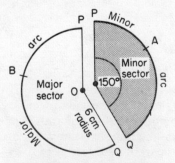

Figure 168. Minor and major sectors and arcs

The angle tells you what fraction of the circle has been removed to form the sector. In a complete circle the angle would be 360°, so the sector area is:

$\frac{150}{360}$ths of the circle area

$= \frac{150}{360} \times \pi \times 6^2$

$= \dfrac{150 \times \pi \times 36}{360} = 47.13\,\text{cm}^2$

In general, with an angle $\alpha°$ (α is the Greek letter alpha) and a circle radius r:

Sector area $= \dfrac{\alpha}{360} \times \pi r^2$

or:

$\dfrac{\pi r^2 \alpha}{360}$

In reverse, suppose you know the radius of the circle and the sector area, but want to find the sector angle, α. The 're-arranging formula' method looks like this. Starting with:

$S = \dfrac{\pi r^2 \alpha}{360}$

ask yourself how the formula has been built up around α, then work backwards to find α on its own.

$S = \dfrac{\pi r^2 \alpha}{360}$

Multiply by 360:

$360S = \pi r^2 \alpha$

Divide by πr^2:

$\dfrac{360S}{\pi r^2} = \alpha$

Sector arc length and angle

In Figure 168 the smaller shaded sector is called the **minor sector** PQ, while the larger unshaded sector is called the **major sector** PQ. The points P and Q are at the ends of two arcs; the **minor arc** PAQ on the right and the **major arc** PBQ on the left (arc simply means part of a curve).

As with the sector area, since angle POQ = 150°, the length of the **minor** arc is:

$\frac{150}{360}$ths of the circumference of this circle

$= \frac{150}{360} \times 2 \times \pi \times 6$

$= 15.7\,\text{cm}$

The angle for the major sector is $360° - 150° = 210°$, so the length of the major arc is:

$\frac{210}{360} \times 2 \times \pi \times 6 = 22.0\,cm$

In general for a circle radius r and sector angle α:

arc length $= \frac{\alpha}{360} \times 2\pi r$

Self-check

1　What is the area of a sector with angle 70° and radius 20 cm?

2　A sector has an area of 20 cm² and is taken from a circle radius 4 cm. What is the sector angle?

3　What is the length of an arc of a circle radius 10 cm where the angle of the sector is 108°?

4　An arc is 12 m long. It forms part of the perimeter of a sector with an angle of 200°. Calculate the circle radius.

ANSWERS

1 244 cm². **2** 143°. **3** 18.9 cm.

4 Arc $= \dfrac{\alpha}{360} \times 2 \times 3.142 \times r$

SO

$12 = \frac{200}{360} \times 6.284 \times r \Rightarrow 3.44\,mm$

Self-check

This includes questions which involve rearranging formulae.

7.5 m

Figure 169.

1　A cylindrical drum (Figure 169) of diameter 7.5 m holds 20 turns of rope. What is the rope length?

Calculate the arc lengths for the following sectors.

2 Angle 40°, radius 15 mm.

3 Angle 243°, radius 214 mm.

4 Calculate the sector angle for the following arc: arc length 7 mm, radius 9 mm.

5 Hot tar is spread on a circular roof of radius 6 m. The tar is carried to the roof in buckets each holding 8 litres. How many buckets are needed to give a depth of 2 mm?

6 A cone has a base radius of 24 cm. How high should it be to have a volume of 12 litres?

ANSWERS

1 $23.57 \times 20 \simeq 471$ m.

2 $\frac{40}{360} \times 2 \times 3.142 \times 15 = 10.5$ mm.

3 908 mm. **4** 44.6°.

5 Working in cm, $V = 3.142 \times 600 \times 600 \times 0.2 = 226\,224$ cm³ $\simeq 226$ litres $= 28.3$ buckets, so at least 29 buckets needed.

6 $h = \dfrac{12\,000}{\frac{1}{3} \times 3.142 \times 24^2} = 19.9$ cm $\simeq 20$ cm

Review

1 In the formula:
$$\frac{\alpha}{360} = \frac{r}{l}$$
make r the subject and find its value when $l = 8$ cm and $\alpha = 135$.

2 Rearrange the formula $A = 2\pi r h$ to make h the subject.

3 A collection of cylinders all have the total of height + diameter = 20 cm. Complete the table below for volume (V) and the total surface area (T).

h (cm)	d (cm)	V (cm³)	T (cm²)
4			
8	12	905	528
12			
16			

4 Use your answers to **3** to estimate the dimensions of two cylinders whose height + diameter = 20 cm and where:

    a one cylinder has the largest volume; and

    b the other cylinder has the smallest total surface area.

11 | Accurate drawing, ratio and scale factors

Topics covered

- Ratio and scale drawing.
- Maps and map scales.
- Enlargement and similar shapes.
- Conditions for similar shapes.
- Accurate drawing of triangles.
- Bisector constructions.
- Bearings and maps.

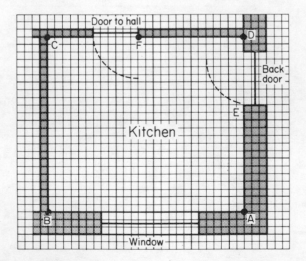

Figure 170. Outline plan of a kitchen drawn to a scale of 1:50

Scale drawing

Figure 170 shows the outline plan of a kitchen in a new house. The plan is drawn **to scale**. This means that you can measure distances on the plan and, knowing the scale, you can convert these into full-size measurements.

Here the scale is 1 to 50 (or 1:50), so 1mm on the plan stands for 50mm full size, 1cm on the plan stands for 50cm full size, etc.

It often helps to draw plans like this on graph paper – here the graph paper has 2mm spacing, so each 2mm square represents a full-size square of $50 \times 2 = 100$mm width.

You can see that the kitchen is 52mm (26 squares) long on the plan – this represents a full-size length of $52 \times 50 = 2600$mm or 2.60m.

Activity

Copy and complete the table below showing plan and full-size measurements. (Give full-size distances correct to the nearest 5cm.)

		Measurement			
	Width AD	Window width	Distance AE	Distance DF	Distance ED
On the plan	23 squares = 46mm				
Full-size:					
mm	2300				
m	2.30				

ANSWERS

AD	Window	AE	DF	ED
23 squares =	13 squares =	14 squares =	14 squares =	9 squares =
46mm	26mm	28mm	28mm	18mm
2300mm	1300mm	1400mm	1400mm	900mm
2.30m	1.30m	1.40m	1.40m	0.90m

You can use the plan to decide on the best layout for sink, cooker, storage units, etc., in the kitchen. In Figure 171 you will see a plan of a sink unit, again to a scale of 1:50.

Figure 171. Plan of a sink to a scale of 1:50

Activity

Make an exact copy of this plan. Use the table below to make scale plans of other units in the kitchen. Try arranging them on the kitchen plan (Figure 170) to get the best layout.

Description	Length (mm)	Depth (mm)
Sink unit	1200	600
Storage unit	1200	600
Refrigerator	560	600
Small table	1000	500
Cooker	500	540

Self-check

Suppose that the scale of the kitchen plan is changed to 1:20. List the lengths and depths of the scale plans for the units above, to a scale of 1:20.

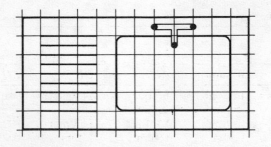

Figure 172. Plan of a sink to a scale of 1:20

ANSWERS

60 mm by 30 mm; 60 mm by 30 mm; 28 mm by 30 mm; 50 mm by 25 mm; 25 mm by 27 mm.

> *Activity*
>
> Draw and cut out another rectangle representing the sink unit, to a scale of 1:20 (see Figure 172).

You can see that your two sink plans are the same shape – it's just that one is an enlargement of the other. In fact *every* measurement on the large plan is $2\frac{1}{2}$ times as much as the matching small length ($2\frac{1}{2} \times 12 = 30$, $2\frac{1}{2} \times 24 = 60$, etc.).

Maps

Many maps are drawn to scale, of course. Sometimes the scale is given as a ratio (e.g. 1:50000), sometimes as a pair of corresponding measurements and sometimes as a length marked to scale, as in Figure 173.

If 2 cm represents 1 km (= 100000 cm) then 1 cm represents 50000 cm, so a scale of 2 cm to the kilometre is the same as 1:50000.

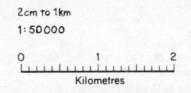

Figure 173. Scale from a 1:50000 map

> *Self-check*
>
> Figure 174 shows part of a map of the area near Gunthorpe, Nottinghamshire, to a scale of 1:25000. You can see the River Trent (bottom left to top right).

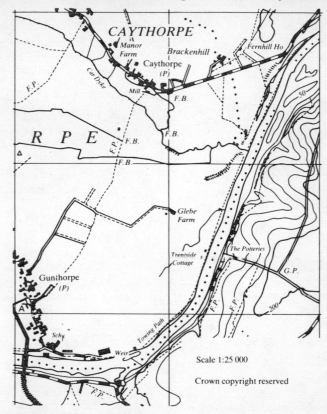

Figure 174.

1 How many centimetres on the map represent 1 kilometre?
2 How many metres are represented by 1 mm on the map?
3 How long is the track leading from Glebe Farm to Gun-
 thorpe village?

Change these full-size distances to map ones.

4 2 km, scale 1:25000.
5 30 km, scale 1:50000.

ANSWERS

1 4 cm. **2** 25 m. **3** About 56 mm, i.e. 1.4 km. **4** 80 mm. **5** 60 cm.

Similar shapes

Let's return to the idea of enlargement. Look at Figure 175.

Network **2** ($A_2B_2C_2D_2E_2F_2H_2$) is an **enlargement** of network **1** ($A_1B_1C_1D_1E_1F_1G_1H_1$). You can see that the shape of the network is unchanged – it's just that the lengths in **2** are twice the matching lengths in network **1**. You can check that by tracing network **1** and putting it on top of network **2**. I could have enlarged the shape further so that all the lengths were multiplied by **3**, or **4**, or reduced it in size (still referred to as an enlargement though) so that lengths were halved. In every case, though, the shape of the picture you see looks the same – it's just that lengths have increased or decreased.

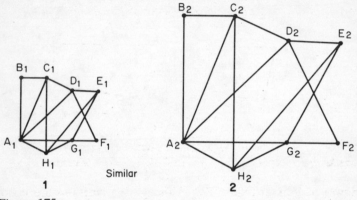

Figure 175.

Notice that **angles** between lines in the shapes **remain the same**. (If you changed the angles, then the shapes would change also.)

Pairs of diagrams, where one is an enlargement of the other, are said to be **similar**, i.e. network **1** is similar to network **2**. In similar diagrams:

- the ratio of corresponding (or matching) pairs of lengths is the same for all pairs;
- corresponding angles are equal.

To be sure that two diagrams are similar, **both conditions must apply**. Some diagrams have corresponding lengths in the same ratio, but corresponding angles are not equal – they are *not similar* (see Figure 176). Other diagrams have corresponding angles equal, but corresponding lengths are not in the same ratio – they are *not similar* (see Figure 177).

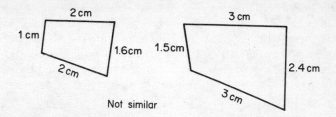

Figure 176. Corresponding lengths are in the same ratio but corresponding angles are not equal – the shapes are not similar

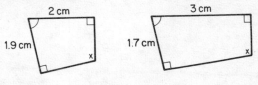

Figure 177. Corresponding angles are equal but corresponding lengths are not in the same ratio – the shapes are not similar

However, look at Figure 178. Although the diagrams are not to scale, the ratios of corresponding lengths are the same:

- 80:60 = 4:3
- 40:30 = 4:3
- 12:9 = 4:3
- 84.8:63.6 = 4:3

and in both diagrams the angles are 90°, 90°, 109° and 71°, so the pair of diagrams *are* similar.

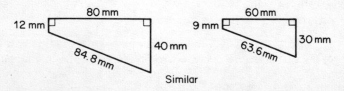

Figure 178. Ratios of corresponding lengths are the same and corresponding angles are the same – the shapes are similar

You can see how in this example each large diagram length is $\frac{4}{3}$ of the matching small diagram length – or each small length is $\frac{3}{4}$ of the matching large diagram length. In other words, pairs to corresponding lengths are in **direct proportion**.

Self-check

The diagrams in Figure 179 are in similar pairs but are not drawn to scale. Calculate the lengths or angles marked with a letter.

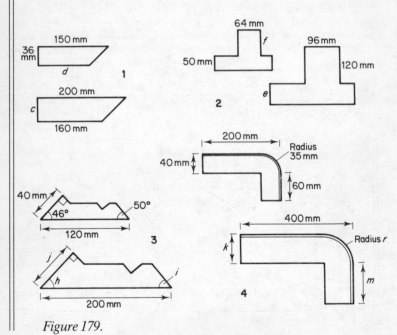

Figure 179.

ANSWERS

1 Ratio = 3:4; $c = 48$ mm; $d = 120$ mm.
2 Ratio = 2:3; $e = 75$ mm; $f = 80$ mm.
3 Ratio = 3:5; $j = 66.7$ mm; $h = 46°$; $i = 50°$.
4 Ratio = 1:2; $k = 80$ mm; $r = 70$ mm; $m = 120$ mm.

Similar triangles

Unlike other shapes, once you alter the angle of a triangle you are bound to alter at least one of the lengths, whilst as soon as you alter a side length in a triangle at least two of the angles change. As a result, for triangles only, the two conditions on page 268 are interconnected, and you can be sure that two triangles are similar if:

1 the ratio of corresponding pairs of side lengths are the same;

or:

2 corresponding angles are equal;

or:

3 one pair of corresponding angles are equal and the sides on each side of the angles are in the same ratio (a mixture of the other conditions);

or:

4 in right-angled triangles only, any two pairs of corresponding sides are in the same ratio.

Self-check

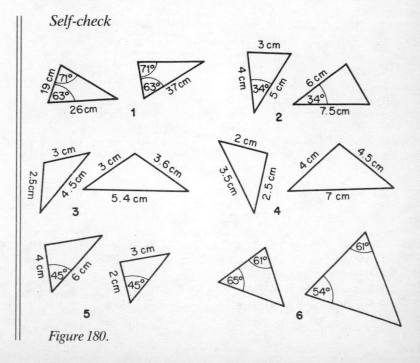

Figure 180.

Look at the pairs of triangles in Figure 180. In each case say if the pair is similar. If so, give the reason (**1**, **2**, **3** or **4** above). The diagrams are not accurately drawn, so rely on the written information only.

ANSWERS

1 Similar, **2**. **2** Similar, **3** (ratio 2:3).

3 Similar, **1** (ratio 5:6). **4** Not similar (sides not in same ratio).

5 Not similar (sides not in corresponding positions).

6 Similar, **2** (as is clear when the third angle in each triangle is calculated – angles of any triangle add to 180°).

Review

1 Figure 181 shows part of a map drawn to a scale of 1:250000. What is the distance (to nearest 0.1 km) from Budby to Ompton?

Crown copyright reserved

Figure 181.

2 Triangles ABC and DEF are similar to each other, with angle A = angle D, angle B = angle E and angle C = angle F. If AB = 6cm, BC = 9cm and EF = 18cm, calculate the length of DE and the ratio of FD to CA.

3 A plan is drawn to a scale of 1:40. What plan length corresponds to a full-size length of 8m?

4 The diagrams in Figure 182 represent two similar shapes. Calculate the sizes of lengths and angles marked with letters.

Figure 182. Diagrams not drawn to scale

Triangle constructions

Many scale drawings are based on rectangular grids or shapes and you can draw them without much difficulty on graph paper. Triangles without right angles prove more difficult and you will require a protractor and compasses as well as a ruler when drawing them accurately.

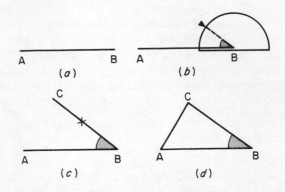

Figure 183. (a) *Draw one side, label the ends.* (b) *Use a protractor to dot in the known angle at the correct end.* (c) *Draw the second side through the dot.* (d) *Join up the side ends to give the third side*

Constructing triangles where you know the lengths of two sides and the size of the angle between them

You are given AB, BC and ∠ABC. You can see the steps in Figure 183.

> *Self-check*
>
> The length or angle you measure after drawing the following triangles enables you to check that your drawing is correct.
> 1 Draw △PQR where PQ = 5 cm, PR = 6 cm and ∠RPQ = 38°. Measure RQ.
> 2 Draw △EFG where EG = 6.4 cm, ∠FEG = 138° and EF = 3.6 cm. Measure FG.

ANSWERS

1 RQ = 3.7 cm. 2 FG = 9.4 cm.

Constructing triangles where you know one side and two angles

If you know the sizes of two angles in a triangle, you can always work out the third, since angles of any triangle add to 180°.

In this construction you first need to know the sizes of the angles at each end of the known side length, so you may have to calculate one angle before you start. Then use the steps in Figure 184.

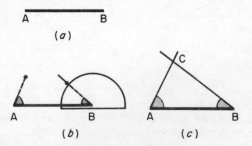

Figure 184. (a) *Draw and label the given side.* (b) *Use a protractor to dot in the known angles at each end of the line.* (c) *Draw lines from the end through the dots to form the triangle*

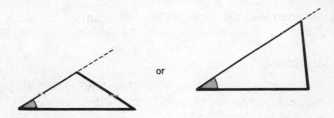

Figure 185.

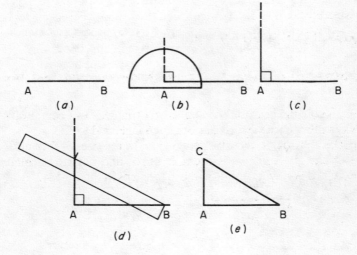

Figure 186. (a) *Draw and label the shorter length.* (b) *Use a protractor to dot in a right angle at the end not meeting the hypotenuse.* (c) *Draw a line through the dot from the right angle.* (d) *Use a ruler to mark in the ends of the hypotenuse.* (e) *Join up to complete the triangle*

Self-check

1 Draw △ABC where AB = 6.5cm, ∠ABC = 34° and ∠CAB = 71°. Measure BC.
2 Draw △EFG where EG = 5.7cm, ∠FEG = 70° and ∠EFG = 73°. Measure FG.

ANSWERS

1 6.4cm. **2** 5.6cm.

Constructing triangles where one angle is 90° and you know two side lengths

If you are given the measurements of two sides and an angle *not* between the sides, you can often construct two different triangles (see Figure 185). This however is *not* possible if the angle is 90°. Now follow the steps in Figure 186. (Stage (*d*) can be carried out with the help of compasses, as in Figure 187.)

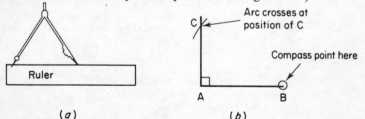

Figure 187. An alternative to Figure 222(d). (a) Set compasses to the length of the hypotenuse. (b) With compasses at the fixed point B, draw an arc to cross the other shorter length at C

Self-check

1 Draw △ABC, where ∠CAB = 90°, AB = 4cm, BC = 5.5cm. Measure AC.
2 Draw △XYZ, where ∠YXZ = 90°, XY = 3.9cm and YZ = 7.4cm. Measure XZ.

ANSWERS

1 3.8cm. **2** 6.3cm.

Constructing triangles where you know all three side lengths

Activity

Draw a line AB, 6cm long. With compass point at A, draw an arc on one side of AB with a radius of 7cm. With compass point at B draw an arc of radius 4cm. Label the point C where the arcs intersect. Now join up A and B to C. You will have constructed triangle ABC, with side lengths of 4cm, 6cm and 7cm (Figure 188).

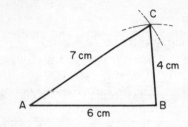

Figure 188.

Self-check

1 Draw △PQR where PQ = 3.6cm, QR = 4.7cm and PR = 5.1cm. Measure ∠PRQ.

2 Draw △MSC where MS = 5.3cm, SC = 4.8cm and MC = 7.9cm. Measure ∠MSC.

ANSWERS

1 43°. **2** 103°.

Two compass constructions

Activity

Mark two points, A and B, on a sheet of paper and draw the line AB. Now fold the paper so that the points are on top of each other.

Notice that the fold line cuts AB in half and that AB and the fold line are at right angles. In other words, the fold line is the

perpendicular (at right angles) **bisector** ('cutter in half') of the line AB.

You can see why this must always be the case from the symmetry produced by folding.

You can construct the perpendicular bisector of a line more accurately just by using a ruler and compasses, as follows.

Perpendicular bisector of a line

Activity

On another sheet of paper make two points, C and D. Now draw an arc of a circle centre C and another arc with the *same* compass setting centred on D. If the compass radius is large enough the arcs will intersect at two points, each an equal distance from C and D. Reset the compasses and repeat several times. You will produce a diagram like Figure 189.

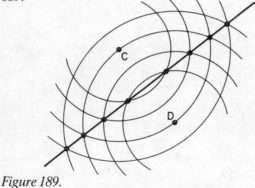

Figure 189.

You can see how all the points where the pairs of equal radius arcs cross lie on a single line, the perpendicular bisector of CD.

Of course a pair of points is sufficient to locate the line so just two equal radius arcs are enough to fix it, but the diagram in Figure 189 shows how points at an equal distance from C and D are *all* situated on the perpendicular bisector of CD.

Activity

1 Draw a triangle ABC, and construct (by using ruler and compasses) the perpendicular bisector of AB.
2 Now construct the perpendicular bisector of AC.
3 Now construct the perpendicular bisector of BC.
4 What do you notice?
Repeat with another triangle.

ANSWERS

In each case the three perpendicular bisectors meet at a single point which is an equal distance from all three vertices of the triangle. You can check that this is correct by placing your compass needle at this point. You will find you can draw a circle centred at this point which passes through all three vertices of the triangle.

Bisector of an angle

You have seen how using compasses to mark off equal distances from fixed points produces diagrams with line symmetry. If you start with two fixed lines instead (as in Figure 190), with P and Q on the two lines an equal distance from the intersection X, then mark off equal radius arcs from these points, crossing at Y, you produce the framework for another diagram. YX is a line of symmetry for the diagram, so XY bisects (cuts in half) the angle PXQ. If you extend the lines PX and QX beyond X to the left, you can use your compasses to construct another line of symmetry. In Figure 191, XY and XZ bisect the angles at X. The angle between the two symmetry lines must be 90°. Can you explain why?

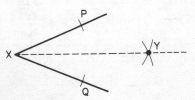

Figure 190.

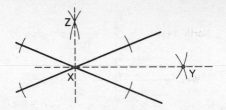

Figure 191.

Activity

1 Draw a triangle ABC and construct using ruler and compasses the bisector of angle BAC.
2 Now construct the bisectors of ∠ABC and ∠ACB.
3 What do you notice?
Repeat with another triangle.

In each case the three angle bisectors meet at a single point (*not* the same as the point of intersection of the three perpendicular bisectors of the sides). This point is an equal distance from each of the three sides of the triangle. You can check this by placing your compass needle at the intersection point. You will find that you can draw a circle centred on this point which just touches all three sides.

Bearings

You are probably familiar with the four main compass directions, **north**, **south**, **east** and **west**. You may also know that other directions can be described by combining these main directions. For instance:

● **south-east** (midway between south and east);
or
● **east-south-east** (midway between east and south-east) – see Figure 192.

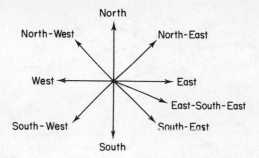

Figure 192. The points of the compass

You can also give directions using **degrees only** and measuring **angles clockwise from north**. Remembering that there are 360° in a complete turn:

- south becomes 180°;
- west is 270°;
- east is 090° (bearing are normally given with 3 figures);
- north is 0°.

So:

- south-east is 90 + 45 = 135°;
- east-south-east is 90 + $\frac{1}{2}$ of 45° = 112.5°.

See Figure 193.

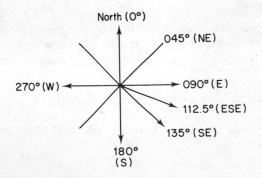

Figure 193. The angles of the compass

Self-check

Re-write these directions using degrees only.
1 North-east. **2** North-west. **3** South-west.

ANSWERS

1 045°. **2** 315°. **3** 225°.

When you are describing the direction (or **bearing**) of one point
from another, imagine that you are standing at one place looking
at the other. For example (see Figure 194), if you are standing at
O looking at A, B, and C in turn, then the:

- bearing of A from O is 071°;
- bearing of B from O is 116° (71 + 45 = 116°);
- bearing of C from O is 332° (360 − 28 = 332°).

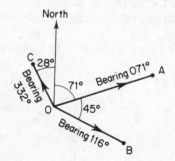

Figure 194.

If you were standing at A, still looking in the direction of 071°, you
would be looking away from O (as shown in Figure 195). Now
imagine that you turn round to look back at O. You would have
turned through 180°, so the:

- bearing of O from A is 071 + 180 = 251°.

In the same way:

- bearing of O from B is 116 + 180 = 296°;
- bearing of O from C is:
    332 + 180 = 512°
                = 360 + 152°
  the same as 152°.

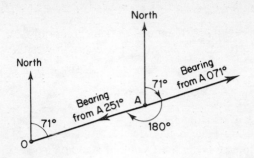

Figure 195.

Self-check

Calculate the following.
1 The bearing of C from B, if the bearing of B from C is 128°.
2 The bearing of A from C, if the bearing of C from A is 275°.
3 The bearing of D from C, if the bearing of C from D is 196°.

ANSWERS

1 308°. **2** 095°. **3** 016°.

Activity

Put your protractor on the map on page 272 (Figure 181), with the 0° line parallel to the vertical north–south lines and the centre point of the protractor over Budby. Check that you can see that the bearing of Ompton from Budby is 125° and the bearing of Budby from Ompton is 305°.

Review

Construct the following triangles.
1 △HGE where HG = 4.3 cm, ∠GHE = 68° and HE = 7.3 cm. Measure EG.

2 △MAG where MA = 5cm, AG = 4cm, MG = 3cm.
Measure ∠MGA.

3 Construct △HKN where HK = 6cm, HN = 8cm and
KN = 5cm. P is a point equally close to H and K but
inside the triangle. Mark in the possible positions for P.

4 On your diagram for **3** above, shade in the location of
points inside the triangle which are closer to K than to
H.

5 Suppose that △MAG in **2** above is a map showing three
places drawn to a scale of 1:100 000, and that G is east of
M. What is the bearing of:

a A from G;

b M from A?

12 | Right-angled triangles

Topics covered

- Right-angled triangles.
- Pythagoras' rule.
- Squares and square roots.
- Problems in right-angled triangles.
- Pythagorean triples.
- Standard form.
- Using your calculator in standard form.
- Harder problems in right-angled triangles.
- Rearranging formulae involving squares and square roots.
- Square roots in standard form.

Pythagoras' rule

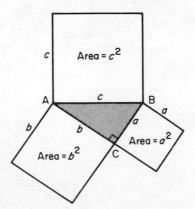

Figure 196.

Over 2000 years ago the Greek mathematician Pythagoras described the rule connecting the lengths of sides in right-angled triangles. He found that if squares were formed on each of the sides, as in Figure 196, then adding the areas of the two smaller squares gave the area of the larger square.

The areas of squares are a^2, b^2 and c^2, so you can write the rule as:

- $a^2 + b^2 = c^2$

This explains why the word **squaring** is often used for multiplying a number by itself. You read this statement as:

- a squared plus b squared equals c squared.

Notice how in the triangle in Figure 196 side a is opposite angle A, b is opposite B, and c is opposite C.

The longest side in a right-angled triangle (c in this diagram) is called the **hypotenuse**, and the associated square is called the **square on the hypotenuse**.

Testing Pythagoras' rule

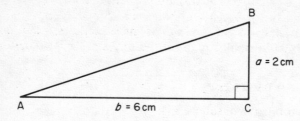

Figure 197.

Figure 197 shows a right-angled triangle with shorter sides of 6 cm and 2 cm. Measure side AB, the hypotenuse. You'll find its length is between 6.3 and 6.4 cm (it's difficult to be any more accurate). Here:

$a^2 + b^2 = 36 + 4 = 40 \text{ cm}^2$

while c^2 is between $6.3^2 = 39.69$ and $6.4^2 = 40.96$, i.e. approximately 40 cm^2, so the rule appears to work.

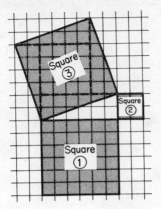

Figure 198.

You can also check the rule by finding areas directly. In Figure 198 you can see that the area of square 1 is 36 and of square 2 is 4, so:

Area 1 + Area 2 = 36 + 4 = 40

Because square 3 is on a slant, it is a little harder to find its area directly, but you can see that you can split the square up into four triangles which are **congruent** (exactly the same as each other) and a small square in the middle. Each triangle has an area of:

$$\frac{6 \times 2}{2} = 6 \text{ squares}$$

so the total area of square 3 is:

6 + 6 + 6 + 6 + 16 = 40

So:

Area 1 + Area 2 = Area 3

Self-check

1 Use Pythagoras' rule to find the length of the hypotenuse in a right-angled triangle with shorter sides of 5 cm and 12 cm.

2 Check your answer to **1** by making an accurate drawing.

ANSWER

1 $5^2 + 12^2 = 169$, so hypotenuse $= 13\,cm$ (because $13 \times 13 = 169$).

Square roots

Just as 25 is the **square** of 5 and 169 is the **square** of 13, in reverse 5 is the **square root** of 25, and 13 is the **square root** of 169.

The symbol $\sqrt{}$ or $\sqrt{}$ means square root, so:

- $\sqrt{25} = 5$
- $\sqrt{169} = 13$

Of course $^-5 \times {}^-5 = 25$ also, so:

- $\sqrt{25} = {}^-5$, as well as 5
- $\sqrt{169} = 13$ or $^-13$.

However, for this chapter you will only need to consider positive square roots.

> ### Self-check
>
> **1** Jot down the positive square roots of 9, 49 and 100.
> **2** What are the positive values of $\sqrt{36}$, $\sqrt{64}$ and $\sqrt{144}$?
> **3** Between which pairs of neighbouring whole numbers do you think the values of the following occur?
> $\sqrt{73}$; $\sqrt{3}$; $\sqrt{45}$.

ANSWERS

1 3, 7 and 10. **2** 6, 8 and 12.
3 8 and 9 ($8^2 = 64$, below 73; $9^2 = 81$, above 73); 1 and 2; 6 and 7.

Let's try to find a more exact value for $\sqrt{73}$. $8.4^2 = 70.56$, $8.5^2 = 72.25$, $8.6^2 = 73.96...$ so $\sqrt{73}$ lies between 8.5 and 8.6. You can repeat this process, finding, for instance, that $8.53^2 = 72.7609$, $8.54^2 = 72.9316$, $8.55^2 = 73.1025...$ so $\sqrt{73}$ lies between 8.54 and 8.55...

You have probably got a $\sqrt{\ }$ key on your calculator. Press:

| 7 | 3 | $\sqrt{\ }$ | |

On my calculator, I obtain 8.544 003 7. However, the accurate value of $(8.544\ 003\ 7)^2$ is 72.999 999 225 613 69, so even the version of $\sqrt{73}$ on my calculator is not exact. In fact, as for many other square roots, an exact decimal value of 73 does not exist.

For practical purposes, though, you rarely need a value of a square root to a greater accuracy than 3 or 4 significant figures.

> *Self-check*
>
> 1 Write down the most accurate values of the following numbers you can, using your calculator square root key.
> $\sqrt{3}$; $\sqrt{45}$; $\sqrt{30}$; $\sqrt{450}$; $\sqrt{4.5}$.
> 2 Give approximate values of your results in 1, correct to 3 s.f.

ANSWERS

1 My calculator gave the following results. Yours may give slightly different results – more or fewer digits for instance.

   1.732 050 8; 6.708 203 9; 5.477 225 6; 21.213 203; 2.121 320 3.

2 1.73; 6.71; 5.48; 21.2; 2.12.

Using Pythagoras' rule

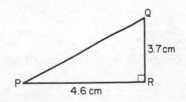

Figure 199.

Here are two further examples.

● In Figure 199:

$$PQ^2 = 4.6^2 + 3.7^2$$
$$= 21.16 + 13.69$$
$$= 34.85$$
So:
$$PQ = \sqrt{34.85}$$
$$\simeq 5.90\,\text{cm} \ (3\,\text{s.f.})$$
● In Figure 200:
$$13^2 = 8.7^2 + b^2$$
So:
$$b^2 = 169 - 75.69$$
$$= 93.31$$
So:
$$b = \sqrt{93.31}$$
$$= 9.66\,\text{cm} \ (3\,\text{s.f.})$$

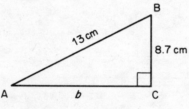

Figure 200.

Self-check

Look at the diagrams in Figure 201. In each case calculate the length of each side marked with a letter, correct to 3 s.f.

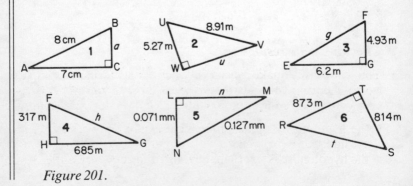

Figure 201.

ANSWERS

1 $a^2 = 15$, $a = 3.87$ cm.
2 $u^2 = 8.91^2 - 5.27^2 \simeq 51.6152$, so $u = 7.18$ m.
3 $g = 7.92$ m.　　**4** $h = 755$ m.
5 $n = 0.105$ mm.　**6** $t = 1190$ m.

Self-check

Look at Figure 202.
1 Write down the formula connecting x, y, and r.
2 Rearrange the formula to make x the subject.
3 Now make y the subject.
4 Find the value of r when $x = 7$, $y = 24$.
5 Find the value of y when $x = 12$, $r = 20$.

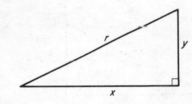

Figure 202.

ANSWERS

1 $x^2 + y^2 = r^2$ or $r = \sqrt{(x^2 + y^2)}$.
2 $x = \sqrt{(r^2 - y^2)}$.
3 $y = \sqrt{(r^2 - x^2)}$.
4 25.　**5** 16.

Checking your results

You can easily make mistakes when using formulae, so it's worth checking your answers to see if they 'seem right', whenever you can. Measure some right-angled triangles and see how:

- the hypotenuse (opposite the right angle) is *always* the longest side; but
- the hypotenuse is *less* than the total of the other two sides.

For instance, in question **4** above:
  hypotenuse = 25, other sides add to 7 + 24 = 31.

Using Pythagoras' rule in harder problems

Now try these problems. At the start:
1 draw a clear diagram, putting in any measurements you know;
2 look for the right-angled triangles you will use in the calculation;
3 label any lengths you are going to calculate with a small letter and make an estimate of the likely value of that length;
4 now write down Pythagoras' rule, using the letters and known lengths from your diagram.

I'll start with an example. A chimney is secured by 15 metre stays like PQ in Figure 203. The total distance PR is 14.7m and the chimney is 0.7m wide. Calculate the height of the collar at Q above the line PR.

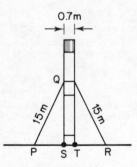

Figure 203.

First of all, PS and TR are equal, so I can find PS by taking 0.7 from 14.7 then halving the remainder:
$$PS = \tfrac{1}{2} \text{ of } (14.7 - 0.7)$$
$$= 7.0\,\text{m}$$
Using h for QS (see Figure 204):
$$h^2 + 7.0^2 = 15^2$$
which leads to:
$$h = 13.3 \text{ metres (to 3 s.f.)}.$$

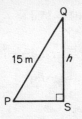

Figure 204.

Self-check

Look at Figure 205.
1 In diagram 1 calculate AB if AD = 3.6 m, DC = 4.1 m and BC = 5.14 m.
2 Diagram 2 shows a rectangle formed of scaffolding poles, braced by diagonals AC and BD. If AD = 2.0 m and DC = 3.5 m, what should be the length DE?

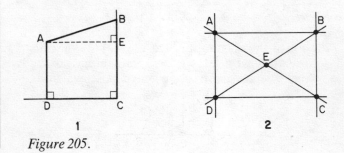

Figure 205.

ANSWERS

1 $AB^2 = 4.1^2 + 1.54^2$, so AB = 4.38 m.
2 AE is half of $\sqrt{16.25}$ = 2.02 m.

Looking at square numbers and right-angled triangles

You may have noticed some right-angled triangles where all three sides are exact whole numbers of units. For instance, a triangle with sides of 3, 4 and 5 metres is right-angled because:

$3^2 + 4^2 = 9 + 16 = 25$ and $5^2 = 25$

This leads to a set of similar triangles such as 6, 8, 10; 30, 40, 50; 0.3, 0.4, 0.5; 1.2, 1.6, 2.0, etc. There are many other such sets of similar right-angled triangles, e.g. the 5, 12, 13 set, the 7, 24, 25 set, the 9, 40, 41 set, etc. You can use your calculator to help you search out further sets if you're interested.

Review

1 Find the lengths marked with small letters in the diagrams (correct to 3 significant figures) in Figure 206.

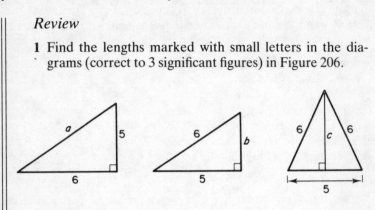

Figure 206.

2 Look at the diagram in Figure 207. Without using your calculator write down two measurements between which you are sure that the length of BC will lie.

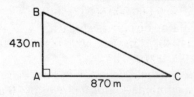

Figure 207.

3 Find the values of the letters in each of these equations.
 a $x^2 = 6^2 + 7^2$
 b $a^2 + 7^2 = 8.2^2$
 c $10^2 = d^2 + 94.81$
4 Rearrange each of these formulae to make y the subject.

$\quad$ **a** $x^2 + y^2 = r^2$
$\quad$ **b** $d^2 - y^2 = a^2$

Large and small numbers – standard index form

Try working out 987654^2 on your calculator. The chances are that if you have an ordinary (non-scientific) calculator, the display will go blank, or a letter E will appear – there's just not enough room in the display for the complete answer. If you have a scientific calculator, the display may read something like:

9	.	7	5	4	6			1	1

What does it mean? In fact:

$\quad 987654^2 = 975\,460\,423\,716$, i.e. over 900 billion

and the calculator display is short for 9.7546×10^{11}. You'll remember from Chapter 4 that 10^{11} means $10 \times 10 \times 10 \times 10 \times 10 \times 10 \times 10 \times 10 \times 10 \times 10 \times 10$ or $100\,000\,000\,000$ – one hundred billion. Thus $9.7546 \times 10^{11} = 975\,460\,000\,000$, an approximate version of $975\,460\,423\,716$.

Now try working out $0.000\,000\,2^2$. Again, if you've got a simple calculator, the display will go blank or show an E, meaning you have exceeded the space available in the display. If you have a scientific calculator, your display will read:

4	.			$^-$	1	4

What does this mean? In fact:

$\quad 0.000\,000\,2^2 = 0.000\,000\,000\,000\,04$

and the calculator display is short for 4×10^{-14}. Again you'll remember that 10^{-14} means $0.000\,000\,000\,000\,01$, so 4×10^{-14} equals $0.000\,000\,000\,000\,04$.

In both cases, the calculator is giving readings in **standard index form**, a combination of a power of 10 and a number with one figure or **digit** in front of the decimal point. It is a convenient and commonly used way of writing very large or very small numbers without having to write lots of 0s.

Here are some more examples:

- $3 \times 10^5 \quad = 3 \times 100\,000 \quad = 300\,000$
- $1.4 \times 10^5 \quad = 1.4 \times 100\,000 \quad = 140\,000$
- $2.83 \times 10^5 \quad = 2.83 \times 100\,000 = 283\,000$

- 3×10^{-3} $= 0.003$ $= 3 \times 0.001$
- 1.4×10^{-3} $= 0.0014$ $= 1.4 \times 0.001$
- 2.83×10^{-3} $= 0.002\,83$ $= 2.83 \times 0.001$

Self-check

See if you can translate these standard index form (or standard form) numbers into ordinary numbers.

1 4×10^6.   **6** 6×10^{-1}.
2 7×10^2.   **7** 8×10^{-4}.
3 1.08×10^4.   **8** 6.1×10^{-1}.
4 6.721×10^5.   **9** 8.42×10^{-4}.
5 2.04×10^1.   **10** 8.042×10^{-4}.

ANSWERS

1 4 000 000.   **5** 20.4.   **8** 0.61.
2 700.   **6** 0.6.   **9** 0.000 842.
3 10 800.   **7** 0.0008.   **10** 0.000 804 2.
4 672 100.

All these may become clearer if you make a table of the values of powers of ten, say from 10^4 down to 10^{-4}.

Power of ten	Ordinary form
10^4	10 000
10^3	1 000
10^2	100
10^1	10
10^0	1
10^{-1}	0.1
10^{-2}	0.01
10^{-3}	0.001
10^{-4}	0.0001

In the table you'll see that $10^0 = 1$ (if you are not sure why this is so, look back to Chapter 4). The table shows how each time you multiply by 10, you add 1 to the **power** (or **index**). At the same time the 1 in 1, 10, 100, etc., moves one place to the left when you multiply by 10. Reversing this process, each time you divide by 10, you subtract 1 from the power – for instance:

- $10^5 \div 10 = 10^4$
- $10^3 \div 10 = 10^2$

At the same time the 1 in the number you start with moves one place to the right. If you extend this process further, you obtain the results in the lower half of the table – for example:

- $1 \div 10 = 0.1$ so $0.1 = 10^{-1}$
- $0.1 \div 10 = 0.01$ so $0.01 = 10^{-2}$
- $0.01 \div 10 = 0.001$ so $0.001 = 10^{-3}$

You will find a fuller explanation of negative powers in Chapter 4.

Here are some further examples of numbers in standard form.

- $700 = 7 \times 100 = 7 \times 10^2$
- $47\,600 = 4.76 \times 10\,000 = 4.76 \times 10^4$
- $0.3 = 3 \times 0.1 = 3 \times 10^{-1}$
- $0.0091 = 9.1 \times 0.001 = 9.1 \times 10^{-3}$

Self-check

Convert the following to standard form.

1 9000.	**2** 23 000.	**3** 4080.
4 67 500 000.	**5** 741.2.	**6** 0.8.
7 0.65.	**8** 0.041.	**9** 0.003 01.
10 2.361.		

ANSWERS

1 9×10^3.   **2** $2.3 \times 10\,000 = 2.3 \times 10^4$.
3 4.08×10^3.   **4** 6.75×10^7.
5 7.412×10^2.   **6** $8 \times 0.1 = 8 \times 10^{-1}$.
7 $6.5 \times 0.1 = 6.5 \times 10^{-1}$.   **8** 4.1×10^{-2}.
9 3.01×10^{-3}.   **10** 2.361 (or 2.361×10^0).

Standard form on your calculator

If you have a **scientific** calculator, it's likely that you will have a key, labelled **Exp** maybe, which enables you to input numbers in standard form. The calculator instruction book will explain how it works.

If you have a **simple** calculator you have to carry out the adding of powers of ten yourself when multiplying, so to calculate 230 000 × 140 000 000 first re-write in standard form, giving:

$2.3 \times 10^5 \times 1.4 \times 10^8$

Now use your calculator to work out 2.3 × 1.4, giving 3.22:

$2.3 \times 10^5 \times 1.4 \times 10^8 = 3.22 \times 10^{13}$

Fractions and standard form

If you have to convert fractions to standard form, the first step is to convert them to decimals (see Chapter 5). Sometimes the fractions will convert easily (especially if they occur in exam papers); usually it is simplest to convert to a decimal using your calculator, and round off to a sensible accuracy, e.g.:

- $\frac{3}{47} = 3 \div 47 = 0.063\,829\,7\ldots \simeq 0.0638 = 6.38 \times 10^{-2}$
- $\frac{1}{500} = 1 \div 500 = 0.002 = 2 \times 10^{-3}$

With some simple fractions you can also use equivalent fractions ideas to change the denominator into a power of 10 (10, 100, 1000, etc.), e.g.:

$\frac{1}{500} = \frac{2}{1000} = 2 \times 1000 = 2 \times 10^{-3}$

Self-check

Convert the following fractions to standard form (correct to 3 significant figures).

1 $\frac{3}{80}$. **2** $\frac{1}{400}$.

Convert the following to fractions in their simplest form.

3 8×10^{-1}. **4** 8.8×10^{-2}.

Check your answers by converting back to standard form, using your calculator.

ANSWERS

1 3.75×10^{-2}. **2** 2.5×10^{-3}.
3 $0.8 = 8 \div 10 = \frac{8}{10} = \frac{4}{5}$. **4** $\frac{11}{125}$.

Area and volume questions which involve square roots

The formula for the area of a circle:

$A = \pi r^2$

involves squaring the radius, then multiplying by π to find the circle area. If, instead, you know the area of a circle and need to find its radius, you reverse these steps, i.e. divide A by π, then find the square root of the result. In effect, you are rearranging the formula to make r the subject:

$\pi r^2 = A$
$r^2 = A/_\pi$
$r = \sqrt{\frac{A}{\pi}}$

For instance, if $A = 100\,\text{cm}^2$, then:

$r = \sqrt{\dfrac{100}{3.142}} = \sqrt{31.83} = 5.64\,\text{cm (to 3 s.f.)}$

You can **check** the result:

- by using this value of r to calculate A:
  $3.142 \times 5.64^2 = 99.95\,\text{cm}^2$
  $\simeq 100\,\text{cm}^2$

or:

- by carrying out a rough check in your head to see if the value of r you obtained is reasonable, e.g. if r is between 5 and 6, then r^2 is between 25 and 36, and so A is roughly between $3 \times 25 = 75$ and $3 \times 36 = 108$; the given value of A is between these values, so your calculated value of r makes sense.

In many ways, standing back a little, as in the second check, is a preferable approach – it's always worth asking yourself if answers make sense. Sometimes carrying out a check in too much detail can lead you to overlook some key error in a calculation.

Here's another example. Suppose you know the volume of a cone and its height, can you calculate its radius? In other words, make r the subject of the formula:

$V = \dfrac{\pi r^2 h}{3}$

As before, it is worth asking yourself what has happened to r to produce V, then undo the steps.

$$\frac{\pi r^2 h}{3} = V$$

$$=> \pi r^2 h = 3V$$

Divide by h and π:

$$r^2 = \frac{3V}{h\pi}$$

$$=> r = \sqrt{\frac{3V}{h\pi}}$$

If $V = 100\,\text{cm}^3$, $h = 6\,\text{cm}$, then:

$$r = \sqrt{\frac{300}{6\pi}}$$

$$= \sqrt{15.91}$$

$$= 3.99\,\text{cm}$$

Again, check back to make sure, starting with $r \simeq 4$ and $\pi \simeq 3$, so then:

$$V \simeq \frac{3 \times 16 \times 6}{3} = 96 \simeq 100$$

Self-check

1 Rearrange the formula $V = \pi r^2 h$ to make r the subject.
2 A cylinder has a radius equal to its height. If its radius is r, write down a formula for the curved surface area of the cylinder, A.
3 Rearrange the formula in 3 to make r the subject.
4 The surface area of a sphere is $25\,\text{m}^2$. What is its radius? Use this value to calculate its volume in litres (to the nearest 250 litres).

ANSWERS

1 $r = \sqrt{\dfrac{V}{\pi h}}$

2 $A = 2\pi r^2$.

3 $r = \sqrt{\dfrac{A}{2\pi}}$

4 $S = 4\pi r^2$

so:

$$r = \sqrt{\frac{25}{4\pi}} = 1.41\,\text{m}$$

$$V = \frac{4\pi r^3}{3} \simeq 11.75\,\text{m}^3$$
$$= 11\,750\,\text{litres}$$

Finding square roots in standard form

When using area or volume formulae in reverse, or Pythagoras' rule, you may be faced with having to calculate the square root of a very large or very small number, possibly in standard form. Here are two examples.

• $\sqrt{9 \times 10^8} = 3 \times 10^4$

because:
$$3 \times 10^4 \times 3 \times 10^4 = 9 \times 10^8$$

• $\sqrt{3.6 \times 10^{15}} = \sqrt{36 \times 10^{14}}$
$$= 6 \times 10^7$$

since:
$$6 \times 10^7 \times 6 \times 10^7 = 36 \times 10^{14}$$

Review

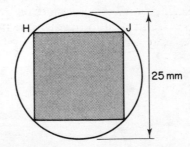

Figure 208.

1 Convert the following to standard form (correct to 3 significant figures):
a 4781; **b** 0.069; **c** $\frac{123}{4600}$; **d** $\frac{1}{20}$.

2 Convert to ordinary numbers:
  a 6.2×10^3; **b** 7.14×10^{-4}.

3 What is the positive square root of 8.4×10^7?

4 A round bar, diameter 25 mm, is filed down at one end to produce a square section as shown in Figure 208. What is the side length HJ?

5 Rearrange the formula:

$$V = \frac{5mr^2}{8}$$

to make r the subject. Hence find the value of r when $V = 600$, $m = 18$.

13 | Circles and angle properties

Chapter 10 dealt with some of the calculations you may meet concerned with length and area properties of circles. This chapter is more concerned with **angle properties of circles** and the ways you can use them in calculations.

Chords and segments

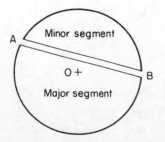

Figure 209. Major and minor segments

A **chord** is a straight line joining two points on the edge of a circle. In Figure 209 the chord AB cuts the circle into two **segments** – large (**major**) and small (**minor**) segments. The **radii** OA and OB divide the circle into two **sectors**, **major** and **minor**, as shown in Figure 210.

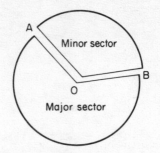

Figure 210. Major and minor sectors

> *Activity*
>
> Draw a circle yourself and mark a point on your paper outside the circle. Label the point P. Now draw straight lines from P towards the circle.
>
> Some will cut the circle in two places – these are called **secants** of the circle. Some will just touch the circle at a single point – these are called **tangents** to the circle. Other lines will miss the circle altogether.

Some symmetry properties of the circle

What makes the circle special is its symmetry – you only have to think of the infinite number of different ways you could fold a circle in half, with each fold line including a diameter of the circle.

> *Activity*
>
> Draw a circle on thin paper and label its centre O and label two points A and B on its circumference (not at the ends of a diameter). Now fold the circle so that the points

A and B are on top of each other. Open out the circle again and draw lines AO, OB and AB. You will obtain a diagram like the one in Figure 211. Triangle AOB is isosceles.

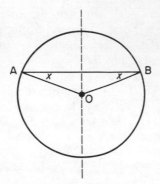

Figure 211.

Self-check

Sketch the diagrams in Figure 212 and calculate the other angles in the triangles.

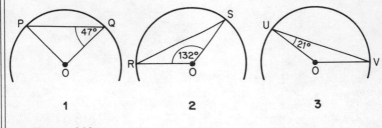

Figure 212.

ANSWERS

1 ∠OPQ = 47°, ∠POQ = 86°.
2 ∠ORS = ∠OSR = 24°.
3 ∠UVO = 21°, ∠UOV = 138°.

Circles and rectangles

Activity

Take your folded circle (Figure 211) and fold the circle in half again so that the new fold is at right angles to the previous one. Mark through the images of A and B, labelling them D and C. Open out the paper and you will find that ABCD is a rectangle, one of many which you could draw inside the circle.

The diagonals of ABCD (or any other rectangle) are diameters of the circle (see Figure 213). In reverse, you could start by drawing a diameter. This forms the diagonal of a family of rectangles, as in Figure 214.

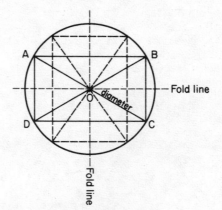

Figure 213.

All this shows how an angle such as ∠ABC in Figure 214, based on a diameter AC, is bound to be a right angle. Test it by using your protractor to check that the angle B, based on (or **subtended by**) the diameter AC, is always 90°, wherever you position B on the circumference. In other words:

● the angle in a semicircle is a right angle.

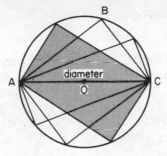

Figure 214. Rectangles based on the same diameter

Self-check

A rectangle measures 5 cm by 12 cm. What is the diameter of the smallest circle which will contain it?

ANSWER

13 cm (use Pythagoras' rule).

Angles at centre and circumference

Look at Figure 215. You'll see that one of the sides of the triangle has been extended (or **produced**) to form a diameter.

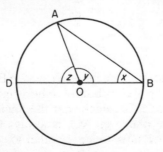

Figure 215.

Activity

Draw the diagram and measure the angles marked x and z. Now repeat with B in a different position on the circumference, again measuring x and z. What do you notice?

When I drew the diagram I found that $x = 34°$ and $z = 68°$ – exactly double. If $x = 34°$, then:

$y = 180 - 2 \times 34 = 180 - 68 = 112°$

and z must be $68°$ because $y + z$ add up to $180°$. Check your measurements in the same way.

In each case, you'll have noticed that $z = 2 \times x$. Now put two triangles together, as shown in Figure 216.

$z_1 = 2x_1$ and $z_2 = 2x_2$

so:

$z_1 + z_2 = 2x_1 + 2x_2$
$\qquad = 2(x_1 + x_2)$

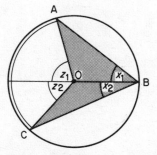

Figure 216.

Self-check

Use this result to calculate angles marked with letters in Figure 217.

ANSWERS

$a = 2(47 + 24) = 142°, b = 154°, c = 180°.$

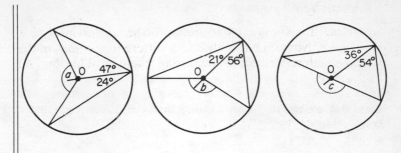

Figure 217.

This illustrates the general result that:

● (Angle at the centre of a circle) = 2 × (Angle at the circumference)

For instance, in Figure 218 the angle at the centre (AOC) is 150°, which is 2 × the angle at the circumference (ABC), which is 75°.

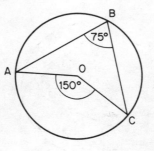

Figure 218.

As a special case, if ∠AOC = 180°, then AC is a straight line – a diameter of the circle. It follows that:

∠ABC = ½ of 180° = 90°

showing another way in which you explain why the angle in a semicircle is 90°.

Tangents and symmetry

In Figure 219 AB is a tangent to the circle, touching it at T. Because of the circle's symmetry, the diameter passing through O and T (shown dotted) meets the tangent at right angles. Now look at Figure 220, which includes another tangent to the circle from B. OB is a line of symmetry, with pairs of equal angles at O and B as shown. If you rotate the diagram you can see this more clearly.

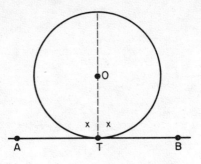

Figure 219.

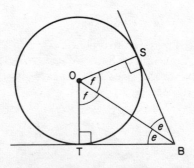

Figure 220.

Self-check

Calculate the following.
1 ∠TOS when $e = 36°$.
2 ∠TBS when $f = 56°$.

3 ∠TOS when ∠TBS = 74°.
4 ∠SOB when ∠SBO = 30°.

ANSWERS

1 2 × 54 = 108°. **2** 2 × 34 = 68°.
3 106°. **4** 60°.

Review

1 Figure 221 shows a pipe held in a V-slot. If angle *a* = 45°, calculate angle *b*.

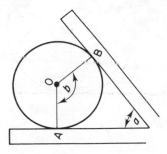

Figure 221.

2 A circle passes through the corners of a rectangle which measures 4 cm by 8 cm. What is the circle radius?

3 Calculate the sizes of the angles marked with letters in Figure 222.

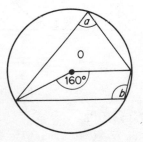

Figure 222.

4 In Figure 223, O is the centre of the circle. PTQ is a tangent touching the circle at T. If $\angle$QTS = 50°, find the sizes of $\angle$PTO and $\angle$TSO.

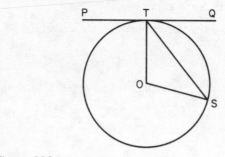

Figure 223.

Angles in the same segment

Figure 224 shows a circle cut into two segments by the chord AB. C is somewhere on the major arc AB – I have shown four possible positions, labelled C_1, C_2, C_3 and C_4.

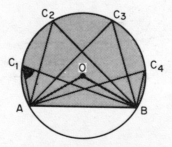

Figure 224.

Activity

Measure $\angle AC_1B$ (I have shaded in the angle). Now measure $\angle AC_2B$, $\angle AC_3B$ and $\angle AC_4B$. Mark in some extra positions for C on the same arc and measure the resulting angles $\angle AC_5B$, $\angle AC_6B$, etc. What do you notice?

All these angles are subtended by (based on) the same chord AB and are in the same segment of the circle.

You can see now why the angles $\angle AC_1B$, $\angle AC_2B$, $\angle AC_3B$, etc., are equal to each other – it is because every one of them is half of angle $\angle AOB$. So in general:

- angles in the same segment are equal to each other.

Activity

1 Mark two points about 6 cm apart. Label them A and B. Join AB.
2 From A, draw a set of lines at angles of 10° to each other. Do the same for B, producing another set of lines.
3 Look at the points where two lines cross at an angle of 60° (two such points are shown). Mark in as many other such points as you can find (see Figure 225).
4 Repeat this for different crossing angles and see what happens.

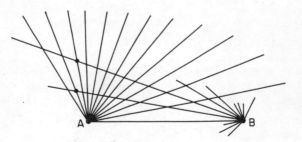

Figure 225.

Self-check

In Figure 226 calculate the sizes of the angles marked with letters. There is a tangent at T and the line BT is a diameter of the circle, centre O.

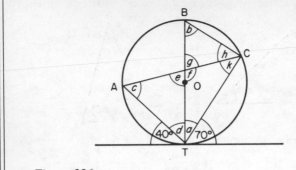

Figure 226.

ANSWERS

$a = 20°$; as TBC is right-angled at C, $b = 70°$; $c = 70°$; $d = 50°$;
$e = 60°$; $f = 120°$; $g = 60°$; $h = 50°$; $k = 40°$.

Similar triangles – a reminder

As you will recall from Chapter 11, when two triangles have matching (or corresponding) angles equal, the triangles are similar to each other. In other words, one triangle is an enlargement of the other.

You can tell which are matching pairs of sides in these triangles when the triangles are drawn facing the same way on the page. Even when this is not so, you can pick out pairs of corresponding sides quite easily – both sides in a pair face a pair of equal angles.

Self-check

In the diagrams in Figure 227:
1 What side corresponds to GH?
2 What side corresponds to KL?
3 If GH = 5 cm, HI = 4 cm and LJ = 15 cm, calculate LK.
4 If GH = 8 cm, JK = 2.4 cm and GI = 9.6 cm, calculate JL.

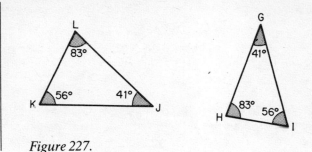

Figure 227.

ANSWERS

1 LJ. **2** HI.
3 Side lengths in triangle LJK are three times side lengths in triangle GHI, because LJ = 3 × GH, so LK = 3 × HI = 3 × 4 = 12 cm.
4 JK corresponds to GI. Here JK × 4 = GI, so JL × 4 = GH. However, GH is 8 cm, so JL is 2 cm long.

Similar triangles and circles

The **angles in the same segment** property of circles leads to pairs of equal angles, which in turn leads to similar triangles. You can see how this works in Figure 228.

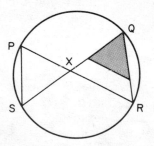

Figure 228.

Activity

Copy Figure 228 and make a tracing of triangle PXS. Turn the tracing over and check that pairs of angles in triangles PXS and QXR are equal by sliding the tracing in turn into each of the angles of triangle QXR, as shown.

You have now checked that the triangles are similar, and you can see that this will always be the case wherever you position P, Q, R and S on the circle. In every case:

- ∠SPR = ∠SQR (angles in the same segment, subtended by SR);
- ∠PSQ = ∠PRQ (angles in the same segment, subtended by PQ);
- ∠PXS = ∠QXR (vertically opposite).

By marking in pairs of equal angles on your diagram, you can pick out pairs of corresponding sides:

- QX corresponds to PX;
- RX corresponds to SX;
- QR corresponds to PS;

so:

$$\frac{QX}{PX} = \frac{RX}{SX} = \frac{QR}{PS}$$

As an example, if QX = 8cm, PX = 4cm and SX = 6cm, then you can calculate RX as follows:

$$\frac{8}{4} = \frac{RX}{6}, \text{ so } RX = 12\,cm$$

Self-check

Using Figure 228:
1 If QR = 9cm, PS = 5cm, XS = 8cm, calculate RX.
2 If PX = 4.5cm, PS = 5cm, SX = 6cm and QR = 8cm, calculate XR and QX.

ANSWERS

1 $\dfrac{RX}{8} = \dfrac{9}{5}$, so RX = 14.4 cm.

2 $\dfrac{XR}{6} = \dfrac{8}{5}$, so XR = $\dfrac{48}{5}$ = 9.6 cm, QX = 7.2 cm.

Angles in the alternate segment

In Figure 229, triangles PQR and POR are as before, with circle centre at O. PS and RS are tangents.

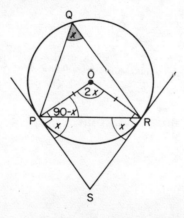

Figure 229.

First, suppose that $\angle$PQR = x. Then $\angle$POR = $2x$ (angle at centre = 2 × angle at circumference). But:

$\angle$OPR = $\angle$ORP

as triangle OPR is isosceles, so each must be $\frac{1}{2}$ of $180 - 2x$, i.e. $90 - x$, and so:

$\angle$SPR = x = $\angle$SRP

Because the angle PQR is in the segment on the other side of the chord PR, i.e. the **alternate segment**, you can say that:

- angle between tangent and chord equals the angle in the alternate segment.

Self-check

Using Figure 229.

1 If ∠SPR = 60°, ∠RPQ = 50°, calculate the sizes of the angles in the triangle PQR.

2 If ∠OPR = 18°, calculate the size of ∠PQR.

3 Calculate values for ∠PSR when ∠PQR = 30°, 40°, 50° and 60°.

4 Use your results from **5** to find a connection between ∠PQR and ∠PSR.

ANSWERS

1 ∠PQR = 60°; ∠RPQ = 50°; ∠PRQ = 70°.
2 ∠POR = 144°, so ∠PQR = 72°.
3 120°; 100°; 80°; 60°.
4 ∠PSR = 180° − 2 × ∠PQR.

Other arrangement of similar triangles

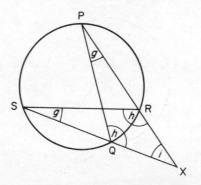

Figure 230.

In Figure 228 the two similar triangles were fixed by the position of the two chords PR and SQ, intersecting **inside** the circle at X. Figure 230 shows two chords PR and SQ intersecting **outside** the circle at X. See how in the triangles PXQ and SXR the angles at P and S are equal (angles in the same segment) while the angle at X is common to both triangles. This means that the remaining angles in each triangle must equal each other as well (as the angles in a triangle always add to 180°). Thus the triangles PXQ and SXR have pairs of matching angles equal, which means that the triangles must be similar to each other.

Self-check

1 Calculate PX if QX = 4cm, RX = 5cm and SX = 10cm.
2 Calculate QX if PX = 6cm, RX = 4cm and SX = 8cm.
3 Calculate PQ if PX = 6cm, SX = 9cm and SR = 6cm.

ANSWERS

1 $\dfrac{PX}{10} = \dfrac{4}{5}$, so PX = 8cm.

2 $\dfrac{QX}{4} = \dfrac{6}{8}$, so QX = 3cm.

3 $\dfrac{6}{9} = \dfrac{PQ}{6}$, so PQ = 4cm.

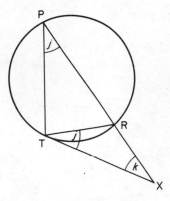

Figure 231.

Now look at Figure 231, where XT is a tangent to the circle, touching it at T. Look at the triangles PTX and TRX. The angle at k is common to both triangles while the angles marked j are equal (angles in the alternate segment). Hence the remaining angles of each triangle equal each other and the triangles are similar. As before, corresponding sides are opposite equal angles.

Self-check

1 Calculate PX when TX = 8 cm, RX = 5 cm.
2 Calculate PT when PX = 10 cm, TX = 6 cm and RT = 4 cm.

ANSWERS

1 $\dfrac{8}{5} = \dfrac{PX}{8}$, so PX $= \dfrac{64}{5} = 12.8$ cm.

2 $\dfrac{10}{6} = \dfrac{PT}{4}$, so PT $= 6\frac{2}{3}$ cm.

Review

Use Figure 232 for questions **1–4**.
1 Calculate NY if NV = 8 cm, NZ = 6 cm and NW = 2 cm.
2 If UT = 5 cm and UV = 2 cm, calculate VW.
3 If YV and ZW meet at P, state the triangle which is similar to triangle YPZ.
4 If ∠UTW = 80°, calculate ∠TYW and ∠WZT.
5 In Figure 233, A, C and B are equally spaced on the arc of a circle. AB = 18 cm and C is 4 cm above AB. Calculate the diameter of the circle.

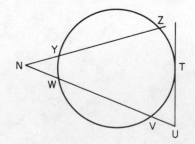

Figure 232.

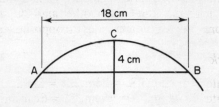

Figure 233.

14 | Introducing statistics

Are longlife batteries worth the extra cost? Which type of car is more likely to break down during a year's motoring? These are just two situations where you depend on what you know about what happened in the past to tell what is likely in the future. Just looking at a battery or a car won't tell you how long it will last or how reliable it is. However, you can start to answer questions like these if you have information about many ordinary and longlife batteries and many cars of each type.

The information you start with (battery life, number of breakdowns in a year, etc.) is called **data**. The branch of mathematics which deals with analysing such data is called **statistics**.

Making a tally table and a frequency chart

Suppose that you kept a check on the lateness of a particular bus for 50 mornings, noting whether it was over 5 minutes late or not, and your results were as below. (O means over 5 minutes late, N means not over 5 minutes late):

O N O O N N N O N O O N N O O N N N O N
O N N N O N O O N O N N N N N O N O N O N
N N N N N N O N N N

You can start to sort out the data by making a **tally table**, working along each line of the data and blocking the tally marks in fives as you go (see Figure 234).

Lateness	Tally	Frequency
Over 5 mins	ЦНГ ЦНГ ЦНГ III	18
Not over 5 mins	ЦНГ ЦНГ ЦНГ ЦНГ ЦНГ ЦНГ II	32

Figure 234. A tally table plus frequency column

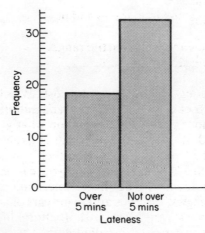

Figure 235. A frequency chart

Marking the tally table like this can seem tedious, but you can be sure of having counted every result. It is all too easy to miss a result or count one twice if you try to pick out all the O results first, then all the Ns.

The number of times a result occurs in a **sample** like this is called its **frequency**, so here the frequencies are 18 and 32, totalling 50 as you would expect.

You can also illustrate the data in a frequency chart, as in Figure 235. See how the frequency scale is upwards, and how both scales are labelled clearly so you can understand the chart at a glance. Normally the columns in a frequency chart are of equal widths, as they are here. Of course, the data won't enable you to tell how late tomorrow's bus will be – it just gives the general picture.

Self-check

1 Overalls are provided for trainees at a training centre. In the last year, 40 trainees were involved, needing the overall sizes listed below. Make a tally table from the data and use it to draw a frequency chart for the different overall sizes.

```
S   L  XL  M   M   L   M   S   M   S
M   L  XL  L   L   M   S   S   M   S
M   M   M   S   L   L   M   S   S   M
M   M   S   L   L   M   M   L   M   S
```

2 At the same centre, safety boots are issued in sizes 4, 5, 6, 7, 8, 9, 10 and 11.

The same trainees needed boots in these sizes.

Make a tally table from the data and use it to draw a frequency chart for the boot sizes.

```
4   7   6   7   6   8   8   9   7   6
5   8   9  11   7   6   8   8   9   9
7   7   9   7   8   8   4   9   7   8
6   5   7  10  10  11   6   7   8   7
```

ANSWERS

See Figure 236.

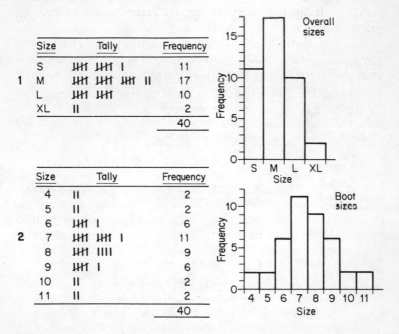

Size	Tally	Frequency
S	ЈНТ ЈНТ I	11
M	ЈНТ ЈНТ ЈНТ II	17
L	ЈНТ ЈНТ	10
XL	II	2
		40

(row group labelled **1**)

Size	Tally	Frequency
4	II	2
5	II	2
6	ЈНТ I	6
7	ЈНТ ЈНТ I	11
8	ЈНТ IIII	9
9	ЈНТ I	6
10	II	2
11	II	2
		40

(row group labelled **2**)

Figure 236

Continuous and discrete data

The data in the two self-check questions could be arranged in a limited number of categories. For instance, with the overall size, there were only four categories or **classes** (S, M, L and XL), while with the boots there were only eight classes (sizes 4, 5, 6, 7, 8, 9, 10 and 11). This type of data is called **discrete**.

Measuring lengths, times, etc., can give rise to **continuous** data. For instance, most adults' heights are between 140 cm and 200 cm, so if you measured the heights of a sample of adults, you could expect *any* height between 140 cm and 200 cm.

Grouped data

The heights of the 40 trainees were measured so as to decide on the best workbench and tool operating heights for them. The measurements were made to the nearest centimetre:

156, 167, 174, 176, 151, 149, 176, 184, 136, 148,
158, 163, 156, 171, 160, 158, 147, 160, 166, 164,
144, 156, 160, 164, 158, 162, 181, 153, 157, 159,
178, 162, 154, 169, 163, 166, 166, 154, 167, 170.

You can get a clearer picture of how the heights are spread out by grouping them, say in 5 cm intervals:

Ht in centimetres	Tally	Frequency
135–9		
140–4		
145–9		
150–4		
155–9		
etc.		

Self-check

1 Copy and fill in the tally table above.
2 Draw the corresponding frequency chart.

ANSWERS

See Figure 237.

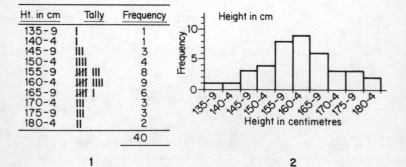

Figure 237.

From your table or chart you can see how most of the trainees had heights between 150 cm and 170 cm – not obvious from the data as first presented. You could well use the information to help you design the benches, etc.

The data could have been grouped in intervals of 10 cm (130–9, 140–9, etc.) or in 2 cm intervals (136–7, 138–9, etc.), giving six columns in the first case and 25 in the second. Probably the original 5 cm interval with ten columns on the frequency chart is about the best compromise between not enough accuracy and too much fine detail obscuring the general picture.

Ways of grouping data

Let's look again at the 'heights of trainees' on page 326. First each height was measured 'to the nearest centimetre' – this means that *all* heights between 135.5 cm and 136.5 cm count as 136 cm, and so on. For the interval or class 135–9 cm the **boundary heights** are 134.5 cm and 139.5 cm, so *any* height between these values is counted in this class.

You have to make a decision about how you will count a height of **exactly** 139.5 cm, say. It could go into the 135–9 cm class or the 140–4 cm one. Often, you **round up** boundary values so you would count 139.5 cm as being in the interval 140–4 cm, but this isn't always the case. You can also describe classes by simply stating the lower bound, so:

- 135–9 cm (to nearest cm) becomes 134.5 cm – measuring 134.5 and over;
- 140–4 cm (to nearest cm) becomes 139.5 cm – measuring 139.5 and over;
- 145–9 cm (to nearest cm) becomes 144.5 cm – measuring 144.5 and over;

and so on.

Self-check

What are the boundary values of these intervals?
160–9 kg
170–9 kg   weighed to nearest kg.
180–9 kg

ANSWERS

159.5 kg, 169.5 kg, 179.5 kg, 189.5 kg.

Samples and populations

The sample of 40 trainees was only a small number compared with all the possible people who *might* have enrolled. In the same way, the 50 days you chose to keep a check on bus lateness is likely to be much less than the total of possible days. In each case, you take a sample from a **population** – the population of possible trainees or of all the times that particular bus has run.

Each sample gives a picture of its population, and in general the larger the sample the more accurate the picture. However, you can get a distorted or **biased** picture of a population if your sample is not random, i.e. if some members of the population are more likely to be chosen than others. For example, noting the times of buses on Mondays only might give a biased picture of the service on all weekdays.

Showing fractions of a whole

Look back to the frequency chart you drew for overall sizes (Figure 236). If the sample gives a fair picture of future trainees, then the manager should order more size M overalls than size XL, and it seems that about the same number of S and L overalls will be needed.

You can explain decisions like this directly by using the frequency chart, which tells you how popular one size was compared with another, but the chart doesn't show how these frequencies compare with the total.

Imagine stacking the columns on top of each other and you obtain a chart like the one in Figure 238. By eye, you can see that about two-thirds of the overalls are in sizes S and M, and so on. To be exact:

- $^{11}/_{40}$ths of the sample needed size S;
- $^{17}/_{40}$ths of the sample needed size M;
- $^{28}/_{40}$ths of the sample needed sizes S or M.

These fractions are called **relative frequencies** and give the fraction of the total in a particular class or classes.

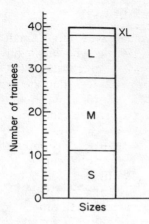

Figure 238.

Self-check

1 What is the relative frequency of the sample of 40 who needed size XL?
2 Using the boot size data, what are the relative frequencies of these classes?
   a People needing size 7.
   b People needing sizes 9 or over.
   c People needing sizes 5, 6 or 7.

ANSWERS

1 $\frac{11}{40}$.
2 **a** $\frac{2}{40}$ (or $\frac{1}{20}$).   **b** $\frac{10}{40}$ (or $\frac{1}{4}$).   **c** $\frac{19}{40}$.

Using percentages

It is often helpful to give relative frequencies as percentages – this makes it easier to compare samples of different sizes. For example:

$^{11}/_{40} = 0.275$
$= 27.5\%$

Self-check

What percentage of the trainees were within 10 cm of 160 cm in height?

ANSWER

67.5%.

Using pie charts

You will also meet relative frequencies shown on a circular **pie chart**. The circle is divided into sectors in proportion to the relative frequencies. Figure 239 shows a pie chart for the data on overall sizes alongside the matching percentage relative frequency bar chart. The sector angles for the pie chart are fractions of 360° (complete turn), so the $^{11}/_{40}$ths needing size S gives a sector angle of $^{11}/_{40} \times 360 = 99°$.

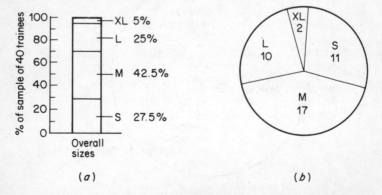

Figure 239. (a) Relative frequency chart and (b) related pie chart

The other three angles are $^{17}/_{40}$ths of 360 = 153°, $^{10}/_{40}$ths of 360 = 90° and $^{2}/_{40}$ths of 360° = 18°. Check that you can work out these angles correctly, either with or without your calculator. Turn back to Chapter 1 if you are not sure how to do it.

Self-check

Agricultural land usage in June 1978 in the UK was approximately as shown below. Draw a pie chart to show this data.

Crop	Million hectares
Wheat	1.3
Barley	2.3
Oats	0.2
Potatoes	0.2
Other arable	0.9
Grass	7.1
Total	12.0

ANSWER

See Figure 240. Angles are 39°, 69°, 6°, 6°, 27°, 213°.

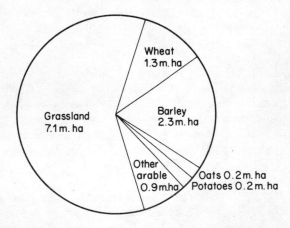

Figure 240.

Pictograms

Sometimes frequencies or percentages are drawn horizontally, while, to provide a more vivid display, the bars are replaced with a series of picture symbols, each representing a given quantity. Charts like this are called **pictograms**. The example in Figure 241 shows average expenditure per person per week on food in families with two adults in the second quarter of 1980.

Family size	Amount spent on food per person
2 adults 0 children	£ £ £ £ £ £ £ £ £
2 adults 1 child	£ £ £ £ £ £ £ £
2 adults 2 children	£ £ £ £ £ £ £
2 adults 3 children	£ £ £ £ £ £
2 adults 4 children	£ £ £ £ £ £

£ represents £ per week

Figure 241.

Review

120 components on a production line were removed as a sample. Their lengths were measured in mm to the nearest 0.1 mm, as shown below.

67.3, 67.6, 67.8, 67.8, 67.1, 67.5, 67.6, 67.3,
67.5, 67.8, 67.3, 67.1, 67.0, 67.9, 67.3, 67.6,
67.8, 68.2, 68.1, 68.0, 67.0, 67.1, 66.9, 67.1,
66.9, 67.2, 67.4, 67.1, 67.8, 67.3, 67.4, 67.4,
67.7, 67.1, 67.0, 67.6, 67.9, 67.4, 67.5, 67.5,
67.5, 67.6, 67.2, 67.1, 67.4, 67.3, 67.3, 67.1,
67.4, 68.2, 68.3, 67.9, 68.0, 67.0, 66.8, 67.1,
67.2, 67.1, 68.0, 67.3, 67.0, 67.0, 66.9, 67.2,
67.3, 67.4, 67.6, 67.1, 67.5, 67.3, 67.4, 67.4,
67.6, 67.2, 67.2, 67.6, 67.3, 67.4, 67.7, 67.8,
67.7, 67.7, 67.7, 67.2, 67.0, 67.6, 67.7, 67.1,
67.5, 67.7, 67.4, 67.2, 67.5, 67.5, 67.3, 67.4,
68.4, 68.5, 66.6, 66.7, 67.2, 67.2, 67.7, 67.5,

68.3, 67.4, 67.5, 67.2, 67.2, 67.2, 67.2, 67.5,
68.1, 67.3, 67.4, 67.4, 67.3, 67.0, 67.7, 67.9.

1 Make a tally table using the classes 66.6–66.7 mm, 66.8–66.9 mm, etc.

2 Components should be at least 67.0 mm long but no longer than 67.7 mm.

   a Find the relative frequencies for 'too short', 'all right' and 'too long'.

   b Convert these fractions to percentages.

3 Draw a percentage frequency chart and a pie chart to illustrate your results from **2**.

Averages

Fifteen people measure their heights. They record what they find and try to answer questions like:

- Which person is the tallest?
- What is the average height?
- Am I taller than average?
- How much more will I have to grow to reach the average height?

By **average** they mean a sort of **middle value**. The word average is widely used when people compare one piece of data (height, salary, etc.) with a collection of data (heights of 15 people, salaries of workers in the UK, etc.). It means a central value which in some way represents the collection of data.

However, there are different types of average used to answer different questions. I'll use the example of the 15 people to explain what I mean.

   Their heights in centimetres were:

160 153 164 176 180
142 167 171 172 166
164 168 173 171 155

Finding the median

1 Arrange the heights in order, smallest to largest – you'll obtain:

142, 153, 155, 160, 164, 164, 166, 167,
168, 171, 171, 172, 173, 176, 180.

2 Now pick out the middle number in this list – it's 167.

3 This middle value is called the **median**, so the median height is 167 cm.

Peter's height is 160 cm, so he is below average height for the group, i.e. in the lower half of the sample. Sue's height is 176 cm, so she is well above average in height for the group.

It's easy to pick out the median height because the sample size of 15 is an odd number:

| 7 below | | 1 | | 7 above | total $7 + 1 + 7 = 15$

However, you can still find a median if the sample size is even – for instance if Peter left the group. The median is then the value halfway between the two central values – in this case the median is midway between 167 cm and 168 cm, i.e. 167.5 cm.

To summarize:

● the median of a sample is the middle value of the sample when the sample values are arranged in order of size.

Finding the mean

Using the same sample of 15 as before:

1 add the 15 values together – you'll obtain 2482 cm;

2 divide the total by 15;

3 this value is called the **mean**:

$$2482 \div 15 = 165.466\ldots \simeq 165.5 \text{ cm}$$

As before, if Peter left the group, the mean would change slightly. The new mean is:

$$2322 \div 14 \simeq 165.9 \text{ cm}$$

Again as before, when below-average Peter leaves, the average of the remainder increases slightly. See how the median and mean calculations, though quite different, give results which are close to each other, though *not* the same.

To summarize:

● Mean of a sample $= \dfrac{\text{Total of values of sample}}{\text{Sample size}}$

Self-check

Find the median and mean times in the following.
1 Journey times to work during one week (in minutes):
    43, 37, 38, 40, 45.
2 Seven people have weekly wages of:
    £89, £93, £104, £105, £105, £170, £195.
    Calculate the median and the mean wage.

ANSWERS

1 Median = 40 minutes, mean = 40.6 minutes.
2 Median = £105, mean = £123.

Which average is used?

The median This is the middle value of a sample, so you can use it to decide whether a particular value is in the lower or upper half of the sample. Extreme values, such as the two higher wages in question 2 above, do not affect it.

You use the median to describe average wages, average weights, etc., which are liable to be distorted by extreme values.

The mean This is the result of sharing out the total of all the values of the sample equally among members. It takes into account every value in the sample. Thus the mean wage in question 2 above is the result of sharing out the total wages of £861 equally among the seven wage earners.

You use the mean when you want to take into account the total of sample values. Although it is a little harder to calculate than the median, it is more often what is meant by the word 'average'. Use it unless told otherwise.

If you know the mean value and size of a sample, you can find the total of values of the sample. For instance, suppose that a sample of nine components has a mean length of 27 mm – this means that the total length of the nine is:

$27 \times 9 = 243$ mm

Self-check

1 The median of a sample of five lengths is 18.0 m. Two further items are included in the sample with lengths of 16.1 m and 19.3 m. What effect does this have on the median?
2 The mean weight of 120 people is 69 kg. What is their total weight?
3 Five items have a mean weight of 8.1 g. A sixth is added and has the effect of reducing the mean to 8.0 g. What is the weight of the sixth item?

ANSWERS

1 No effect.   2 8280 kg = 8.28 t.
3 Total weight of six items is 6 × 8 = 48 g, but weight of five is 5 × 8.1 = 40.5 g, so sixth weight is 7.5 g.

Working with grouped frequencies

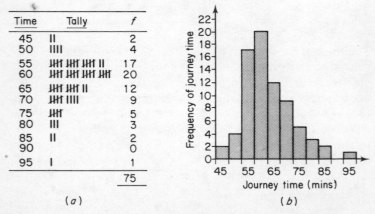

Figure 242. (a) Tally table and (b) frequency chart for bus journey time

A bus company is revising its bus timetables in the light of changing traffic conditions in the rush hour. On a particular route, the rush hour journey times for 75 bus journeys were noted to the nearest five minutes. The bus company want to find:

- the average journey time;
- the slowest and fastest journey time;
- some idea of how close the majority of journey times are to the average;
- what the new schedule time should be for the journey.

The first step is to make a tally table and draw the matching frequency chart (see Figure 242).

Finding the median

Imagine the 75 journey times arranged in order – you can use the table or chart to help you. Two journeys took 45 minutes, four took 50 minutes – that's six so far. Seventeen took 55 minutes – that's 23 so far, and so on. Figure 243 shows all 75 journey times in order.

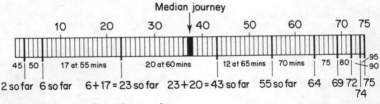

Figure 243. Finding the median

You can see that the middle time (37 below and 37 above) is in the 60 minutes class, so the median time is approximately 60 minutes.

Finding the mean

As you'll remember from page 334, calculating the mean time involves totalling up all the 75 journey times, then dividing the total by 75. Extending the frequency (tally) table will help you do this.

- There are two 45 minute journeys making 90 minutes.
- There are four 50 minute journeys making 200 minutes.

These are entered in the right-hand column of the table.

t	f	ft
45	2	90
50	4	200
55	17	935
60	20	1200
65	12	780
70	9	630
75	5	375
80	3	240
85	2	170
90	0	0
95	1	95
Totals	75	4715

So the mean journey time is:

$$\frac{\text{Total of times}}{\text{Number of journeys}} = \frac{4715}{75} = 62.9 \text{ minutes}$$

Notice that the mean and median are close to each other.

The mode

The sample value which occurs most often (corresponding to the highest column in Figure 242(*b*)) is called the **mode** of the sample. Here the mode is 60 minutes.

You can pick out the mode straight away from a frequency chart and usually its value is close to the median and mean. For this reason, the mode value of a grouped sample is also described as an average, along with the mean and median. (However, there is no reason why a sample should not have several modes, corresponding to several columns of the same height.)

Looking at spread – range and interquartile range

Knowing an average for a sample doesn't tell you anything about how the sample values are spread out. For instance, just looking at the mean bus time of 62.9 minutes does not tell you how close the individual times are to this figure. One simple way of describing this spread is to find the difference between the lowest and highest sample values. This is called the **range** of the sample. In this example the range is:

97.5 − 42.5 = 55 minutes

The range only takes into account the two extreme values of the sample and tells you little about how closely bunched the majority of the sample is. For this reason, a better way of describing the spread of a sample is to find the spread of the 'middle half' of the sample, ignoring the lowest quarter and the highest quarter (see Figure 244).

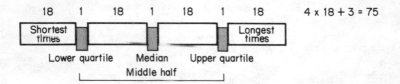

Figure 244. Lower quartile, median and upper quartile

You can see how the 75 times have been arranged from shortest to longest. It is as in Figure 243 but this time arranged in four blocks rather than two. Just as the median value separated the lower and higher blocks of values in the sample, so the **lower quartile**, **median** and **upper quartile** are at the boundaries between the four blocks of values.

● The lower quartile time is:
    18 + 1 = 19th
  time of approx. 55 minutes.
● The upper quartile time is:
    18 + 1 + 18 + 1 + 18 + 1 = 57th
  time of approx. 70 minutes.

Thus half of all the journey times were within approximately 70 − 55 = 15 minutes of each other, that is the **interquartile range** is approximately 15 minutes. In other words half of all the bus journeys are within about 8 minutes of the median time.

With other sample sizes, the sizes of the four blocks do not always work out so easily but you use the same general approach.

Using results from samples

You have already seen how you can use averages and the interquartile range as well as frequency charts to obtain a picture of a population from a sample. With the bus example, it is reasonable to suppose that the average journey times will be just over 60 minutes and that three-quarters of the journeys will last 70 minutes or less, so a scheduled time of 70 minutes would allow about three-quarters of the buses to run to time. Extending the scheduled journey time to, say, 85 minutes would allow practically every bus to run to time, but might be unacceptable because of extra wasted time before the next journey starts. It's a question of balance, but at least the data and your analysis gives you a clear picture of what is happening and so a clear basis for making decisions.

All depends on how fair you have been in choosing your sample, that is how free your sample is from **bias**.

Self-check

Each of these methods of selecting samples is likely to produce bias. Can you say why?
1 Interviewing people on the street on Tuesday afternoons to find out what fraction of people is unemployed.
2 Asking people on trains if they find the train times convenient.

ANSWERS

1 Most employed people will be at work, so the sample could well give an artificially high fraction.
2 The people who do not find the times convenient are less likely to be asked.

Review

1 Using the data from the Review on page 332 and the frequency table in Figure 245, find:
a the median length;
b the lower and upper quartile lengths;

c the interquartile range.
2 Using the frequency table in Figure 245 calculate the
mean length.

Length (mm)	Tally	Frequency
66.6 - 66.7	II	2
66.8 - 66.9	JHT	5
67.0 - 67.1	JHT JHT JHT IIII	19
67.2 - 67.3	JHT JHT JHT JHT JHT III	28
67.4 - 67.5	JHT JHT JHT JHT JHT II	27
67.6 - 67.7	JHT JHT JHT III	18
67.8 - 67.9	JHT JHT	10
68.0 - 68.1	JHT	5
68.2 - 68.3	IIII	4
68.4 - 68.5	II	2
		120

Figure 245.

15 | Introducing trigonometry

Topics covered

- Measuring slopes.
- Gradients.
- Connections between gradients and slope angles.
- Tangents, sines and cosines.
- Using sines, cosines and tangents in problems involving angles of elevation.

Measuring slopes

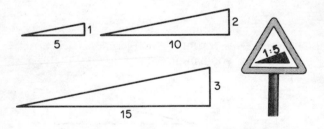

Figure 246. Gradients of 1:5

As you travel around hilly areas of the country you are bound to come across road signs which tell you the steepness of a hill. Often these signs give the steepness or **gradient** as a ratio, e.g. 1:5 (read as 1 in 5) means that you rise or fall by 1 unit (say 1 metre) for every five units you move horizontally. Figure 246 shows this. Of course moving 10 metres horizontally will mean you rise by 2 metres, for every 15 metres horizontally you rise 3 metres and so on, as the diagram shows.

You can also describe gradients by fractions, just as you did with graphs. For example, a gradient of $\frac{1}{5}$ is the same as 1:5. You can change these fractions to decimals or percentages, of course. For instance:

- $\frac{1}{5} = 0.2 = 20\%$
- $\frac{1}{8} = 0.125 = 12.5\%$

Thus a gradient of 12.5% is the same as one of 1:8. In reverse:
    1 in 7 = $\frac{1}{7} \simeq 14\%$
You'll probably have seen newer road signs on steep hills, with the gradients given in percentages.

Self-check

1 Put these gradients in order from steepest to shallowest.

- 1 in 8.
- $\frac{2}{18}$.
- 8 centimetres up for 1 metre horizontally.
- 1:6.

2 Look at the diagrams in Figure 247. For each slope, give its gradient as a simple fraction and as a percentage (to the nearest whole number).

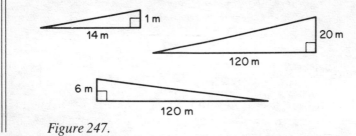

Figure 247.

2 $\frac{1}{14} \simeq 0.07$ or 7%; $\frac{20}{120} = \frac{1}{6} \simeq 17\%$; $\frac{6}{120} = \frac{1}{20} = 5\%$.

Angles of elevation

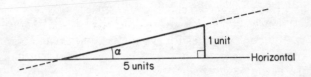

Figure 248.

In Figure 248 the angle marked α (alpha) is called an **angle of elevation**. It is the angle of slope measured from the horizontal. Here the gradient of the slope is $\frac{1}{5}$ or 0.2.

> ### Activity
>
> Draw the right-angled triangle accurately (say 5 cm across and 1 cm high) and use your protractor to measure α. You may find graph paper a help here. What do you find? Did you find the angle was about 11°?   Now draw triangles with gradients of 0.1, 0.3, 0.4 and 0.5. Measure α in each case.
> Now check your results in this table.
>
> | Gradient | Angle of elevation (to nearest degree) |
> |:--------:|:--------------------------------------:|
> | 0.1 | 6° |
> | 0.2 | 11° |
> | 0.3 | 17° |
> | 0.4 | 22° |
> | 0.5 | 27° |

Increasing the gradient

Look back at the table above. Maybe you can see how the table would extend for gradients over 0.5. The gradients would go 0.6, 0.7, 0.8, 0.9, 1.0, 1.1... How would the angles go?

Activity

What would you expect the angle to be for gradients of 1, 1.5 and 2? Write down your estimates now. Now draw accurate triangles to check your estimates.

I have sketched two possible triangles in Figure 249. Were your estimates for the angles on the high side? Can you see how, as the gradients increase, so equal changes in the gradients give **smaller** changes in the angle? Thus the values of gradients and α are **not proportional**.

You can see this in the table below, which shows changes in angle in the column on the right. A gradient of zero means no change in height, so the matching angle of elevation is 0°.

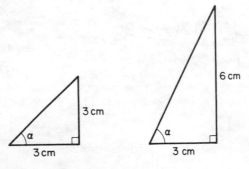

Figure 249.

Gradient	Angle of elevation (to nearest degree)	Approx. angle change
0	0°	—
0.5	27°	27°
1	45°	18°
1.5	56°	11°
2	63°	7°
2.5	68°	5°
3	72°	4°

You can use tables like this to avoid having to make accurate drawings each time you want to calculate an angle in a right-angled triangle when you know a gradient – or the other way round.

Trigonometry is the branch of mathematics which deals with calculations like these, which connect angles and lengths in triangles and other shapes.

More complex shapes can often be split up into triangles, particularly right-angled triangles, so the study of right-angled triangles forms the foundation for calculations connecting angles and lengths in many different shapes.

Self-check

Look at Figure 250, which shows rough sketches of right-angled triangles. In each case there is an angle or side length marked with a letter. Use the tables on pages 344 and 345 to find the values of the letters.

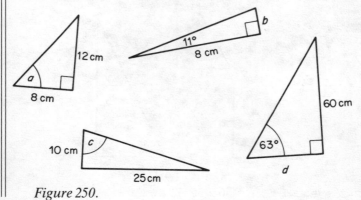

Figure 250.

ANSWERS

$a = 56°$ because $\frac{12}{8} = 1.5$.

$b = 1.6$ because $\frac{1.6}{8} = 0.2$.

$c = 68°$ because $\frac{25}{10} = 2.5$.

$d = 30$ cm because $\frac{60}{30} = 2$.

Tangents of angles

It is rather a mouthful to say, for instance, that 'the gradient matching an angle of elevation of 27° is about 0.5', or 'the gradient matching an angle of 60° is 1.732', so normally this is shortened to

- tangent of 27° ≃ 0.5
- tangent of 60° = 1.732

There are various reasons which explain why the word **tangent** is used in this way, which date from several hundred years ago. Just think of it as corresponding to gradient, so tangent of 60° = 1.732 (often further shortened to tan 60° = 1.732) means that the gradient corresponding to a slope angle of 60° is 1.732.

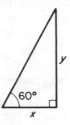

Figure 251.

In Figure 251, because the marked angle is 60°:
$$y = 1.732 \times x$$
So:

- if x is 1 m, then $y = 1.732$ m;
- if x is 36 cm, then $y = 36 \times 1.732 = 62.4$ cm;
  and so on.

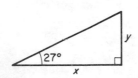

Figure 252.

In Figure 252, using the more accurate value of tan 27° = 0.510:

- when $x = 10$ cm, $y = 10 \times 0.510 = 5.1$ cm;

- when $x = 3\,\text{km}$, $y = 3 \times 0.510 = 1.53\,\text{km}$.

You can summarize all this as follows. Referring to Figure 253, with an angle of elevation of α and gradient of y/x:

- $\tan \alpha = y/x$

or:

- $y = x \tan \alpha$

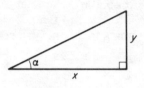

Figure 253.

You could make a table of tangent values for different angles by accurately drawing lots of triangles. Normally, though, you either use ready-prepared tangent tables or a scientific calculator to find the gradient which matches a given angle, or vice versa. Armed with these, you can then calculate unknown lengths or angles of right-angled triangles, without having to make accurate drawings.

Figure 254 shows part of a three-figure tangent table, where angles are given to the nearest $0.1°$ and tangent values are given to three significant figures. It shows, for example, that:

- $\tan 13° = 0.231$
- $\tan 13.2° = 0.235$

In reverse, you can find the angle which corresponds most closely with a known tangent value by spotting it in the tables and then reading off the matching angle. For instance, if $x = 13$ and $y = 3$, then:

$$\frac{y}{x} = \frac{3}{13} \simeq 0.231$$

so:

$$\tan \alpha = 0.231$$

and:

$$\alpha = 13°$$

Angle in degrees	0.0	0.1	0.2	0.3	0.4
0	0.000	0.002	0.003	0.005	0.00
1	0.017	0.019	0.021	0.023	0.0
2	0.035	0.037	0.038	0.040	0.4
3	0.052	0.054	0.056	0.058	0.
4	0.070	0.072	0.073	0.075	0.0
5	0.087	0.089	0.091	0.093	0.09
6	0.105	0.107	0.109	0.110	0.11
7	0.123	0.125	0.126	0.128	0.130
8	0.141	0.142	0.144	0.146	0.148
9	0.158	0.160	0.162	0.164	0.166
10	0.176	0.178	0.180	0.182	0.184
11	0.194	0.196	0.198	0.200	0.202
12	0.213	0.214	0.216	0.218	0.220
13	0.231	0.233	0.235	0.236	0.238
14	0.249	0.251	0.253	0.255	0.25

Figure 254. Part of a tangent table

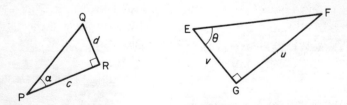

Figure 255.

Although I have used x, y and α in the diagrams so far, I could
have used any symbols I chose, though usually people use small

letters (like a, b, c, x, y, etc.) to stand for unknown side lengths and Greek letters like α, β, θ (alpha, beta, theta) for angles. Thus in triangle PQR in Figure 255:

$\tan \alpha = \frac{d}{c}$

and in triangle EFG:

$\tan \theta = \frac{u}{v}$

Often the side facing the marked angle is called the **opposite** side and the side between the marked angle and the right angle is called the **adjacent** side (see Figure 256), so you can say:

- $\tan (\text{Angle}) = \dfrac{\text{Opposite side}}{\text{Adjacent side}}$
- Opposite side = Adjacent side $\times$ tan (Angle)

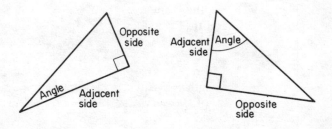

Figure 256. Adjacent and opposite sides

In Figure 255, d and u are opposite α and θ, while c and v are adjacent to α and θ.

Self-check

Use your tables or your calculator.
1 Write down (correct to 3 s.f.) the values of:
    tan 40°; tan 60.5°; tan 76.4°; tan 5.7°.
2 Write down (correct to 0.1°) the angles whose tangent values are:
    0.682; 1.76; 6.04; 0.072.
3 Using the diagrams in Figure 255, what is the value of α if $c = 7$ cm and $d = 2.59$ cm?
4 In Figure 255 what is the value of θ if $u = 9.8$ cm and $v = 5$ cm?

5 Using the diagram in Figure 253, calculate y when $x =$ 8 cm and $\alpha = 42°$.

ANSWERS

Using 3 significant figure tables.
1 0.839; 1.77; 4.13; 0.100.
2 34.3°; 60.4°; 80.6°; 4.1°.
3 $\tan \alpha = \frac{d}{c}$, so $\tan \alpha = \frac{2.59}{7} = 0.370$, so $\alpha = 20.3°$.
4 $\tan \theta = \frac{u}{v} = \frac{9.8}{5} = 1.96$, so $\theta = 63.0°$.
5 $y = 8 \tan 42° = 8 \times 0.900 = 7.2$ cm.

Using the hypotenuse – sines and cosines

Tangent values give you the connection between an angle in a right-angled triangle and the two sides which are opposite and adjacent to the angle. The longest side (the hypotenuse) is not involved.

Look at Figure 257. Here you know the lengths of the hypotenuse (8 cm) and the length opposite the marked angle (5 cm), so to calculate the size of θ you would first need to find the length of the adjacent side EG before you used tangent values to find θ. This would involve using Pythagoras' rule. However, you can find θ directly by using the **sine** tables. The sine of an angle in a right-angled triangle tells you how big the **opposite side is compared with the hypotenuse**, so here:

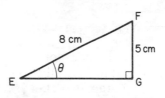

Figure 257.

sine $\theta = \frac{5}{8} = 0.625$

Using your calculator or tables you can find the angle whose sine is closest to 0.625 – it's 38.7°, so the required angle, θ, is 38.7°.

In general:

- sine (Angle) $= \dfrac{\text{Opposite side}}{\text{Hypotenuse}}$
- Opposite side $=$ Hypotenuse $\times$ sine (Angle)

Cosine values tell you how big the adjacent side is compared with the hypotenuse, so:

- cosine (Angle) $= \dfrac{\text{Adjacent side}}{\text{Hypotenuse}}$
- Adjacent side $=$ Hypotenuse $\times$ cosine (Angle)

In Figure 258 the hypotenuse is the longest side (4 cm) and the adjacent side to β is 3.5 cm (between β and the right angle). Because you know the lengths of the hypotenuse and of the adjacent side to β, you can use the cosines to calculate β:

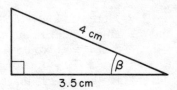

Figure 258.

cosine β $= \frac{3.5}{4} = 0.875$

so:

β $\simeq 29.0°$

This means that the remaining angle in the triangle is 61° (29 + 61 + 90 = 180). Of course the 3.5 cm is opposite the 61°, so sine

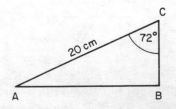

Figure 259

61° should equal 0.875. You can check this in your tables or on your calculator.

Here is another example. I want to calculate length AB in Figure 259. The hypotenuse is 20cm and the angle at C is 72°. As AB is opposite the angle of 72°, it's straightforward to use sines. Remember:

Opposite side = Hypotenuse × sine (Angle)

AB = 20 × sine 72°

= 20 × 0.951

= 19.02 ≃ 19 cm

Self-check

Refer to Figure 260. Make a sketch of each of the triangles, then use tangents, sines or cosines to calculate sides or angles marked with letters as accurately as you can.

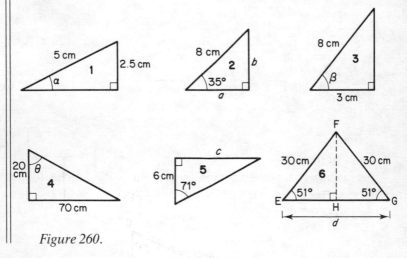

Figure 260.

1 sine $\alpha = \frac{2.5}{5} = 0.5$, so $\alpha = 30°$.

2 $a = 8 \times \cos 35° = 8 \times 0.819 \simeq 6.55$ cm.

$b = 8 \times \sin 35° = 8 \times 0.574 \simeq 4.59$ cm.

3 $\cos \beta = \frac{3}{8} = 0.375$, so $\beta = 68°$.

4 $\tan \theta = \frac{70}{20} = 3.5$, so $\theta = 74°$.

5 $c = 6 \tan 71° = 6 \times 2.90 = 17.4$ cm.

6 EH $= 30 \cos 51° = 30 \times 0.629 = 18.87$, so $d = 2 \times 18.87 = 37.74 \simeq 37.7$ cm.

A note on accuracy

Your results may differ slightly from these, depending on the tables or calculator you use. Four-figure tables are more accurate than three-figure ones, but are more complicated to use. In any case, the accuracy of your final result can be no greater than the accuracy of the original information.

Review

1 Calculate the lengths marked with letters in Figure 261.
2 Calculate the angles marked with letters in Figure 261.
3 A slope has an angle of elevation of 8°. What is the gradient of the slope as a percentage?
4 A hill has a gradient of 1 in 6. What is the gradient of the hill as a percentage? What is its angle of elevation?

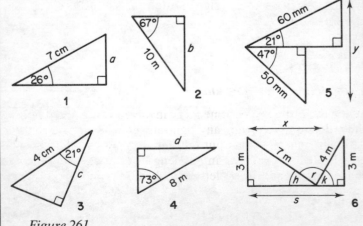

Figure 261.

Using sines, cosines and tangents

In this section the accent is on using sines, cosines and tangents – the trignometric functions – in more involved situations. As before, I will assume that you are using three-figure tables. If you are not, your answers may differ slightly.

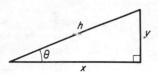

Figure 262.

Referring to Figure 262, to calculate side lengths:

- $y = h \times \sin \theta$
- $x = h \times \cos \theta$
- $y = x \times \tan \theta$

To calculate angles:

- $\frac{y}{h} = \sin \theta$
- $\frac{x}{h} = \cos \theta$
- $\frac{y}{x} = \tan \theta$

Often you will find the $\times$ sign omitted, so for instance:

    $h \sin \theta$

means:

    $h \times$ sine of θ

Using letters and diagrams

When the problems become more involved you'll find it helps to draw diagrams, showing any right-angled triangle you're using. This will help you think out the steps in your calculations more clearly. It's worth filling in any lengths or angles you know on the diagram, and using letters to label anything you are calculating.

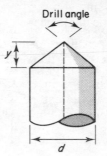

Figure 263.

For example, from Figure 263 calculate the drill angle when d = 18mm and y = 7mm. You can see that the diagram is made up of two identical right-angled triangles 7mm by 9mm, and that the drill angle = 2α (see Figure 264). The problem is thus to calculate α, then double it. Looking from α:

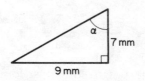

Figure 264

the opposite side is 9mm (y in Figure 262);
the adjacent side is 7mm (x in Figure 262).
So you use tangents to find:
   $\tan \alpha = \frac{9}{7} = 1.2857...$
   $\Rightarrow \alpha = 52.1°$
and the drill angle is $2 \times 52.1 = 104.2°$, say 104°.

Self-check

1 Repeat the calculation above but with d = 25mm, y = 9mm.
2 A drill, as above, has a diameter d of 16mm. Calculate the value of y which will give an angle θ of 100°.
3 Figure 265 shows an earth bank with a slope of 35°.

Calculate the angle θ and use it to find the depth *d* if the bank's height is 12 m.

4 What will the slope angle be if the depth *d* is reduced by 1 m?

5 A road up a hill is in three stages: first a horizontal distance of 150 m at a slope of 1 in 10; then 100 m at 1 in 8; and finally 200 m at 1 in 15. It is replaced by a new road at a steady gradient all the way. What is the percentage gradient of the new hill? What is its angle of elevation?

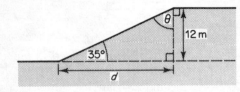

Figure 265

1 108°. **2** $y = 6.7$ mm. **3** 55°. **4** 17.1 m.
5 Increases in height at each stage are:
$\frac{1}{20} \times 150$; $\frac{1}{8} \times 100$; $\frac{1}{15} \times 200$
i.e.:
   $7.5 + 12.5 + 13.33$ m $= 33.33$ m
so new gradient is:
$\frac{33.33}{450} = 0.074 = 7.4\%$ (or 1 in 13.5)
Angle of elevation is 4.2°.

Review

Read this problem through, then write down a rough estimate for the answers before you do any calculating. Then carry out the calculations.

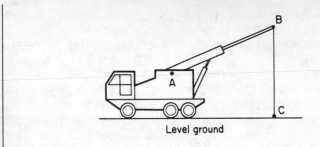

Figure 266.

A mobile crane (see Figure 266) has an extending jib AB, pivoted at A. A is 3.2m above ground level. Calculate the angle of elevation of the jib when AB = 12m and BC = 8m.

Review answers

Chapter 1, page 31.

1 £1.63.   **2** 61.5, 17.02.   **3** 100, 10, 0.1, 0.042.
4 17.5, 36.0.   **5** 2.4, 4.7.   **6** 19g.   **7** 5 tins.   **8** 6.6p.

Chapter 2, page 47.

1 9.   **2** 14, 20.   **3** 10.5.   **4** 27, 81.
5 $y=11, 15, 17, 23.8, 28.6$; $z=4, 5, 5.5, 7.2, 8.4$.   **6** $20-3$.
7 $20-3\times2$.   **8** $(20-3)2$.   **9** $20(3-2)$.   **10** $(20+3)/2$.
11 $20\times3\div2$.

Page 66.

1 $d=6.1, 46.1, 66.1, 86.1, 126.1$.   **2** 62 kg.
3 $h={}^-10, {}^-4, 2, 8, 14, 20, 26, 32$.   **4** ${}^-1, {}^-3, 9, 15$.

Chapter 3, page 80.

1 225°.   **2** 78.8°.   **3** Isosceles.   **4** Two of 78°, one of 102°.
5 144°, 106°.   **6** p and t or u and q.   **7** y.

Page 89.

1 0 or 2.   **2** 40°.   **3** rhombus.
4 a polygon with one or more vertices pointing inwards.

Chapter 4, page 110.

1 14, 700, 9, 16.   **2** **a**(8), **b** (480), **d**, **f**.   **3** 64, $3\times16=48$, 10, 1, a.

Chapter 5, page 126.

1 35m, 18000m, 0.48m, 21m, 4.0m. **2** 6656kg.
3 0.538, 0.571, 0.600, 0.625; 0.647. **4** $^{16}/_5$, $^{191}/_{11}$. **5** $8^4/_{10}$, $6^8/_{15}$,
$46^1/_{31}$. **6** 21, $^8/_{15}$, 7. **7** 337, 27, $^{49}/_{165} \simeq 0.30$.

Page 142.

1 $\frac{1}{2}$, $\frac{9}{10}$, $\frac{4}{5}$, $\frac{7}{8}$, $\frac{6}{7}$, $\frac{2}{3}$. **2** $\frac{a}{b} \times \frac{p}{q} = \frac{ap}{bq}$, $\frac{h}{k} \times \frac{mh}{mk}$, $\frac{a}{b} \div \frac{a}{p} = \frac{ap}{bq}$. **3** $x = \frac{5}{36}$, $y = \frac{3}{4}$, $z = \frac{3}{20}$,
$w = 2^1/_{16}$. **4** $\frac{2}{3} \times \frac{7}{8} = \frac{7}{12}$ or 0.583, $\frac{2}{3} \div \frac{7}{8} = \frac{16}{21}$ or 0.762, $\frac{7}{8} \div \frac{2}{3} = \frac{21}{16}$ or 1.3125.

Chapter 6, page 152.

1 34 41 41 39   **2** £300, 23%.   **3** £41.68   **4** B (£142.40).
  57 49 53 52
   8 10   6   8

Page 157.

1 $^1/_{12}$m.   **2** Sugar beet 32ha., barley 30ha., wheat 58ha.
3 $\frac{1}{2} + \frac{2}{5} = \frac{9}{10} = 0.9$, $\frac{2}{3} + 1\frac{1}{5} = 1\frac{13}{15}$ (not $\frac{13}{12}$), $\frac{1}{8} - \frac{1}{10} = \frac{2}{80} = \frac{1}{40}$, $\frac{5}{8} - \frac{1}{10} =$
$^{21}/_{40} = 0.525$, $0.8 \div 0.5 = 1.6 = 1\frac{3}{5}$, $0.8 + 0.05 = \frac{85}{100} = \frac{17}{20}$, $0.8 \times 0.5 = 0.40 = \frac{4}{10}$.

Chapter 7, page 188.

1 **a** $^-18$, **b** $^-9$, **c** 9, **d** 18, **e** $^-9$, **f** $^-9$, **g** $^-18$, **h** 18.   **2** $\frac{1}{2}$, $1\frac{1}{3}$, $^3/_d$, $^1/_{3y}$.
3 36, $^-6$, 20, 2.   **4** $26 - 2y$, $5 - y$.   **5** $x = 9$, $x = ^-3$.

Chapter 8, page 211.

1 4.8m².   **2** 7.13cm².   **3** 683cm².
4 20000cm², 1.60cm², 6500cm².   **5** 0.32m²   **6** 42.7l
7 148ml, 0.014ml, 1400ml.

Page 218.

1 12.5cm.   **2** at least 2.09m.   **3** $x = ^T/_w$, 0.8.   **4** $y = ^{4M}/_p$, 32.
5 $^{4h^3}/_3 = 5$. By repeated guesses, $h \simeq 1.55$m.

Chapter 9, page 226.

1 54°F, 6°C, 23°F, $^-7$°C.   **2** 0.186, 0.465, 0.93, 1.86, 2.79.
3 2.98m², 21.5sq ft, 0.67m², 6.99sq ft.
4 Lo − Not − Le − Ed − Ca − Br − Lo or reverse, 882 miles.

Page 238.

1 125mm², 10.8m/s.   **2** 4.16t, 333mm².
3 2.5, No (not through origin).

Chapter 10, page 261.

1 $r=\frac{\alpha l}{360}$, 3cm.   **2** $h=\frac{A}{2\pi r}$ **3**

4	16	804	603
12	8	603	402
16	4	201	226

4 d=13.3, **h**=6.7, as thin as possible.

Chapter 11, page 272.

1 8.8km.   **2** 18cm, 2:1.   **3** 20cm.
4 a=72mm, b=48mm, c=20mm, d=64°, e=73°.

Page 283.

1 EG=6.9cm.   **2** 90°.
3 Check ∠H=38.6°, P is on perpendicular bisector of HK (cuts HK 3cm from H, and cuts HN 3.8cm from H).

Chapter 12, page 294.

1 7.81m, 3.32m, 5.45m.   **2** Between 870 and 1300m.
3 9.22, 4.27, 2.28.   **4** $y=\sqrt{r^2-x^2}$, $y=\sqrt{d^2-a^2}$.

Page 301.

1 4.781×10^3, 6.9×10^{-2}, 2.67×10^{-2}, 5×10^{-2}.   **2** 6200, 0.000714.
3 9170.   **4** 17.7mm.   **5** $r=\sqrt{\frac{8V}{5m}}$, 7.30.

Chapter 13, page 311.

1 135°.   **2** 4.47cm.   **3** a=80°, b=100°.   **4** 90°, 40°.

Page 320.

1 2.67cm.   **2** 10.5cm.   **3** WPV.   **4** 80°, 80°.   **5** 24.25cm.

Chapter 14, page 332.

1 see p.341.   **2** $^7/_{120}$=5.8%, $^{92}/_{120}$=76.7%,
$^{21}/_{120}$=17.5%, not shown, pie chart angles are 21°, 276°, 63°.

Page 340.

1 $\simeq 67.45$ mm, $\simeq 67.25$ mm, $\simeq 67.65$ mm, $\simeq 0.4$ mm.
2 67.43 mm.

Chapter 15, page 354.

1 $a = 3.07$ cm, $b = 9.21$ m, $c = 3.73$ cm, $d = 7.65$ m, $x = 6.32$ m, $s = 8.97$ m, $y = 58.1$ mm.　　**2** $\mathbf{h} = 25.4°$, $\mathbf{k} = 48.6°$, $r = 106°$.
3 14.1%, 16.7%, 9.5°.

Page 358.

23.6°

Index